JUNGLE PILOT
The Life and Witness of Nate Saint

This edition is dedicated to
YOU

Because of friends like you,
Mission Aviation services have multiplied
eighteen-fold since this story took place.
Countless people have come to Christ,
churches have been established,
and lives saved.

Thank you.
Thank God!

MISSION AVIATION FELLOWSHIP
Box 202
Redlands, CA 92373

JUNGLE PILOT

The Life and Witness of
NATE SAINT

by RUSSELL T. HITT

ZONDERVAN
PUBLISHING HOUSE
OF THE ZONDERVAN CORPORATION
GRAND RAPIDS, MICHIGAN 49506

To MARJ SAINT
in whose wedding ring was engraved
a Scripture reference, Psalm 34:3,
chosen by Nate —
"O magnify the Lord with me,
and let us exalt his name together."

JUNGLE PILOT: *The Life and Witness of Nate Saint*
Copyright © 1959 by The Fields, Inc.

Photos by Cornell Capa, Magnum Photos,
appear on pages 92, 95 and 96.
Washington Cathedral Photo (page 83) by Horydczak.

Reprinted by arrangement with Harper & Row, Publishers

Zondervan Books edition   1973
Tenth printing   1980

Library of Congress Catalog Card Number 59-10335
ISBN 0-310-26082-5

Printed in the United States of America

CONTENTS

PREFACE

WHEN Nate Saint first went to Ecuador in 1948 he wrote a letter to Charles Mellis of the Missionary Aviation Fellowship:

"I don't want to be a great writer but I long to express myself— just as I've often longed to be able to sit down at a big pipe organ and express myself.

"I want to share the stories that are unfolding all around us. Mine would only be attempts, to be sure, but these attempts plus helpful criticism from others may allow me eventually to be able to tell stories with the flavor that can come only from an eyewitness."

So it was that Nate wrote to his good friend, Charlie, who had offered "helpful criticism" in connection with one of the first brief accounts that Nate had written shortly after he had reached the field.

It was a part of his creative nature to set down on paper the experiences through which he was passing. A keen observer and a "born" writer, Nate continued to express himself in letters, in articles for Christian magazines, in journals, and in unpublished manuscripts.

It was from the vast treasury of Nate's own written accounts that this book came into being.

To those involved in gathering together his letters and papers, it seemed providential that nearly all the letters he wrote to his parents during more than three years in the Army had been kept.

It was just as remarkable that the files of the Missionary Aviation Fellowship had not been "cleaned out" by 1958 when formal research was begun on *Jungle Pilot*. All of Nate's correspondence over a period of twelve years had been preserved.

Carbon copies of letters sent to friends as well as business firms during the seven years of missionary service had not been destroyed. All this seemed beyond coincidence.

Nate, the capable chronicler of events during the planning stages of Operation Auca and the diarist of "Palm Beach," contributed largely to our knowledge of those fateful days. Those logs were the normal culmination of a lifetime of "expressing himself."

When Nate's papers were examined after his death, it was apparent that there was more than enough material for a book. The request for weaving these writings into a biographical account came soon after.

No effort was spared to track down everything available about Nate Saint. Literally scores of people were interviewed—missionaries, Ecuadorians, and Indians on a trip that took the author to Ecuador and the heart of the eastern jungle. It was important to learn at first hand the conditions under which Nate Saint lived and worked; to visit Shell Mera and examine the hydro plant on the little stream; to see the yellow planes in the hangar; to talk to members of his Bible class; to hear the reminiscences of missionaries who had worked shoulder to shoulder with Nate.

There were visits to the Jivaro stations and outstations; to the Quichua settlements; and to the Atshuara village. There were flights in threatening weather and over dangerous jungle terrain. There was the visit deep in the jungle to call on Betty Elliot and Rachel Saint at Limon Cocha, and to meet Dayuma and Mankamu and Mintaka. The high spot of the trip was the spine-tingling, low-altitude flight over the Auca settlements, and then the aerial survey of Palm Beach with an unuttered shout of victory that the wind forced back into a tightened throat.

There was a trip to California that included time in the files of MAF.

There were visits, too, to Huntingdon Valley, Pennsylvania, and interviews with relatives, neighbors, and boyhood friends.

This book is constructed largely of genuine "stories with flavor that can come only from an eyewitness"—Nate Saint himself.

ACKNOWLEDGMENTS

No ONE is more keenly aware than the one listed as the author that this book has been the work of many.

Right from the start, when the assignment came from Harper & Brothers and from the Saint family, it was understood that Nate's own writings would make up the bulk of the book. For in addition to his many other gifts, Nate was a writer of rare ability. The reader will find thrilling passages that are his untouched handiwork.

After him first credit goes to Nate's wife Marj, for compiling the storehouse of original letters, private papers, and miscellaneous writings of her husband. During months of research in California and in Ecuador she culled out choice material that has found its place in the book. Finally, she journeyed from Quito to New York and Philadelphia for the final job of checking and editing the manuscript, working closely with the author and the staff of Harper & Brothers.

Sam Saint, Nate's brother, masterminded the operation from the time the biography was conceived right until it reached the final stages of writing and editing. Lawrence and Katherine Saint, the parents of our "Jungle Pilot," were helpful aides, as were Nate's sister Rachel and others of the family.

Deep thanks are due to the officers of the Missionary Aviation Fellowship for opening their confidential files to the author and giving him full co-operation in gathering material. MAF pilots Johnny Keenan and Dan Derr flew the author and Marj Saint to the jungle mission stations in Ecuador and over Auca territory, including the hallowed final resting place of the five martyred missionaries at "Palm Beach" on the River Curaray.

There are so many others, too, who gave invaluable help and counsel, including Betty Elliot, the missionaries of the Oriente, and even the ham-radio operators who made short-wave communication possible between Ecuador and the United States. Volunteers from the Christian Business Women's Association in New York typed the final draft of the manuscript.

Permission to use portions of articles which appeared earlier in their publications was granted by the editors of *Christian Life*, *The Sunday School Times*, and *Moody Monthly*.

The author is especially grateful to Donald Grey Barnhouse and the trustees of The Evangelical Foundation, Inc., for making it possible for him to take off needed time as the book neared completion.

Seclusion—that rarest of all commodities in these mad days—was provided by George and Martha Ayers, who gave the use of their summer home at Ocean City, New Jersey.

Lillian, a patient and capable wife, proved to be a constant source of help and counsel, besides typing the original manuscript and aiding in the proofreading.

And a final word of sincere thanks goes to Melvin Arnold of the publishing house, who had the temerity to think that I could write a book.

RUSSELL T. HITT

Merion Station, Pennsylvania
April 14, 1959

1

"TACASTA!"

. . . they fly away as an eagle toward heaven. PROVERBS 23:5

A SMALL group of Indians and one lone white man swung axes and machetes, hacking away at the tangled forest, cutting down trees, slashing back bejuco vines, tearing the chirichiri from the black mucky earth. Gradually the thick mat of jungle vegetation was rolled back—pushed into piles higher than a man's head by the side of the unfinished airstrip.

The lone white man, a tall, gaunt, hollow-eyed young missionary, was digging out stumps. He worked on the smaller stumps—trying not to think of the one big stump that stood like the Rock of Gibraltar right where the airplane's wheels should touch down.

More and more often the white man and the Indians with him paused, leaning on their tools—paused to scan the western sky and listen for the faint hum that would announce the coming of Nate Saint in the little yellow airplane.

The unfinished airstrip was a mere pockmark in the deep deceptive forest of Ecuador's eastern jungle. At the end of the airstrip was a native village dominated by a huge thatch-roofed communal house. The village lay some four days by canoe and jungle trail southeast of the mission station at Macuma. It was from Macuma that Roger Youderian had come to help the Indians complete the airstrip.

As Roger and Frank Drown, his missionary co-worker, and Nate Saint, the jungle pilot, had planned the clearing of an airstrip at the village of the Atshuara Indians, the project had seemed routine.

True enough, the Atshuaras had kept missionaries out of their territory for years by threatening death to any intruder within their borders. But in the Lord's time Santiaku their chief had come out

11

to the mission station seeking medicine to cure him of a hideous and disfiguring jungle disease. After being cured, Santiaku invited Roger and Frank to make the long trail trip to his village for a visit.

On their first visit the missionaries took in tools and succeeded in getting the Atshuaras to start clearing an airstrip. No airstrip— no medicine. It was that simple. Roger and Frank stayed with the Indians for three days, giving them medicinal care and the simple gospel message before returning to their base at Macuma.

During the months that followed, Nate Saint flew over periodically to watch progress on the new airstrip. Finally it became apparent that the Indians needed help, so Roger decided he would go in and push the project to completion. It seemed the only thing to do. No serious problems were anticipated as Roger took off down the trail to the country of the Atshuaras.

Unknown to those back at Roger's base, however, an unforeseen complication had arisen. When Roger arrived at Santiaku's house, he discovered that many in the village had contracted flu from soldiers who had been through the area. It was a deadly virus to which these Indians had not previously been exposed. They had no resistance to it and Roger knew they could start dying like flies. This, of course, might close the door to missionary effort among this group of Indians for years to come.

It was typical of Roger Youderian, an ex-paratrooper, that he took command at once. In the providence of God he had brought along a small supply of penicillin. He used it all on the first day, giving shots to the worst cases in the hope this would stem the tide. In the following days these cases did recover somewhat and it seemed as though no more serious ones would develop. But it was clear to Roger that a solid and safe relationship with the Atshuaras would not be achieved until a doctor and other help could be flown in whenever needed. He knew he had to get Nate and the yellow plane onto the ground here in this isolated clearing at the earliest possible moment.

The air was warmer now. Clouds of black gnats, stirred up by the slashing machetes, swarmed over Roger's sweating body as he worked with the Indians on the airstrip. The tall young missionary, his shoulders sagging with fatigue, lifted the edge of his torn and dirty T-shirt and mopped the perspiration from his face and the black stubble of his beard. He studied the thin layer of morning fog that hung like a shroud above this remote part of the great forest. He bowed his head and closed his eyes. "Lord, **break away these clouds and send** Nate soon," he breathed fervently in English. The group of unconverted Atshuaras, inscrutable killers of the forest, glanced at one another uneasily.

Roger's prayer was short, but it came from the bottom of his heart. He was in a precarious position with the savage and somewhat unpredictable Atshuaras. It was important to talk with Nate to arrange the first landing earlier than they had originally intended and to get more penicillin lined up—just in case.

The airplane could not land, Roger knew. The strip was far from finished. But he felt sure that Nate, when he arrived overhead, would lower his unique, air-to-ground telephone-in-a-bucket, developed for just such emergencies. *"Tacasta!"* ("Get going!") Roger called, urging the Indians back to work.

After a time the fog began to break and the morning sun made a pattern of light and shadow on the yuca patches where the women worked nearby. Children played in the holes where stumps had been dug out, preferring to be near where the men were working.

Roger moved over to study the big stump. He dug a little around the great buttress roots. The tree had been felled a long time before, but the wood of the stump remained solid. Stubborn . . . unyielding . . . defiant . . . were words that came to Roger's weary mind. It almost seemed the stump was there to test his strength of will. The stump stood between the Atshuaras and the missionaries who longed to bring them the gospel that could lift them out of heathen darkness. The stump had to go. Roger had just begun to dig seriously when a shout stopped all work on the airstrip.

Warush, youngest of the Atshuara men, was pointing excitedly with his machete. "I hear! I hear!" And in a few more seconds they all heard the airplane coming.

Roger was concerned for fear Nate might not find the clearing.

13

The country of the Atshuaras is east of the last foothills of the Andes Mountains. There are no natural landmarks; this part of Ecuador's jungle stretches eastward, flat as the sea, to the distant horizon. The remnants of the early morning ground fog, Roger realized, could easily camouflage this tiny spot in the unmarked forest.

Then through a break in the mist they saw the sun glint on the yellow wings. Nate was flying a straight course, a little to the south, going right by—but no! Abruptly the engine was cut and the plane turned sharply, coming straight toward the clearing, losing altitude fast.

As Nate buzzed the clearing, Santiaku came out of his house and stood apart, watching silently. His bright feathered headband and painted face were set off by long black hair hanging in braids.

Nate turned and came back across the clearing, this time with the engine throttled back to idling speed. His voice floated down to the men below as he passed close overhead. *"Clear the strip for a drop!"* Roger rounded up the Indians and got them off the strip. In four passes overhead Nate dropped packages of food, and axheads and cloth for the Indians.

While the Indians scrambled for the packages strewn along the strip, Roger stood waiting for what he hoped would happen next. The airplane was circling now, holding steadily in a tight turn. As Roger watched, he saw a tiny black speck detach itself from the airplane and move slowly out behind. He breathed a prayer of thanks to the Lord he knew was guiding in the whole operation. Soon the tiny speck was far behind the airplane, following it around in its circle. After a turn or two the speck began sliding in toward the center of the circle and, as it did, it began to drop toward the ground, rapidly growing larger. The speck became a canvas bucket and the twisted pair of wires that connected it to the airplane above was now visible. The bucket was hanging almost motionless, just above the treetops, hanging at the vortex of an inverted cone. It drifted in slightly erratic fashion. Then it dropped slowly almost into Roger's hands—and suddenly went zooming up again. Roger realized that Nate was having trouble with the layer of broken clouds. When Nate couldn't see what the bucket was doing, he pulled it up clear of the trees until he could see it again. On the next time around the bucket dropped fast all the way to the ground. It bounced along a hundred feet or so and banged up against a log where it held until Roger raced over to grab it.

In the bucket Roger found the phone wrapped in thick padding for protection. He tore off the wrappings and a moment later was talking to Frank Drown who was riding with Nate in the airplane.

"Hello, Roj; hello, Roj." Frank's voice came down the spiraling wire, faint but clearly readable. "How are things going down there?"

"I'm sure glad you fellows came over," Roger answered. "Things are under control now, but you should have seen this place four days ago. When I got here half this crowd were down with the flu."

"Did you have enough penicillin?" Frank asked.

"Used it all," Roger answered, "but I think we're all right for the moment. How are Barb and the children?"

"She said to tell you they are all fine. She'll be glad to see you back. Got a schedule worked out yet?"

Roger looked down the airstrip at that big stump for a moment, knowing that the Lord would have to give the strength to get it out of there. "Tell Nate we'll be ready for the first landing Friday. We'll be ready for him Friday morning. And tell him he'd better bring me another supply of penicillin."

"Maybe you'd better let us drop you some more penicillin tomorrow," Frank said; "—you might need it before Friday."

Roger hesitated; he knew Nate's normal rounds kept him on the go from early morning until dark every day the weather was flyable. "No need for a special trip," he finally decided, "just tell him to bring it when he comes Friday."

A large loop of the phone line lay on the ground, twisting with the motion of the plane overhead. One of the Indians grabbed the twisted wire with delight and held it against the airplane's pull like a boy flying a kite.

Frank's voice came again from the airplane:

"Nate says to remind you that your life won't be worth a

plugged nickel if a few of those characters have relapses and die before Friday. He thinks he should bring you some more penicillin right away—unless you're sure things are going to be okay."

"No," Roger said. "We'll make it okay until Friday. Friday is good. Tell Nate we'll see him on Friday, Lord willing."

They talked for a few minutes longer while the airplane circled. When they had said all that needed to be said, Nate put a little tension on the line. Roger let go of the bucket and it soared up out of the clearing. Nate waggled his wings and the plane straightened out toward Macuma.

The gifts from the sky and the excitement of the occasion put new life into Santiaku's men for a time. Roger pushed the work on the strip at an even harder pace. In spite of this, however, Tuesday's progress was too slow. Roger put off the real push on the big stump, hoping for a stronger work force on Wednesday. But Tuesday evening one of the Indians had a serious relapse and by noon on Wednesday there were three more cases of flu in the village. Roger was stunned by this new blow. If only he had taken the fellows' advice. Now he had no way to call for the penicillin he needed. He prayed to the Lord who had sent him into the village—he prayed that none would die before the penicillin arrived on Friday.

Wednesday Roger had misgivings about finishing the strip by the Friday deadline. The Indians seemed willing, but only a handful remained well enough to work and two or three of these were too weak for the heavier jobs. Roger drove himself to the point of collapse. Again he put off tackling the big stump, praying for more manpower on Thursday.

On Thursday morning, however, two more came down with flu. Some of the men grumbled because Roger's needle had no more medicine. At the end of the day the stump remained. They had dug around it and cut some of the big buttress roots, but it seemed as big and firm as ever. There would be no landing on Friday, but at least Nate would have the penicillin and could drop it into the clearing. That night Roger slept the sleep of utter exhaustion.

By morning the weather had changed. Low-lying clouds and

fitful rain would keep Nate grounded. All day Roger worked at the stump with grim determination. He realized now that he had used up his physical reserve to a dangerous point. He was committing all to completion of the strip, for he felt sure he would not have strength enough left to minister to the village, even after the penicillin came. There was only one answer. The stump had to be moved so the airplane could take him out and bring others in.

In the last fading light of Friday Roger surveyed the strip. The stump was still there, but they had got out the big old crosscut saw Roger had brought and sawed the thing down through the middle so the two halves were loose, and would certainly yield in the first effort of the morning. The strip was short and the trees were tall and close on either side, but Nate could make it, Roger decided. He had flown with Nate many times and watched with admiration as he maneuvered his little plane like a master playing a Stradivarius. Nate could do it, Roger decided, once that stump was out of the way.

The rain and low clouds had cleared by Saturday morning. Roger, promising medicine when the yellow bird arrived, got every able person on the poles and levers he had rigged around the stump. The women, strong from working in the yuca patches, crowded in to help. Even some of the sick ones left their beds and tried to move that stump. Finally it yielded and they dragged it off to the side of the strip. The hole was filled and tamped and smoothed. Roger marked the safe landing area with strips of white cloth.

Then they waited with all hearts turned toward the sky and the yellow plane and the jungle pilot who now played such a key role in the lives of missionaries and Indians alike in this lonely headwater region of the Amazon River.

As the day began to wear on, Roger's concern grew, because a few of the Indians were desperately ill. He was afraid he was going to lose some of them and so he too was listening, anxiously waiting for the airplane. Four o'clock came and he began to get discouraged. It was so late in the day. Then finally they heard it— there it was, they heard it come and they heard it turn and go away. Roger's heart fell to his shoetops. And, well, you can

17

imagine, he was just completely "rendered," as they say in Spanish. He was completely shot from physical exhaustion.

A half hour later they heard it coming again, coming closer and closer. It came quite close this time—then again it began to fade away. By running down to the yuca patch and getting right in line with an opening in the trees, they saw the airplane off in the distance, saw it disappearing. Roger was puzzled. Why was Nate having trouble finding the clearing this time?

Roger felt sure this was the last chance because it was getting so late. He gave up then, and called the Indians together. Out there in the middle of nowhere with nightfall coming on and the need of those sick people heavy on his heart—Roger started having a gospel service. And the service was interrupted. The airplane was coming back. This time the yellow plane was in a long dive straight for the clearing. There was no mistake now.

As the plane banked sharply overhead, they all saw Nate's angular form straining forward to take in every detail of the strip below. Roger could almost read Nate's mind as he watched the tiny plane circle again and again. He knew Nate was hesitating to come in. Then Nate turned in toward the strip, swinging around and diving in close over Santiaku's big thatch-roofed house. He was coming much too fast to land—just coming in for a real close look with obviously no intention of landing. With engine wide open, Nate passed within forty feet of the little group by the edge of the airstrip. Children scattered toward the forest. Women stepped back, but the Atshuara men stood firm, showing momentary fear only in their eyes. With a wave of his hand, Nate pulled up and out of there in a steep climbing turn.

The airplane circled away then and for a few minutes appeared to be making aimless turns. It seemed to Roger that Nate had decided the trees were still too close—that it was too tight to land. But why didn't he drop the penicillin? Or let down the phone? Then he realized the airplane was flying again with obvious purpose. It swung carefully into line with the strip, slow this time. The flaps were down. A little gasp escaped Roger's lips as the plane missed the top ridge of the big house by about fifteen feet, slewing into a steep side slip that looked for three seconds like certain disaster, then, slick as a whistle Nate eased it out of the slip and the wheels touched down light as a feather only a plane's length beyond the white cloth marking the beginning of the strip.

As Nate taxied back to where Roger and the Indians waited, he cut the engine, rolling toward them, easing his lanky frame out of the pilot's seat to hit the ground as the wheels stopped. Tall and lean, with sandy hair cropped short for convenience, Nate's sunburned face, as usual, was covered with a boyish grin—a grin that faded as Roger came running up.

"What's up, Roj, boy," Nate started. "I knew you'd be beat, but I didn't expect—"

Roger looked at Nate out of eyes deep-set in his emaciated face. "Have you got any medicine?" he interrupted. Nate tossed Roger the package padded for an aerial drop. Roger tore it open, laid the syringe out on the seat of the airplane, and shouted orders to the Indians over his shoulder.

Nate followed with the bottles of medicine as Roger made the rounds, shooting nearly everyone in sight with penicillin. Finally the medicine was gone. Everybody that needed it had felt the jab of Roger's needle. For the first time Roger smiled, the pressure was off. He let down then and Nate took charge from there on. They made the rounds saying good-by. Santiaku, sitting on a log, stoop-shouldered, looking sick, painted up fit to kill, was doing his best to look like a chief. Nate, who did not speak the dialect of the Atshuaras, said good-by in English, his expressive blue eyes and infectious white-toothed smile interpreting his words for the chief.

Nate Saint recorded in vivid detail the events of that day:

"I looked at my watch and I said, 'Do you know, Roj, we're not really through—we're still in a rush, man.' The sun was sinking fast, the shadows high on the trees. The air was getting cooler by the minute.

"Roj started grabbing his stuff. I said, 'No, Roj, we can't take one extra pound.' I did let him take his syringe and his camera. The rest of his stuff we threw in a gunnysack and tossed to the chief until we could get back.

"We headed for the airplane, fired the thing up, checked the engine well and started the take-off run. A bump tossed us into the air at about the 160-yard point. After that we touched the turf once more, lightly, then we were airborne."

Nate explained to Roger that he had just enough gas in the tank to make Wambimi, a place where prospecting crews of the Shell Oil Company had abandoned some shacks and an airstrip a few years before. The strip at Wambimi was on the edge of the Atshuara territory about halfway to Macuma. Roger and Barbara had fixed up the strip at Wambimi and spent some time there in outstation work among the Jivaros in that area.

"Frank is waiting for us at Wambimi," Nate explained. "We've got some gas there in a jeep can. Didn't want any extra weight for the landing at Santiaku's place."

"You'll never know how hard we worked," Roger said.

"Brother, you don't need to say a word," Nate said, "your face says it better than any of Mr. Webster's words ever could."

"For a while I thought you weren't going to land," Roger confessed. "Thought you'd throw me the medicine and beat it for home. I nearly died at the thought. Don't know if I could have made it another day."

"I almost did pass you up," Nate agreed. "That isn't exactly what you'd call an airstrip yet. But I knew you'd be needing to get out of there."

Nate's record continues:

"Roger was slumped in the seat, his eyes closed, obviously letting the fatigue drain out of his worn body. Then he opened his eyes again and asked me how come I had so much trouble finding the place this time. I told him I couldn't understand it myself at first. Thought I had that spot nailed. But finally figured it was because I had never been over that country in the late afternoon before. The shadow patterns were all different at that time of day.

"On the way to Wambimi I reeled out the antenna to call in the good word and what do you know—the receiver had gone out. But the transmitter was working, so from there on over to Wambimi I transmitted, repeating several times, that I had Roj with me and we were both headed for Wambimi. Well, it was a beautiful clear evening and I found we'd have time to land, dump in five gallons of gas and the three of us could get on to Macuma before dark. So we really rolled. Landed straight in at Wambimi, cut the engine as soon as we were on the ground, rolled up toward where Frank was waiting. Before we got stopped I shouted to Frank: 'Get the gear. Get the gas and the gear. We've got to get out of here fast.'

"We got the gas in the tank, piled the other stuff in, and we piled in after it. At the end of the strip I stopped and tried the engine. It accelerated rapidly—then cut out. Well, that did it! If everything had been fine, why we probably would have made it on to Macuma, but as it was, we thanked God we were on the ground and not in the air. I told the fellows, 'It's no soap; I think we're here for the night.'

"There was only one thing I could think of doing to that engine, so I got out the tools. It was getting dark fast. I couldn't get the plug out of the carburetor, or the float-chamber drain because the engine was so hot—it was really hot—because we'd come in there plenty fast.

"The wrench wouldn't budge it. We knew we were there for the night anyway; so we decided to let it go till morning."

The fellows then turned to the problem of notifying their wives they were all together and safely out of the Atshuara country. Frank had a hand-crank radio that he had kept with him when Nate dropped him off at Wambimi on the trip down. This was their only hope since the airplane receiver was out of commission. So they strung the antenna up between two saplings. "By that time," Nate reported, "we were stumbling around in the dark. The moon, this time of the month, doesn't come up till later. We got the radio hooked up and we got transmitting to Shell Mera where I knew my wife, Marj, would have her receiver cranked up to full volume. Well, we kept on transmitting, but we couldn't hear a thing—we couldn't get any confirmation on our calls.

"We decided we ought to stay there by the airplane and try again at seven o'clock. We expected all the wives would be listening on the circuit by then and maybe one of them would pick up our call.

"While we were waiting, we got to thinking over our situation. It wasn't particularly ideal. We had no flashlight aboard, and through a chain of circumstances we didn't have the emergency kit in the airplane. I might say right here those missing items caused me to make some powerful resolutions for the future. We didn't even have the means of starting a fire.

"We began calling again at seven. Called and called. And finally Frank got hold of Shell Mera. We heard him answering Marj while Roj and I turned the cranks on the transmitter. He finally got the message to her that all three of us were on the ground at Wambimi.

"Well, that was a great relief. Now our only worry was our own personal circumstances and how we'd spend the night. We were all in a good mood. The Lord had certainly been good to us, getting us out of that place with no accident—and the medicine that got in there in the nick of time to save those lives. And this whole thing will probably open the door over there in that country to the gospel.

"We closed up the radio and put it in the airplane so that it wouldn't get rained on in the night and sort of took stock of our predicament. The abandoned Shell Company shacks were down the strip and off to one side—somewhere out there in the dark. Roj and Frank had both camped there at various times doing outstation work. So when they decided we ought to spend the night in the buildings—well, I didn't give them a hard time; what with a bunch of bugs swarming around us and the evening starting to get really cool, I was game for anything they wanted to do.

"So we started for the shacks. Frank and his wife Marie had been there last and Frank said they had left some provisions locked up in a room. We needed to get a fire going, but what we needed most of all was a light. And by Harry, a light is a light; there is no darkness like darkness.

"Well, these two characters I was with scattered down the trail a way. I didn't know whether they were guiding me or just trying to get themselves down the trail as fast as possible. In the darkness all I could see was their white shirts. It seemed to me that they were practically running. Roj was in the lead, swinging a machete back and forth in the grass to wake up any snakes and get them out of the way. But he was going so fast, I don't know how a snake would have had time to clear out of his way. Apparently he knew the path quite well and he was really making knots. With a little stumbling around, off the edge of the path now and then, we finally got down to the shack.

"It wasn't a welcome little cabin in the woods, with a candle in the window, unfortunately. It was a grim kind of thing there in the gloom. We got inside and it was really dark, no sky at all in there, and Frank reached out a hand in the dark and I got hold of his hand and he guided me through a narrow doorway from one room into another and led me to a chair. I was happy to sit down and stay put. And I just wished like everything that there was some way to reproduce the dialogue I heard as I sat there in the darkness, listening to those two fellows rummaging around, stumbling over stuff, discussing whether to just bash down the door to the locked room, or take it off the hinges, or to work on the lock with a piece of pipe or just what they'd do. Well, it was something like the old radio dramas that I used to listen to when I was a kid; Bobby Benson and the cowboys going into dark caves. Then I heard something give way—Roj said, 'The top hinge is loose.' Then about that time the whole door came off and I heard them walk into the room. The room had a cement floor. It was an old shower room in the Shell days and this was one of the very few buildings that were still surviving in some sort of decent shape. The others were all decayed and grown over with trees and vines. I heard them moving around in the room and I heard Frank say, 'Look Roj, how do we keep from stepping on the snakes in this place?'

"And Roj said, 'Don't worry about that: I fixed this room up so that it's snake-proof. There's a hole over in the corner. I put a board over that the last time I was here.' There was a moment of absolute silence. Then Frank said, kind of quiet and humblelike, 'I took that board off when I was here; I didn't know what it was for.'

"Well, the thing went on like that. It was so dark I couldn't see my hand in front of my face. I heard tin cans rattling around. And Frank called, 'Roj, come over here and feel in this can; see if you can find some matches.' And Roj said, 'What's the matter with you? I'm not sticking *my* hand down in that thing.' He was afraid there might be a scorpion in it. I don't know whose hand went in the can, but at any rate, they kept rattling cans and announcing what they thought they were finding. The lid came off one can and Roj said, 'This is coffee!' Another can would be lentils, another a can of beans, dried beans, but no matches. Finally Frank said, 'Here's a matchbox.' He had found a matchbox somewhere, but when he opened it, it had nails in it. What a disappointment. It was getting miserably cold. We had one blanket with us. I got hold of it and was wrapped up sitting in my chair, listening to this dialogue and thinking of the humorous side of the situation, which would seem a lot more humorous if we could find a match or two. Then Roj stumbled on an old radio B battery, which might have enough voltage left to make a spark. They had already found a little tin of kerosene and another of gasoline. Maybe if that battery would make a spark I could light some gasoline. It was a long shot, but it just might work. So I felt my way over and got hold of this battery. They finally found a little piece of wire and they handed it to me so I went back to my chair and huddled up in this blanket. I was fiddling around Braille method, trying to find the outlets on the battery to stick those wires in and see if I could produce a spark.

"While I was doing that Roj walked over and without changing his tone at all, said, 'Take heart, boys, I've got some matches.' I couldn't believe it; I thought he was kidding us until I saw that match flare. And I'm telling you, that match had as much light in it as a 100-watt bulb, there in that darkness. Boy, it was a beautiful bright light just flooding that whole room but I was sort of afraid he would let the thing go out, and maybe there wouldn't be any more matches, or they'd be wet, or something. Then they found a few candles, a whole box of them as a matter of fact, and the first thing you know, they had several candles going and we had light all over the place.

"We quickly found there in the storeroom canned preserves, a quart of beef, succotash, pears, pickled beets, and some other things. We marched triumphantly off to the kitchen in the other end of the shack.

"There we found a couple of plates and a big wooden spoon. We bent jar lids to make two more spoons. Frank put a handful of lentils in a pot of water, and we got a fire going in the stove—a brick stove with a sheet of metal over it. We made a stew out of the succotash and meat. That stew really went down well, slid right down. We heated up some water in a tin can and threw some coffee in it, and that coffee went down very nicely. We found a jar of sugar and, boy, just everything you could ask for. It was just like the Lord had prepared a table before us in the presence of our enemies. There it was—and our cup was surely running over. No meal was ever more appreciated, I'm sure. Especially for Roj— although he did say that the Indians fed him pretty well over there. Even though most of them were sick, they saw to it that he got well fed."

Roger told his two missionary teammates of the frantic days in Santiaku's village, of the sickness, and how one key man of the tribe had died the day before he arrived. Nate and Frank lived with Roger again "the battle of the stump" as they sat there in the candlelight gulping home-canned pears.

Roger kept saying, "The Lord was in this whole thing! We've got a solid opening with those fellows and we can get in there now with the gospel."

"We had our last cup of coffee around midnight," Nate recorded, "then it was time to turn in. We had one blanket and had to sleep Indian style, three on one big chonta wood bed. I'm not a very good double-sleeper, but I was almost beyond feeling by that time, so I crawled in between those two characters on the hard chonta boards, double-sleeper or no."

The boys were up at five-thirty and Nate soon had the airplane fixed. He flew it first alone, then loaded in the others and the extra paraphernalia, and, as Nate described it, "We took off and made a bee-line for Macuma, and when we got to Macuma people were pretty glad to see people—on both sides of the fence."

A few minutes later Nate took off alone for Shell Mera. It was still early on that beautiful Sunday morning. He loved to fly the airplane empty—without its usual capacity load it climbed so fast and free into the clear blue sky. He recorded the special thrill he got that morning at seeing the snow-capped peaks, Tunguragua and El Altar in the distance as he flew toward his home base in the foothills. He saw Chimborazo (two hundred miles away) and the active volcano Sangay.

It was a time for summarizing, a time for reflection. He would get someone with more medicine back into the Atshuara village, probably tomorrow. And the Indians would hear the gospel and have their eyes turned toward Calvary.

Nate was glad to be a part of the overall missionary effort in this remote part of God's vineyard. He had come to Ecuador as a pilot for a growing organization known as the Missionary Aviation Fellowship. MAF had been started by a small group of World War II pilots. These dedicated young men, with rare vision, had foreseen what airplanes and radio could do to extend the arms of missionaries in out-of-the-way places. Their little yellow planes, better adapted to tiny jungle airstrips than larger planes, were active in the skies over many countries.

Nate Saint was one of the earliest of MAF's circuit riders, his parish covering an ever-increasing number of Protestant mission stations in the eastern jungle of Ecuador. His was the task of providing logistic support for the missionaries who labored patiently in their lonely outposts, taking in mail, fresh meat and vegetables, and all the hundred and one items needed for jungle living. He took in medicine and flew the sick out to a doctor.

Nate was a pilot and a mechanic, but he was a missionary too, one in mind and spirit with the missionary families of the jungle. Some time before he had written of his feeling for the pioneering missionaries he loved to serve:

"Their call of God is to the regions beyond the ends of civilization's roads—where there is no other form of transportation. They have probed the frontiers to the limit of physical capacity and prayed for a means of reaching the regions beyond—a land of witch doctors and evil spirits—a land where the woman has no soul; she's just a beast of burden—a land where there's no word for love in their vocabulary—no word to express the love of a father for his son. In order to reach these people for whom Christ died, pioneer missionaries slug it out on the jungle trails day after day, sometimes for weeks, often in mud up to their knees, while up above them the towering tropical trees push upward in a never-ending struggle for light.

"It is our task," Nate's record continues, "to lift these missionaries up off those rigorous, life-consuming, and morale-breaking jungle trails—lift them up to where five minutes in a plane equals twenty-four hours on foot. The reason for all this is not a matter of bringing comfort to the missionaries. They don't go to the steaming, tropical jungles looking for comfort in the first place. It's a matter of gaining precious time, of redeeming days and weeks, months and even years that can be spent in giving the Word of Life to primitive people."

Winging toward Shell Mera on that crystal-clear Sunday morning, Nate Saint's gaze swept the horizon to the northeastward where lived the savage Auca Indians, a Stone Age tribe who kill swiftly and silently from ambush—a tribe which no white man or Indian had entered peacefully in more than three hundred years. Nate's heart went out to those unknown wraiths of the jungle. They too were men for whom Christ died. "Some one of these days we'll find a way to reach them too," Nate thought to himself.

In a few more minutes Nate was over his home base at Shell Mera, circling to land. There, near the end of the airstrip, he saw the sun shining on the aluminum roof of the wide-eaved rambling house where he knew Marj would be waiting with hot coffee and a generous breakfast. It would be good to see Kathy, and Stevie and little Philip too. He had been gone only twenty-four hours but it seemed like days.

Nate closed the throttle and dipped a wing in a gliding turn toward the runway.

2

IN THE EAGLE'S NEST

. . . I bare you on eagles' wings. . . . EXODUS 19:4

NATHANAEL SAINT, born August 30, 1923, was the seventh child in a family of eight children, all with Bible names. This reflected, in measure, the deep religious conviction of his parents who operated their household on a combination of Old Testament law and New Testament grace.

Lawrence Bradford Saint, Nate's father, always had been a sort of anomaly. An accomplished designer of stained-glass windows, his red beard, large nose, and bright blue eyes called to mind someone out of the Old Testament. Always a bit uncertain and never able to cope with the swift complexities of the modern age, whose God is Mammon, artist Saint was never quite at home in the twentieth century. He was a born artist whose soul had been enraptured by the glories of Chartres, Canterbury Cathedral, and Sainte Chapelle in Paris.

Lawrence Saint inherited his talent for art from his father, Joseph A. Saint, who continued to paint until he was eighty-six.

The atmosphere of Lawrence's home in Huntingdon Valley, north of Philadelphia, was steeped in art and religion. This was his life.

Katherine Wright Proctor, who married Lawrence Saint and became Nate's mother, was a Wellesley graduate and daughter of a successful inventor and manufacturer. She had met her future husband while both worked in their spare time in a South Philadelphia gospel mission.

At Wellesley College, Katherine had specialized in the history of art. With this background and their common interest in Christian work, it was easy for her to fall in love with gentle Lawrence Saint, the art student.

28

Katherine came from strict New England stock that maintained the firm testimony of their Puritan forebears. One of her ancestors was Prudence Wright, whose exploits of valor in the American Revolution won her a monument in Pepperell, Massachusetts. One of her grandmothers made it a practice to read an entire gospel every Sunday.

Married in 1910, the Saints spent their honeymoon in Europe where Lawrence made sketches and color studies of the stained glass in the ancient cathedrals. In the back of his mind was the hope that one day he might be able to approximate the riches of these centuries-old windows.

Together they climbed narrow ladders and spiral stairways so Saint could copy and make tracings of the windows. They clung to ledges where one false step would have meant sudden death on the stone floor far below. While Lawrence was busy with his work, his wife translated French and managed business details.

So excellent were his drawings of these windows that the Victoria and Albert Royal Museum asked him to make copies of most of them which were later included in the book *Stained Glass of the Middle Ages in England and France.*

Returning to America, Lawrence and Katherine settled in Huntingdon Valley, a small town near Philadelphia.

In the years of child-bearing and child-rearing, Katherine Saint turned her back on Chestnut Hill culture patterns, Wellesley which she felt nearly upset her faith, and all worldly social ambitions for herself and her family. She set about in her own way to live for her husband and the children God gave them. She earnestly sought to implant in her children a love for the Savior and the Bible, and at the same time encouraged them to read history and literature. She demonstrated considerable ability in the writing of poetry.

Katherine was slavishly loyal to her husband and his profession and equally devoted to the family of seven boys and one girl that clustered about them in unconventional but loving disarray.

If Lawrence Saint was "law" to his children, certainly Katherine Saint was the embodiment of "grace" and self-effacement. She gave herself freely and completely to the family, encouraging the children to develop their natural abilities and talents. She ran a rather strange household. Meals were served at odd hours, and often members of the family would eat in relays. "There was always a big pot of soup on the stove and dish washing was constantly in progress," one of the family recalls. The children were not punished for failing to make their beds, or being late to school. "Sometimes the younger boys looked pretty shabby and unkempt as they played around the house," one neighbor reported.

By the time Nate was a small boy, his father had learned the secret of making his own glass in his backyard studio furnaces. He had discovered that glass of proper color and texture, the basis of the finest stained glass, was impossible to obtain on the commercial market.

The Metropolitan Museum of Art in New York filmed an educational movie in the Saint studio. Little tow-headed Nate can be seen scampering across the studio in one of these scenes.

The peak of Lawrence Saint's artistic career came when he was commissioned to make stained-glass windows for the Washington Cathedral in the nation's capital—among them the Great North Transept Rose Window. For seven years Lawrence Saint headed the Cathedral's Department of Stained Glass. During this time he designed and made glass for fifteen windows—windows that Andrew Mellon said have "reproduced the finest work of the old world." Significant was the fact that Nate was the five-year-old model for the lad with the five barley loaves and two fishes in Christ's parable of feeding the five thousand, a panel in one of the windows in St. John's Chapel of the Cathedral. It augured the day when Nate would have a part in feeding the Indian tribespeople of the South American jungle.

With a deep sense of conviction, Lawrence Saint ruled that Sunday in the Saint household was to be rigidly observed as the Lord's Day. That meant the whole family would be in Sunday school, the morning church service, and at least one more service in the evening. Then there was prayer meeting Wednesdays.

"We didn't encourage the children's friends to come and play with them on Sunday except rarely," Lawrence Saint explains. "The family altar was the big event of Sunday afternoon. I read the Bible and each of the children prayed, beginning with the eldest. They learned from one another."

Sometimes the prayers of the smaller children were more amusing than devout. After all the others had had first chance, it was a bit difficult for little minds to think of new objects of prayer. Other times a deep kinship of family interest entered every heart. There was the time when Sam, the oldest of the eight, was having difficulties in his love affair with Jeanne Castor, and he confided it to the family. After the subject had been thoroughly covered in the family's prayers, little Nate piped up, "If Sam doesn't marry her, I will."

Dan Saint recalls how Nate used to pray slowly and thoughtfully, "Lord, show us the right way."

On Sunday, the Saint children were not permitted to study their lessons, nor were the Sunday papers allowed in the home. When the boys wanted to play baseball, or wrestle in the yard, Lawrence Saint consistently vetoed it. However, tossing a ball, and long hikes in the country were always in order any time.

The rules were not always strictly obeyed, Sam confesses today. Occasionally the boys slipped away over the back fence to read the Sunday "funnies" at a neighbor's house. Then there was the time the boys climbed to the peak of the roof to watch World War I airplanes performing at a nearby airmeet.

Outside the special Sunday rules the children were permitted to do almost anything they pleased. No one panicked when an eight-year-old boy shinnied up to the peak of the barn roof, or was found studying the gears at the top of the windmill. On warm summer evenings the dinner bell often called the boys and Rachel from the top branches of the tallest tree.

The parents taught their children that alcohol and tobacco were poisons, that movies glamorized crime and stunted the imagination. Dancing and gambling of every sort were taboo for the Saint children. Television had not yet arrived but radio programs were carefully censored.

"We held up Christ as Savior and tried in every way to get the Bible into them," Lawrence Saint recalls. "I dramatized the Bible stories, working out models with flour and matchsticks. To encourage Bible reading a penny a chapter was offered the children. They could pay themselves out of the big glass jar of pennies kept for that purpose."

A favorite aunt, with different ideas about the social amenities, never quite understood the carefree operation of her sister's household. She chided the Saints gently for forcing religion down the throats of their children. She told of meeting little Sam on the street one day and asking him where he was going. "To prayer meeting, darn it," the little fellow replied.

Whether Aunt Jane was right or wrong in thinking the Saint children were getting their religion like castor oil can be debated. Some would explain the Saints' method as legalistic Christianity but they were deeply concerned about living for Christ, and keeping themselves and their children "unspotted from the world." For the record, it is worth noting that three of the eight children became missionaries and a fourth became a preacher.

All eight, without exception, in adult life remained firm believers in the conservative Christian theology of their parents.

The Saints felt it was deceitful to tell their children anything but the truth about Santa Claus or the stork. Instead they reverently told them about human birth even when the children were quite young. The evolutionary theory, anathema to Bible-believing Christians, was denounced.

Lawrence and Katherine Saint counterbalanced all this strict regimen with elaborately planned wholesome recreation. In the backyard Lawrence Saint constructed a double-tracked roller coaster, complete with humps and curves. He also erected a fifty-foot rope swing from a tall tree. Even though it attracted children from the entire neighborhood, the Saints were happy because it was the kind of fun they wanted for the children.

Then there were trips to the Jersey Shore at Ocean City where the whole family enjoyed the beach together. There were picnics and hymn sings and sailing on the Delaware River. The boys went fishing and swimming in the summer, tramping barefoot over the hill, down across the open fields and through the woods to the old swimming hole. The boys hid their clothes in a thicket and swam "in the raw" the way boys were meant to swim in the quiet water of the Pennypack under the branches of overhanging trees. And the last one in was always a rotten egg. This was one phase of family life that Nate's sister Rachel did not get in on. Sledding, skating, and trapping filled the winter months. Two of the older boys once pulled a skunk out from under a porch by a trap on one of his hind legs!

When the children asked to sleep on the roof of the rambling old house, their mother was game. She called in a carpenter to build bunk beds out of board slats and put a fence around a flat roof on the back of the house over the kitchen. Lawrence was seldom consulted on such mundane matters. But he did occasionally climb through the second-floor window onto the "sleeping porch" to lie with the rest of the family, listening to the crickets and counting falling stars as they all drifted off to sleep. Even today, Sam says, "If you have never been awakened at 2 A.M. by that first drop of rain on your cheek—well, you just haven't lived."

This was the atmosphere in which Nate grew up—the household in which he came to live. His home "nest" was the strongest influence on his life but there were other influences upon him in those childhood years in Huntingdon Valley.

3

BOY IN A HURRY

As an eagle stirreth up her nest. . . . Deuteronomy 32:11

"Thanny," as Nate was called during his early years, had long wavy golden hair, rosy cheeks, blue eyes, and dark lashes. People exclaimed about his flawless complexion and the perfection of his features. He was an unusually beautiful child.

It was a shock to his mother when he received his first haircut. She wept; then, in family tradition, wrote a poem that began:

Gone are those curls that framed a face so sweet . . .

Whether her verse was free or incomplete, she had expressed her grieved feelings. Little Thanny was growing up.

Once when the Saints were leaving a Billy Sunday meeting, Lawrence lifted Nate high in his arms. The evangelist leaned over and picked up the little boy and gave him an affectionate pat on the head.

Rachel, Nate's only sister, who was nine years older than he, gave him her special care. She took him for walks and remembers still the picture of the small boy trudging off to the creek with his fishing pole over his shoulder and a can of worms in his hand.

Rachel filled Nate's mind with missionary stories, telling him about John Paton among the cannibals; Livingstone, Judson, and others. These she read from his favorite book, *Fifty Missionary Stories Every Child Should Know*.

But all was not sweetness and light. Like everyone Nate had an Adamic nature too, his parents said. His father asked him one day to pick up a piece of paper that he had thrown on the floor. Nate refused, even though the request was repeated several times. "But I don't wants to," he told his father. Lawrence Saint missed both

34

Sunday school and church that morning in his attempt to make the child obey. Nate submitted only after several whippings with a little green whip that hung in a handy place in the Saint home. They were strong believers in corporal punishment. Nate's father often quoted: "Spare the rod and spoil the child."

Nate's brother Phil recalls some of the setting of Nate's childhood:

"There was seldom a time when there was no sickness in our home. There were weeks when measles and chicken pox went from one to another. Dad was an invalid for a number of years and the family income suffered. Clothes were patched and handed down from one to another."

In those years, Phil remembers, Nate "became so bashful that he would often hide under a bed or in a closet when visitors came to our home. As a lad he was no doubt as mischievous as any of us, but one of the characteristics of his boyhood was his hatred of anything mean or sordid. Even as a child he took his stand as a little Christian soldier."

The missionary who would one day contact the Aucas was not always so brave. He was playing with a neighbor boy with a small wagon on a steep driveway of the Presbyterian Church in Huntingdon Valley. As the wagon was coasting down the grade toward the pike, with Stan up front, Nate grabbed for the back of the wagon and missed. He felt sure that Stan would be hit by a car he saw approaching. Through the quick action of Russell Barrett, driver of the car, Stan suffered only a broken leg.

But Nate, terrified, had not waited to see what would happen. Instead he raced across the lawns for home and shut himself in his room like a frightened animal.

When Nate was seven years old something happened that changed the whole course of his life. His brother Sam took him for an airplane ride at the nearby airport. The little fellow could barely see over the edge of the open cockpit. Later, when Nate was about ten, Sam let him take the controls of another airplane, a larger cabin plane where they sat side by side at the controls. Nate's eyes shone as he felt the airplane respond to his tug on the wheel. From then on he could never get enough of airplanes. They were

35

even more thrilling to Nate than his father's studio and the glass furnaces in the backyard where the secrets of thirteenth-century glass-making were being unveiled.

"Thanny is a dear boy," his father wrote to a friend in France. "He is now eleven years old, and leans toward aviation. Sometimes he works in my tiny bedroom and fills the room with the smell of banana oil, but I am happy if he is happy. He has an interest in financial things which is most fortunate, as no one else in the family has much concern for money. Rachel, who helped in the management of the home, gave Nate one of three tiny bedrooms that had been added to the back of the house. She assigned this room to Nate as a special place for his 'operations.' Characteristically Nate posted a sign on the door that said, 'MESS OUT EVERYBODY!!'"

Nate's younger brother Ben, the youngest of the eight children, remembers some of Nate's childhood peccadilloes. For one thing, he did not think that Nate was like the biblical Nathanael who was without guile. "He'd tease me and then I'd lose my temper and we would have a fight. I remember Nate came along and found me enjoying an ice cream cone. 'Come on, stingy, give me a lick of your ice cream,' he said. I held it out to him, and he took one big bite, leaving an empty cone. He ran off choking, with me half crying, half laughing, trying to catch him to punch him in the nose.

"Nate, right or wrong," Ben adds, "never was a quitter. He often wrestled and boxed. I remember one evening in the playroom when we were wrestling. For a change I was on the top and had a good hold. He could not break out of it but he wouldn't give up. I thought he might break a blood vessel so I finally let go."

Ben also describes Nate's skill in shopping. Before Christmas they would go shopping together for electric train equipment. Nate would not buy, but would take careful note of the prices. After Christmas when prices were down, Nate would do his buying. "Get-a-penny-Than," his brothers called him.

What the Saints lacked in money they made up in ingenuity. During the depression years Phil and Nate often worked together on the electric train they called the "B and T and P Depression

Railroad." (The letters stood for Ben, Thanny, and Phil.) They had sufficient track for the trains but no money for scenery or extras. They wadded wet newspapers and squeezed it into shapes for surrounding scenery which was then painted by artist brother Phil. Nate's brother Dave describes him as "the kid who always had a project." Several years running he won prizes at the annual hobby show held in nearby Abington. A major project was the construction of a miniature railroad locomotive and tender out of scrap brass.

Daniel Saint, fourth child of the family, recalls the six-foot glider Nate made from a drawing in a magazine. They flew it like a kite at the local high school athletic field, holding it with heavy cord.

Brother Steve, sixth in line and next older than Nate, remembers best the sailboat Nate designed and built. There never was another like it. It was about eight feet long and nearly as wide. Nate lettered the name *Sinbad* on the transom and listed its home port as Bagdad. The odd little boat reminded Steve of the bit about "Three Men in a Tub." To the surprise of everyone, Nate's unique boat with its wide beam and unusually large sail would lift out of the water and skim along on the Delaware River, often leaving the sailors of more conventional craft talking to themselves in the *Sinbad's* wake.

On his own Nate found ways of soaking and bending the mahogany boards to fit the careful plans he had drawn. He sewed the sails on his mother's sewing machine and made all the metal fittings by hand.

Nate liked to tell of the time when he was permitted to take the only family car apart. No one, including Nate himself, was sure it would ever operate again, but after three days and several skinned knuckles it ran almost as well as before.

One of his companions of those years was Merle Ivins. They played with model railroads and airplanes and took radios apart. Both were newsboys and often swapped customers in line with the territory and their respective routes.

Merle tells about the time he and Nate sneaked up to a house in the neighborhood while its occupants were celebrating loudly.

They tied the doorknobs to porch posts so the doors could not be opened from inside. On another occasion guests of the same home came out after a party and found strange things happening as they tried to drive off in their cars. Heads muddled by drink, they finally realized the cars were tied together with ropes around their bumpers. The two boys peering through the hedge thought this was a great piece of business.

The Saints for many years attended the Presbyterian Church in Huntingdon Valley. Later they transferred their membership to the Bethany Baptist Church in Fox Chase. Sometimes the church seemed dull to the line of youngsters in the second row on the right. Nate was usually by the side of his sister Rachel. But there came a day when he wanted to sit with the boys, especially his friend Carey Ballbach, the pastor's son. On a certain Sunday morning Rachel noticed that Nate and Carey were giggling in church. After the service she reprimanded her brother, who stoutly said, "You'd laugh too if you had seen what we saw. Deacon Amby had his wig on crooked."

Up to the time he was thirteen Nate had not publicly professed his faith in Christ. In the summer of 1936 he went to Percy Crawford's Pinebrook camp in the Poconos. There, at one of the Saturday night fireside meetings, he testified to his trust in Christ.

That same year he gave a talk at a young people's meeting in the Bethany Church. The following notes were saved by his mother.

"1. Paul said in Acts, 'Believe on the Lord Jesus Christ, and thou shalt be saved, and thy house.' I believe, therefore I am saved and heaven-bound.

"2. Being saved, I have a purpose because Jesus said, 'Go ye into all the world and preach the gospel to every creature.'

"3. Having a purpose, being in the fight against Satan, and belonging to God's army of Christian soldiers, I must be in training. This training I get at Bethany. Here the Word of God is opened wide and taught clearly, wholly, and simply.

"4. I enjoy school because it further prepares me to serve Jesus and enter into his work of winning souls.

"5. To me Bible school means more than silver or gold because these are corruptible, but salvation is eternal.

"6. I want this Bible training so I can say later, like the Apostle Paul, 'I have fought a good fight, I have finished my course, I have kept the faith: Henceforth there is laid up for me a crown of righteousness, which the Lord, the righteous judge, shall give me at that day: and not to me only, but unto all them also that love his appearing.'"

When he was fourteen Nate was stricken with osteomyelitis. The infection centered in his right leg. It kept him in bed for several months. Even when he was confined to his bed with much pain, Rachel recalls, he kept up his various projects. He made a huge papier-mâché head of Mussolini in caricature, big enough to wear over his head. Some of the time, he had to creep about on all fours because he could not walk.

Whenever the pain became unbearable Nate talked with the Lord in the quiet of his bedchamber. He told Him that he was ready to die, but if the Lord permitted him to live he would turn over his whole life to Him. It was only a boy's declaration of spiritual intention, but it was a promise Nate never forgot—a promise that had a bearing on the turning-point decisions of his later life.

In time Nate recovered and suffered no lameness. He soon took a Sunday school class and taught boys who were only a few years younger than he. He served as president of the Baptist Young People's Union.

While Nate was in high school, evangelist Anthony Zeoli conducted a series of meetings at Bethany Church. Nate was so taken with Zeoli's messages that he had to choose between eligibility for the basketball team and attendance at the meetings. He chose the latter and lost his chance to make the team because he missed practice.

Grounded in the belief that social dancing was sinful, Nate would not attend school parties. He was called before the principal but refused to budge on his convictions. Eventually he was excused but not without considerable joshing from his classmates.

"High school was getting extremely dull by the time my senior year rolled around," Nate wrote. "I had been trying to work at night while going to school during the day, so I dropped out of school, took a daytime job in a machine-welding and iron-forging shop, and finished off the high school work in a couple of months at night school in Philadelphia."

On Nate's first time away from home, he delivered a truck to the mountain country in the far southwest corner of Virginia for a family of home missionaries. On the way back he got tired of hitchhiking. He had been told how to hop a freight. Unfortunately he had not been briefed on when to hop off a freight, so at Bluefield, Virginia, he was arrested with several hoboes.

Brought before the judge he was fined ten dollars and ten days. Nate spoke up, and when the judge saw that he was not a professional hobo, he changed the sentence to ten dollars *or* ten days. "Get-a-penny-Than" decided he would save his money and go to jail. From the jail he wrote a series of three postcards to the folks at home. Concerning the food: "The potatoes are so hard I can bounce them on the floor." On the second card, he sketched a rope ladder from the window; said he wished he had his Bible. On the third card he had written: "FREE!" in huge capital letters. It was the nearest Nate ever came to a brush with the law.

Nate worked as a tree trimmer, and then in a gas station. In 1941, when he was eighteen, he went to work at the Flying Dutchman Air Service on the outskirts of Philadelphia. He took his first flying lesson on June 16 of that year. From then on planes became as much a part of him as his two capable hands or his mop of blond hair. He bought a small plane to build up flying experience and took his brothers up for rides.

His brother Sam, now an American Airlines captain, had kept an eye on Nate. He knew that Nate had mechanical aptitudes and was interested in airplanes, so he helped him obtain a job as apprentice mechanic for American Airlines at LaGuardia Field.

"I'll never forget the day I left home to work in New York," Nate wrote. "Mother and Dad had seen the older ones leave home and return and could hide their feelings somewhat, but Ben was different. He bit his lip and tried like everything but when he ducked out of the kitchen with his eyes full of water and his face straining to hide what he figured he was too old for now, I knew how he felt. Well, you know how it is—we grew up together. I couldn't swallow all the way over to New York, and the wind from that old roadster of mine watered my ears with the tears I couldn't hold back."

Sam's wife Jeanne records Nate's arrival in New York:

"When Nate first came to work for American Airlines he lived with us on Long Island. 'Kelly,' as we called him then, was a boy who constantly appeared as though he had important things on his mind and was eager to get to them. Table conversation was full of airplanes. I wearied of nuts and bolts for dinner.

"He loved our four-year-old daughter Eileen, and typical of the one-for-all-and-all-for-one tradition of the Saint family, he entered into her upbringing with seriousness and enthusiasm. He used to take her into the den and close the door and talk to her about her behavior. Eileen, a grown-up teenager today, still remembers those sessions with Uncle Kelly.

"When Nate was hungry it was with real urgency. If dinner was not ready when he was, he would hang around the kitchen, making it very plain that if things weren't hurried up, it was likely he wouldn't survive."

Because of his odd working hours Nate rented a basement room near the airport. He was careful with the money he earned, ironing his own clothes and cooking his own meals in his tiny room. The money he saved went into the purchase of tools.

"Working inside for a year in New York—even though it was in a big hangar opening on the airport, bay, and New York skyline—was almost unbearable," Nate said, "so I mapped out an escape that involved joining the Air Corps. The fact that fathers were being drafted and that I had no dependents made the idea make sense to me."

4

EVOLUTION OF A
YARDBIRD

Oh that I had wings. . . . PSALM 55:6

NATE was just nineteen when he voluntarily renounced his draft-free status and was reclassified "1-A without appeal." He was sharply reprimanded for this action by his employers. But Nate was unperturbed.

"It looked like the Eagle was about to lay the golden egg— $25,000 worth of pilot training," Nate wrote to a friend. His ambition to become a flier consumed all lesser lusts in his life.

After storing away his mechanic's tools in the family home at Huntingdon Valley, Nate spent the Christmas holidays of 1942 visiting friends and making the rounds of church-sponsored parties.

He pulled many wires to enlist in the Army Air Corps, but each of his persistent efforts failed. He even made two fruitless trips to Washington. Waiting for his induction papers increased Nate's impatience. Finally, he visited the draft board offices in Jackson Heights, New York, and found that his papers were ready to be mailed. He grabbed them eagerly, jubilantly. Formal induction took place at Grand Central Palace in New York on December 30, 1942.

There was just one hitch. After his six-hour physical, Nate's draft papers were marked: "Accepted limited service." The doctors had found the scars of the attack of osteomyelitis that had nearly caused the loss of his right leg five years earlier.

Although it was an advance warning of a future experience that would change his entire life, there was nothing to indicate that Nate was upset by the restriction placed upon him by the Army. On New Year's Day he took his girl friend, whom we shall call

Alice Brown, to the 1943 Ice Follies in Philadelphia's Arena. Earlier in the day he had gone horseback riding with some of his brothers and their friends.

Nate's sincere interest in spiritual matters is revealed by his diary which records that he listened on the radio to the Old Fashioned Revival Hour in the course of his final weekend at his Huntingdon Valley home, and two nights before he was drafted joined a Bethany Church group in conducting a service at the Brotherhood Mission, Philadelphia.

After bidding his parents good-by, Nate went to New York City, then out to Port Washington to spend the night at the home of his brother Sam. On January 6, 1943, he was "herded to Penn Station, New York, with about seventy others." There the draftees boarded World War I-style passenger coaches and headed for Camp Upton, New York, some sixty miles to the east on Long Island.

Marching to the music of the camp band, the draftees entered the reception hall to wait long hours for their processing. During a quick snack in the mess hall, canny Nate hid a frankfurter in his pocket for any "emergency." That night Soldier Saint slept in his clothes in the "half-cabin, half-tent" to which he had been assigned. It was bitter cold and the potbellied stove in the cabin just wasn't up to its job.

"Have been 'processed' and I do mean processed," he wrote Sam and Jeanne. "Boy, oh boy, no wonder these birds get tough. It's quite exciting to discover that you are a number and one in thousands at that. Took I.Q., and was interviewed yesterday. . . . They wanted me to give up flying but I didn't weaken.

"Medical Officer said that if I ask for re-exam I can get rid of 'limited service.' Am going to see where I'm shipped and wait until I get a chance to think."

To his mother he wrote:

"Keep on praying. The Lord is blessing above measure. . . . Surely is a different life, but I'm convinced will prove plenty toughening. . . . My shoes don't match—one is a stern-wheeler and the other is a schooner. Bought some after-shave lotion. After you shave with a G.I. razor and cold water, you need something to take the place of your skin!"

To his father, who was then fifty-eight, he quipped:

"Pop, ya better watch out or the draft will get ya! You ought to see some of the specimens of humanity that are dragging uniforms around. . . . Nobody's safe now unless they are proclaimed half-dead."

In other letters and in his diary there were evidences that he maintained a quiet but faithful Christian witness.

"Had a very interesting chat with three Jewish fellows, one Orthodox. . . . Am reading Bible regularly," he said.

"I visited Catholic mass and got a preview of Protestant meetings by talking to the chaplain's assistant. . . . On Sunday afternoon I took a walk and read my Bible in a clearing in the woods, leaning on a pine tree. I finished Matthew."

In most of his letters Nate praised Army food, but he confided to his sister Rachel that the chow at Camp Upton was pretty bad. "I'll bet the Army could teach a guy to think dish water was delicious."

Army discipline brought no terror to Nate. "You get a feeling of confidence out of being able to stand at attention for five minutes without moving your eyes," he told his sister.

Thus began the three years of Army life that would mean so much in the formation of Nate's character. There were rough times ahead that would prepare him for the greater disciplines of Christian warfare. But at this stage in his life, Nate still had his heart set on a flying career.

"I was a Christian, read my Bible every day, but I was awfully ambitious for a fellow that thought he was about to be a hot pilot," he later admitted. "All the ambitions of the last ten years were wrapped up and focused on the prospect of becoming a flier."

On January 15, Sam and Jeanne Saint bade Nate farewell as he left New York for Camp Luna in Las Vegas, New Mexico. "Maybe Sam didn't tell you what awful canal boat shoes he wore," Jeanne wrote Nate's mother. "His coat looked as though it had been slept in for a week. He had been living in a tent and everything had to be kept in two duffel bags. But he looked quite handsome—in spite of his nose—in his little cap.

"He was tired, but content, I think, and excited about the long trip ahead. He was shipped out as a specialist and not herded into a troop train with two thousand others."

The trip west permitted a stop-off in Chicago where Nate discovered the Pacific Garden Mission on South State Street. His diary mentions nothing else about Chicago.

"I had visions of lying on the sand with my shirt off, getting a nice tan," Nate wrote when he reached the New Mexico camp. "When we arrived, there were about three inches of snow and the first night the temperature dipped to 23 below zero. We are about 800 feet higher than the town which is at a 6,400-foot elevation.

"I'm in the airline pool here, among nearly a dozen 'American' men. . . . Classification officers here seemed impressed with my I.Q., student pilot certificate, airplane mechanic's license, experience, etc. . . . They have recommended to the C.O. that I be reexamined to get rid of the 'limited service.' Am now carrying out that Army expression, 'Hurry up and wait.'

"I'll only apply for flight training if there is a good chance in maintaining connection with the A.T.C. (Air Transport Command). If that doesn't look good, I am eligible for Officers Candidate School. . . . I'll be here for basic training."

First assignment for the aspiring Army pilot: latrine duty. But he took it in his stride without griping. "It's like the fellows say . . . 'If you don't like it here (in the Army) why don'tcha resign?'"

On the third day at Camp Luna, Nate "saw a worn Bible on the table at mess last night. Found it belongs to a big southern, square-jawed sergeant . . . the kind of 'sarge' fellows hope for." This was the beginning of dozens of friendships he made during his Army years. Some he met in the Army already were vital Christians, or they were soon moving in that direction under Nate's influence.

"All the Lord has to do to get me into flying is give me permission by opening the door," he wrote his mother. "From the way I bumped around when first trying to enlist, I know that without His approval I can't do anything, and with His permission, 'I can do all things through Christ which strengtheneth me.'"

45

As was to be his custom whenever his duties would permit, Nate was a regular church attendant. "Went to church in town with the mess sarge," he wrote home. "Soldier boy that went with us got saved!"

To his mother who had written about a family friend who was concerned about the spiritual status of her soldier son, Nate advised:

"Point out to Mrs. M—— that although thousands of miles separate her from him, she can still fill a responsibility by getting right with the Lord herself and then plead for her son. . . . I think he knows well what the score is but I'll do my best by letter to get him to make a decision for the Lord. We grew up together and he knows I'm no angel. Yet he must have noticed that when I accepted the Lord, we no longer had common interests. . . . Mrs. M——'s only opportunity now is on her knees."

Meanwhile the urge to fly was still strong. "Pray that the Lord will have His way in this flying business. Seems as though His stamp of approval is 100 per cent 'go ahead,' but I'm not calling personal interests the Lord's will."

It appeared he was one step nearer his goal when on February 5 he received an application for Air Corps Cadet Training which he promptly filled out and sent home for parental consent.

Then on Valentine's Day came the word that he would be shipped out the following day. "Whoopee! I'm shipping again," he wrote in his diary.

Nate was assigned to the Douglas Service School and quartered in the Grand Hotel at Santa Monica. Studies were to be centered on C-47s, the large cargo planes that played such an important part in World War II's logistics. School hours were from 2 P.M. to 1 A.M.

True to form, while he was in the Los Angeles area, Nate hunted up the evangelical churches.

Since the classroom work was easy for him and the Southern California climate mild, Nate felt that he had moved in on Utopia. He wrote home: "If I could describe this beautiful country justly, I'm afraid you'd all enlist so I won't even try."

But his concern was always on the coveted goal: "Pray about my cadet exams. It now seems that I won't be able to take them here because things are so rushed. But I want to be accepted before I get to Africa or somewhere!"

He was graduated from the Douglas Service School on March 23, and transferred to the Long Beach barracks for a week before being sent to the Modification Center at Daggett in the Mojave Desert.

One of the wartime workers at the Center was a cultured woman, Mrs. Clayton Montgomery, mother of four daughters and wife of an ordained Presbyterian minister, turned schoolteacher. When Nate attended the Community Church at Daggett, Sadie Montgomery invited him to her home. This was the beginning of a friendship—between this motherly woman and Nate—that was to last throughout his Army service. Furthermore, the friendship was to play an important part in Nate's future happiness.

But at this juncture Nate was interested chiefly in his new flying clothes that had just been issued. "You ought to see the outfit we get! Complete fleece-lined flying suit and helmet, fleece-lined leather flying boots coated with waterproof vulcanized rubber, plain leather helmet and a beautiful leather jacket and gloves. Pair of suitcases (Air Corps style)!" His letters fairly radiated: "Don't think about cookies, Mom, not as long as you can write. Without a letter from 'Mom' once in a while the best cookies in the world are tasteless. Besides I'd have to shoulder my rifle to walk guard duty by 'em till they were gone! I won't complain if you'll pass around my address. I haven't heard from 'civilization' for quite awhile. I don't even know how the war is progressing."

Yet there were lurking fears about his old leg trouble. In one letter to his mother Nate described a fellow soldier who survived an intricate operation to a leg that had been broken in fifteen places. "Mom, I'll never again worry about my leg," he said.

Then came shipping orders to Jefferson Barracks, just outside St. Louis. Like many another G.I. in World War II Nate was touring the country at government expense. He had been in the Army but four months and had gone from New York to New

Mexico, to three centers in California, and now he was in Missouri. "Please note change of address," he wrote. "Never get bored in this man's army."

A few days after he arrived at the Barracks, he was sent out on parade. Even though the Saints were rock-ribbed Republicans, it was understandable that he recorded in his diary: "President Roosevelt passed within ten feet."

Family letters among the Saints were simple, frank, and direct to the point. It was perfectly natural that he should tell his mother, who was always health-conscious, the state of his well-being. (She had a package of dates waiting for him on his arrival at Camp Luna.)

"Was constipated on arrival but calisthenics loosened me up and sent me to the chow house as hungry as a bear," he dutifully reported.

The tempo of World War II had reached full strength as the United States and her Allies were hitting the enemy hard on two fronts. Of Jefferson Barracks Nate wrote:

"This place is literally a madhouse. They're sending too many men here for the permanent personnel to handle. Basic pools are being broken up and reassembled into overseas pools which have overflowed into tents. It spells clearly 'Big Push' and the push to the finish. We may not be in the Solomons but we know this is serious business and these 30-30s aren't made to hoe potatoes.

"I know that the Lord is still running things, but sometimes I'm so shortsighted. The coming months are going to be hard on guys like me everywhere. Pray for us. We need patience and faith. I'm the army's own—lock, stock, and barrel—but I'm the Lord's own —heart, soul, and spirit.

"Why doesn't someone write to me? No news of the gang at home makes me a bit of an orphan. Maybe if you could see the mail line I sweat out looking for your little postal full of odds 'n' ends, it would speak more honestly than my moody pen. I'm in the mood that's only excusable for a guy who's just been given the cold shoulder by his best gal . . . but I've been given nothing from nobody. The Army is like a jailhouse for a guy who likes to make plans and do things. I'm convinced that the Lord works things out for our good. Sometimes I wonder whether I've learned in whatsoever state I am, therewith to be content?"

Nate's humor constantly sparkled in the flow of letters that sped home to Huntingdon Valley and were passed around for the whole family to read.

"The fellow doing laundry in the sink next to me got a kick out of this so I'll pass it on," he reported. "Beside the mess kit, I had a pair of old socks to wash. Method? First you wash the socks and then use one of them for a wash cloth to do the mess kit. I said, 'If only Mom could see me now—last month's sock in tomorrow's mess kit!'"

In a more sober tone he described some of the camp activity:

"Did I tell you that we went through the gas chamber again? The Allies seriously expect gas warfare to come with invasion. Of all the diabolical ways to fight, I guess gas is the worst. The lectures and instruction here take on a more serious attitude every day. These guys aren't here for a tea party and they all know it.

"So much for that—now to get sentimental and wish for someone else's vocabulary so I could describe the fairyland I just walked through. Rows and rows of tents standing still and straight in the moonlight. Dim lights in some. Air fresh, clear, and snappy. Long passenger train with long rows of lighted windows pointing toward a ghostlike, twisting column of steam. The engineer probably doesn't even know the destination of the train. The boys, hundreds of them, with their duffel bags on their shoulders are filing past the cars—no idea where they'll be before the sun comes over the hill."

Nate's dexterity and understanding of things mechanical showed up in classes dealing with weapons. He described instruction in dismantling a Colt 45 Army pistol:

"The instructor showed us how to 'field strip' it. (Take it apart as far as possible without special equipment.) When I got hold of one I did the same thing I did yesterday with the Tommy gun. Took it apart, studied it, and *put it together again with my eyes closed.*

"I think it boils down to the fact that I've always been curious about the theory of mechanical gadgets and from having pulled stuff apart since I've been old enough to be curious. I remember pulling the Olds apart—guess you folks thought I knew something about it—I did after I got it together and saw it run, almost to my hidden surprise. It sure has been good to have been trusted with anything I wanted to tinker with. . . . When I watch other fellows struggle, push, tug, jam, hammer, and swear at things that should fall together, I feel I should say thanks for your willingness to lay your household gadgets on the altar of chance and call it sacrifice to education."

There followed letters telling about a persistent cough that was annoying him. He described his ailment in minute detail, asking his mother to send him medicine. That was because the Saints, in addition to being ardent followers of health foods, were strong believers in homeopathic medicine. Nate wrote to his mother:

"Three guesses as to what ails me. I don't know either but like some others around here I'm getting mighty suspicious because I'm in a scarlet fever ward! That accounts for that cold, bum appetite, fever, and weakness."

Then came Nate's jubilant letter announcing that he had been accepted for cadet training. He had appeared before an examining board but kept it secret until he had heard he was accepted. He described his gaucherie before the board.

"It was so funny even the Major smiled," Nate told his parents. "Airplanes I know but this military courtesy and formality just about kill me. When reporting to the board of officers you have to walk in without turning your back on the officers to close the door, walk to within one pace of the desk, snap to attention, salute and hold the salute while you say, 'Saint, Nathanael, 28th Training Group, reporting to Aviation Cadet Board, Sir.' When the salute is returned, you drop it and stand at attention until given, 'At ease.' Well, with saying my name backward and being afraid I'd slip somewhere, I managed to go blank in the middle of my report. Instead of standing at attention like a good military dunce, I hauled down my salute and went to 'at ease' without being told. I knew I had muffed up the military procedure, so I just looked at the Major with an involuntary smile that said, 'I know I've muffed; now what?' He just smiled approvingly at my consciousness of my errors and said, 'Suppose you go out and try to do it right once.'

"The next time I came in serious and determined, and sailed through the rigmarole in great style. . . . After he had returned my salute and asked me to sit down, I relaxed and another grin shot across my mush that must have looked like, 'I did it this time! Wow!'

"All the officers were smiling through the brief interview. They seemed more interested in my unique military performance than my knowledge of airplanes. I couldn't help laughing once. The Captain had leaned back and paused to think up another question to heave at me; then he broke out in a big grin and said, 'You're a bit nervous, aren't you?' I broke out with a bigger grin and said, 'I sure am nervous, Sir.' They got a big kick out of that.

"They probably were in a good mood because I got about the highest score in our group on the written exam.

"While I still didn't know the outcome of the interview, I talked to a classification man who told me that they wash fellows out for a 'lack of military bearing' which made me wonder very seriously whether I'd make it."

While he was still at Jefferson Barracks Nate received his medal for marksmanship. "Looks okay," he said, "hanging under my wings like something from a five-and-ten-cent store."

There were few references to Nate's love life during the months at Jefferson Barracks except for two mentions of dating Alice while he was home on furlough during the spring of 1943. There were short diary notations: "Went for a stroll with Alice after choir practice" and "Took Alice riding and to Willow Grove Park."

Again: "Took Alice to the Planetarium ('Music of the Spheres') and said a six-months' goodnight!"

But his real love was airplanes—and cadet training lay just ahead.

5

SHATTERING OF A DREAM

. . . the wings thereof were plucked. . . . DANIEL 7:4

NATE's hopes were high when he left Jefferson Barracks to board a troop train bound for Sioux City, Iowa.

Several days before he had written his mother: "Am all packed up and ready to leave. I'm almost afraid to be too jubilant until I'm on the train and rolling along. . . . My bags are packed and locked in the shipping warehouse."

When the troop train pulled into Sioux City, Nate, with fifty others, was taken to Morningside College where he was enrolled in the Air Cadet Training Program. Nate had reached the goal for which he had planned, schemed, and worked so hard. He was entering the last lap in the race to become an Army pilot.

"These tailor-fitted shirts are plenty snazzy," he told his mother. "They fit like a corset."

In the midst of his exhilaration Nate, according to his lifelong habits, found time for spiritual things. "My two roommates read their Bibles. The older fellow is a Lutheran—a real Christian."

The Lutheran was Robert Bjorklund of Duluth and the third cadet was Ralph McCready from Pennsylvania.

"There were several times when Nate and I had devotions and on our knees had prayer together," Bjorklund later recalled. "I consider this one of the most enjoyable times of my stay in the aviation cadets program. Meeting Nate strengthened my Christian belief."

Nate passed his college entrance examinations and plunged into the heavy schedule that characterized the wartime cadet training programs. There were lectures, drilling, calisthenics—a strenuous regimen, but Nate seemed to thrive on it. "I was on K.P. today," Nate wrote, "or 'mess manager,' as they call it here."

On August 27 Nate with the other cadets of his class engaged in a two-mile cross-country hike as a part of their regular physical training program. Before he retired that night, Nate noticed a reddening around the scar on his right leg caused by the osteomyelitis attack when he was fourteen. He also noticed that the gland in his groin was slightly enlarged and tender.

In one heart-sickening moment Nate realized that all his plans had been thwarted. This was the sudden thud of circumstances that would put away forever his hope of becoming an Army pilot.

"I didn't say a word to my roommate," Nate recounted, "but jumped into bed and turned out the light without a word. There I barred myself tightly into the small, dark confines of my heart, which had now become a dungeon for solitary confinement. Except for the tossing, and choking, and sighing, no one would have known the thing that was almost overwhelming me. . . . I was heartbroken. There wasn't any escape."

That night Nate wrote in his diary: "Disappointment—lessons—resolutions—new horizons."

Then at the bottom of the page: "May His will be done."

To his "dearest Mama," a term he used only when he was ill, Nate wrote a characteristic letter:

"The way the situation has changed during the last couple of days reminds me of that dog in Bryn Athyn, that used to chase me when I rode past with my newspapers. I remember how he put it in reverse the day I dropped a firecracker in front of him. He skidded about ten feet forward while running backward before he stopped.

"I've just stopped—which direction I'll take off I don't know. I've had it in reverse since Friday evening when I noticed a slight enlargement of that gland in the groin. Almost immediately I noticed a slight reddening on my bum leg which since has all but disappeared including gland swelling, but the doc says I can't fly for the Army and that's that!!

"Saturday A.M. while in 'quarters' one of the boys told me I'd been moved up a class with nine others out of eighty men, which meant I was to have been flying by now. Had a good record—no gigs (demerits), not delinquent in class work, etc.

"I've spent three days loafing and getting used to the new perspective. After a month of tense concentration on winged hopes, an eclipse of those hopes left me in a sort of daze . . .

"I'm not forgetting, 'Boast not thyself of tomorrow; for thou knowest not what a day may bring forth,' but I think the Lord wants us to pray and plan to the very best of our ability, using what He has given us, even if He has to reverse those plans.

"Turned twenty yesterday. . . . It was a kind of rough birthday present to be told that instead of going to the airport for my first day of flying that I was going to the base for an X-ray."

Nate who was no musician himself jokingly wrote to Ben:

"Grease up that old trombone, boy, because one of these days I might breeze in and give you a few pointers."

The end of Nate's flying career was a milestone in his spiritual history. From the human standpoint it was a tragedy, but Nate later could look back and realize that it was the hand of God upon his life.

"In the following days pending hospitalization," he told a friend several years later, "I fought bitterly to surrender my monster will to the One I knew it belonged to. The attempt was a failure, and I slumped into a sort of dazed numbness, not caring much for anything."

But Nate showed emotional and spiritual resiliency as he soon began to reorient himself to the changed circumstances. He thought at first that he might be discharged on disability grounds. He also had hoped that he might be transferred to the Air Transport Command at some station near his home in the East, but neither of these plans worked out.

After a few days Nate was sent to the Sioux City Army Air Base for hospitalization.

"Put that soup back in the Frigidaire because I'm returning to duty, but not flying duty," he wrote his mother who thought he was coming home. "This reversal of events is driving me nuts but I'm getting pliable and mentally adaptable."

For a month Nate was attached to the 354th Base Squadron of the Army Air Corps and assigned to nonflying duties at Morning-side College.

In response to a letter from his sister Rachel who had written that maybe the Lord wanted to use him "to bring life rather than death to others," Nate wrote:

"We're here to give our lives that folks at home might live physically as Jesus gave His life that we might live spiritually. Though few soldiers see it this way, here is the Christian soldier's outlook: He's not going over to kill but to safeguard life at home; to give his life if necessary. . . . I guess there are dozens of physical-spiritual parallels but remember nobody's going anywhere to kill.

"If the Lord wants me to preach . . . He hasn't shown me yet, and I know He can make it clear if it is His will. If you think, as Mother seems to, that I should be somewhere else, pray to the only One who can remodel me or lead me, not to me . . .

"I'm here because the Lord wants me to be here. A lot of preachers waste their time walking up and down throwing seeds that won't grow because they've walked over that ground until it's packed hard—gospel hardened. I may be just carrying a seed bag with a small hole in it and maybe those few seeds are falling on some pretty rough, weedy, and stony ground. But the Lord giveth the increase."

There was something touching about his letter enclosing a snapshot. "Enclosed is a picture of my outfit. I've marked with an 'X' the spot I'd be in had I not left for the hospital a few hours earlier."

While Nate was waiting for a transfer, he found his duties any-thing but difficult. It was a life of comparative ease—up to a point.

"This A.M. I slept through breakfast, was half awake at 8:45 when I heard the lieutenant's voice. I was startled into the sudden realization that Saturday A.M. inspection was under way just up the hall a few doors. Wow! You'd have laughed yourself silly at what took place in the next sixty seconds. Had the bed made up in about twenty seconds. Tucked hospital corners only on the visible sides. One scoop got clothing into closet. Another swept this letter and everything else into barracks bag."

In another letter home Nate included an article from the August, 1943, issue of *The Reader's Digest* describing the magic of newly discovered penicillin, and, ironically enough, its effectiveness in treating osteomyelitis.

"Ben, I doubt if you'll be taken into the Army, but if you are, when you take your physical and they ask about the scars on your arm, tell them; it's your Christian duty to be honest about it. I patriotically talked myself out of 'limited service' but when my leg went bad on me I became a burden to the war effort. You'll learn that the docs know more about osteo than you and I. It's not serious, nor a handicap under the right conditions but you might pay dearly, as I did, for a lowered physical resistance. The foregoing is a short sermon so just put a nickel in the collection plate instead of the usual six cents. I hope you'll weigh carefully everything I say because, although I'm neither the beginning nor the end of wisdom, I'm a couple of years farther down the road and am thinking only of you and for you. True you have your own life to live but I'd be foolish to let you make any avoidable mistakes."

Then came word that Nate was to be transferred to Amarillo Field in Texas where he was to spend three months.

Within a brief period at Amarillo he was made barracks chief in charge of fifty men.

"If you think getting these guys out of bed is fun, guess again. . . . Only three fellows made trouble this morning but with prospects of all-day passes tomorrow after having been restricted today, they're sweetening up."

In experiences like this Nate was learning to get along with men and to assert leadership.

From a soldier shipping out Nate bought a guitar for two dollars —worth perhaps twenty-five or thirty dollars. After a time he tired of it so posted a notice in the latrine:

> Cash & carry . . . no credit department
> Good guitar cheap
> Slightly beat up
> Almost for free
> Won't accept over 5 bucks.

Later Sam and Jeanne sent him a ukelele that he described as bringing lots of fun.

There were several Christians who became Nate's buddies during the three-month stay at Amarillo Air Base, including Lester Pontius, Clifford Taylor, Leslie Lombard, William Lyons, Kenneth Adlam, and a lad named Cole. Lester, Cliff, and Nate were often together. They enjoyed the preaching of a certain Chaplain Allen, at the base hospital.

"We had a swell time in the chapel last night," Nate wrote home. "The chaplain is the real McCoy and hasn't let the Army take the ring out of his gospel message. I've run into so many phonies lately and am so closely acquainted with those who need a stirring message that I've become very critical, maybe too critical, but I think that we as Christians should be, at least, what unbelievers expect of us. You can't take a newcomer and preach a ten-minute collection sermon and then expect him to think that a fifteen-minute message about a literal hell is your primary interest. That's a grain of sand against Gibraltar and I think our interests dedicated to each should be somewhat proportional. Inconsistency in our appreciation of values is doing a wonderful job for the enemy of men's souls.

"When I take an unsaved fellow to hear a man preach and the message is diluted with secondary things I always feel like telling the preacher he's an unfaithful steward and a traitor.

"It's easy to brand a phony before he's rambled ten minutes. They all preach the same thing—nothing. They do quite a fancy job of streamlining and rubberizing our 'religion.' I'm aware of the fact that criticism by remote control isn't worth much but here I sit with nothing else to do and 'out of the fulness of the heart the mouth speaketh.' Enough said—maybe too much."

"Nate was continuously involved in barracks bull sessions which were usually centered on religion," Pontius said. "He had a deep concern for his fellow soldiers and his life was always consistent with the things he spoke."

"My Christian life wasn't too sharp," Cliff Taylor confessed, "but Nate's knowledge of Scripture plus his personal testimony helped to get me straightened out with the Lord."

While Nate was always dead in earnest when he was talking about spiritual matters, there seems to have been time for normal barracks horseplay. In his diary Nate recorded:

"Piled Meek's bed up with seven or eight mattresses and woke up at 3 A.M. with four of them on me."

During the days at Amarillo Nate developed a love for photography that was to serve him well in the future. He spent many hours in the darkroom at the Amarillo U.S.O. where the materials and equipment were free to men in uniform.

Nate's first Christmas in the service was at Amarillo. One of his most poetic letters was written on Christmas Eve, 1943, to his good friend Sadie Montgomery, then living in Alhambra:

"Two fellows just closed the barracks door, leaving me alone. . . . They left a radio on and I can hear distantly, 'O Come Let Us Adore Him.' There's snow on the ground and the stars are glittering clearly—like gems on black velvet, illuminated by a great hidden light. . . .

"If you've ever been curious to know how a fellow like me spends Christmas Eve in camp, I would tell you except that I haven't the words. . . . I've never discovered the words for a throat that's tight and dry and has a big lump in it. Maybe there aren't any. The Psalmist comes as close as anyone to expressing those feelings that are almost too deep . . . '*As the hart panteth after the water brooks, so panteth my soul after thee, O God.*'

"The Lord has given me plenty of time to see things differently from the view I had when I went to the hospital while all my buddies went to the airport for their first time off the ground. He has taught me a lot about patience. . . . He's a wonderful Teacher —patient and forgiving. . . .

"They have made up special orders for me to proceed to Fort Wayne, Indiana. If flying is 'out,' I want to be useful in some way. It will feel good to get greasy, get a few callouses, skin my knuckles on a gadget, hurry to get 'er ready to go on time, and go to bed really tired again."

A few days later Nate left for home on a ten-day furlough before starting his new tour of duty at Baer Field, Fort Wayne. In the eighteen months he was to spend at Baer Field would come another climactic experience in the progress of his soul.

6

A VOICE FROM HEAVEN

. . . that which hath wings shall tell the matter. ECCLESIASTES 10:20

AT BAER FIELD Nate was classified "Crew Chief, C-47," which he felt was "just what I've been praying for. . . . Today I saw my card stamped 'Disqualified for combat crew duty.'"

But Nate was content with his lot. "The work is swell—just what I like. Now comes the 'bug'—the desire for something to do, hobby or whatever you care to call it. One of the fellows just took an exam for his engine mechanic's license and that cinched it. I didn't know you could take those exams while in the Army, but now I'm going to take a shot at it—don't know what the future holds but that 'E' license is in my lap and I'd be very foolish not to grab it."

In the summer of 1944 he was a frequent visitor at Winona Lake Bible Conference Grounds and heard his brother Phil, a widely known artist-evangelist, who later became a missionary to Argentina.

By this time the Allies had invaded France and the wartime tempo at Baer Field was in full pitch. For some months Nate and his crew worked twelve hours a day and seven days a week. It was strenuous toil. On July 6 he was made a sergeant. Because of his old leg trouble, Nate was forced to spend five weeks in the hospital, but this seemed to be the last serious flare-up ever to develop.

Brought up in a home dedicated to the strict observance of the Lord's Day, Nate developed a sense of guilt because of his long record of working every day of the week at Baer Field.

In his diary during the latter part of November, 1944, he wrote: "I have felt that it would be wise to write a ten-year advanced reprimand based on lessons learned during the time represented in foregoing pages [i.e., in the period spent at Baer Field presumably].

"1. I would be foolish to forget to keep Sunday as a day of rest.

"2. Family altar, daily Bible reading, and regular church attendance with high priority are invaluable even when practiced as a mechanical habit, that is without particular spur-of-the-moment desire for them.

"3. Overwork to excess is sin.

"4. I should never walk in the counsel of the ungodly nor of religious quacks but in His will, remembering always that in a multitude of counselors there is safety."

These moralizations were a part of Nate's deep-seated respect for God's commandments which he honored as immutable. While his tendency to codify his thinking in matters of conduct at times led Nate to what many would regard as legalistic extremes, there was no denying his own self-discipline.

Only a few days after he had entered these comments in his diary Nate was sent to the Willow Run plant of the Ford Motor Company to study the characteristics of the latest airplane engines being produced there. While it may have appeared to be an interesting assignment, Nate's sojourn in the Detroit area marked him for life. He was soon to experience one of the peaks of his spiritual history.

He sought out the Zoller Gospel Tabernacle in Detroit as a result of hearing Dr. John Zoller's radio broadcast on his barracks radio.

After attending several services at the Tabernacle, Nate met a warmhearted motherly woman, Mrs. Albert Shuell. Not without some misgivings about the wisdom or propriety of her act, Mrs. Shuell invited the soldier with the flashing smile to spend Christmas with her family. The Shuells, like the Montgomerys of Daggett, had four daughters and no sons, and for a brief interval there was considerable speculation as to whether Nate would feel at home.

But in short order, Nate and the Shuells launched into an animated conversation that went on for hours. They shared their views on many subjects and eventually Nate told them that he probably would follow his brother into commercial aviation after the war was over.

Sixteen-year-old Miriam, already planning to become a missionary, sensed that Nate was not settled in his own mind, she later reported.

"I felt that there was going to be a great need for missionary pilots," she said, "but I agreed with Nate that God could certainly use an all-out Christian pilot in the business world."

Miriam, deeply attracted by the earnest sandy-haired soldier, found it hard to sleep that night. She longed that Nate's obvious talents might be fully used for the Lord. The following week she met him again at a Youth for Christ meeting and he spent the last Sunday of the year in their home.

Miriam had prepared a message to give to a young people's group. "With fear and trembling, I put away the notes I had so carefully prepared," she said. "I could not get away from the idea the Lord was prompting me to give my personal testimony. . . . I had no idea . . . that Nate was even listening but apparently he was in the midst of making the greatest decision of his life."

Nate was back again to attend the New Year's Eve service at the Tabernacle. After the benediction, instead of lingering around to talk with the young people, he left the church. In his hurry he forgot his hat. Coming back to get it, he saw Mrs. Shuell. His only words to her as he slipped out of the church door were, "Pray for this boy."

Describing the experience later in a letter to Maeva Park Dobner, whom he met in the Army, he said:

"Stationed in Detroit, I found myself in a New Year's Eve service, taking inventory and philosophizing. Everything was in terms of questions that only God could answer. What was going on in the church service wasn't important. I wasn't hearing anything with my ears, anyhow.

"I doubt whether I even framed the question, but I pleaded helplessly with my Heavenly Father for the answer that stood between me and the peace that Jesus said should be ours. Now, you've heard people tell about God speaking to them, haven't you? I don't know about the other fellow, but that night I saw things differently . . . BING . . . like that. Just as though a different Kodachrome slide had been tossed onto the screen between my ears.

"As soon as I could, I stepped out of the building to get away from people and things, so that I could see what the deal was. It was snowing and there was already a deep virgin snow on the ground, and the moan of city traffic was muffled as it is when deep snow is around. A joy, such as I had never known since the night I accepted Jesus' forgiveness for my sins, seemed to leave me almost weak with gratitude. I was completely relaxed and happy again. The verse that fitted itself to my thoughts was the one that says, 'And they found the man . . . sitting . . . clothed, and in his right mind.' The old life of chasing things that are of a temporal sort seemed absolutely insane, once the Lord had shown me the new plan.

"From that time to this, the happiness that has been encountered on every hand, stops me cold. Oh, sure . . . there have been and will be rough places, but the things that mean the most . . . spiritual things . . . mean a lot more in the tough places.

"Before this experience we've been talking about, I had no idea of the real truth of the statement, 'He that loveth his life shall lose it. . . .' Now it seems quite clear."

Nate's decision in Detroit changed the course of his life and led him to the mission field.

"I've always believed that if the Lord wants a guy in full-time service on the mission field," he soon wrote his mother and sister, "He would make him unbearably miserable in the pursuit of any other end. So, methinks the aircraft industry has suffered the loss of a 'big operator' and the Lord has won for Himself a 'li'l operator.'

"An evolution too long to go into brought me to this place but the 'status quo' is that I'm very happily contemplating missionary training if it's His will. The Lord clipped my wings. It was over a year ago that it seemed logical to suppose that an inherent yen to fly defined the Lord's will, but He said 'no!' Only door left open to a curious kid was book larnin'. If I'm going to buckle down to a couple of years of college anyway, there's no longer the 'I hate school' excuse.

"The whole deal has opened up an entirely new world to me. I've seen enough of airplanes 'n' stuff to be convinced that somehow the world will get by without my help, and have lived just about long enough to realize that a little plugging for the Lord now will pay compound interest 'til the old horn blows and clocks become obsolete. Then untold joys should be ours—with Him.

"The Lord has given me no desire to preach but I'd like some day to be able to tell somebody who has never heard. . . . Please pray that I'll be kept from useless side tracks."

When Nate returned to Baer Field in the middle of January, 1945, he wrote in his diary:

"Have experienced a full and overflowing joy while contemplating the job of being His bondservant."

Unaware of his son's decision to serve the Lord on the mission field, Lawrence Saint had forwarded to him an article in *The Sunday School Times* written by Ensign James C. Truxton, president of the Christian Airmen's Missionary Fellowship (the original name of the Missionary Aviation Fellowship). It was entitled "On Wings of the Wind," and dealt with the formation of the CAMF as a means of serving missionaries in remote areas. It was Nate's first realization that such an organization existed.

"In a way the clipping was a slight disappointment at first," Nate wrote. "Being a grease monkey for the Lord seemed like an inferior sort of call. It seemed to me that there must be a flock of laymen and that the big need was for men who could break the Bread of Life. Nevertheless, 'What is that in thine hand?' could, for me, be answered only one way: a mechanic's license and a private pilot's ticket."

Truxton in his article had invited interested Christian airmen to contact the CAMF office in Los Angeles.

Accordingly on January 15 Nate wrote the Fellowship from Baer Field:

"Have just finished reading your article in *The Sunday School*

Times and feel that it was sent to me as a definite answer to prayer.

"Last New Year's Eve in a watch-night service I responded to the missionary challenge. Have been interested in missionary work for some time but the Lord owned only my finances. He now has my life."

Nate then listed in detail his qualifications and educational background. He concluded by saying:

"I'm not making any air castle assumptions, but want to further the cause of Christ in any way I can, so please count me in and keep me informed of the goings on.

"Your vision is one that is shared by many mission-minded Christians. We're praying for this work and anxious to be 'fustus with the mostus' for Jesus."

The die was cast. Nate's face from that point on was set as a flint toward service as God's missionary, using his airplane as the rod in his hand to do God's bidding.

7

MISSIONARY IN KHAKI

. . . under whose wings thou art come to trust. RUTH 2:12

WHILE Nate was home on a short furlough, he bought an E-2 Cub. He flew the plane back to Fort Wayne and used it to build up hours for his private license. After two months, having flown for more than one hundred hours, he sold the plane for six hundred and fifty dollars.

Working again with his crew, Nate reported:

"The work on the line seems light right now. It gives me time to fly. The way the Lord lays out and accomplishes *His* purposes makes me glad I'm on His band wagon."

Describing his duties:

"I'm now getting paid to do what I used to do on my own time—hunt down new gadgets on the ships as they come through. My job consists of briefing combat crews. They fly the pond from here so briefing is mostly made up of maintenance hints, tricks and last-minute instructions."

He was pleased because he now had his Sundays off and had his own office and classroom. For a time he was engaged in the instruction of Chinese pilots some of whom spoke no English, so he was required to teach through an interpreter.

To Mrs. Montgomery he reported:

"The Lord has been blessing in a way that challenges my faith; another of my buddies has been redeemed and is a child of the King now! A few of us have a Bible study fellowship here on the base. I was overjoyed last night when the fellow I work with took a stand for Christ without any coaxing.

"Since throwing in with the Christian Airmen's Missionary Fellowship, the past years of aero curiosity are beginning to make sense. . . . Selfish ambition is a dull and ungrateful pursuit. I'm glad that the Lord finally got some sense through my thick head. The mission field pays such wonderful dividends!

"As far as I can tell, my work in coming years will be the marrying of the possibilities of aviation to the needs of missionaries. We feel that time is at a premium now and that the return of Christ might not be too far distant. In any case, He told us to watch for His coming and to redeem the time."

Then on June 19 Nate ended his eighteen-month stay at Baer Field and flew west in an Army plane. His new assignment was destined to be the Air Base at Salinas, California. He continued a deep interest in his maintenance work but the surrender of Japan in August foreshadowed the end of his Army days.

Yet the three months Nate spent at Salinas and the subsequent time spent at Castle Field, Merced, were from a spiritual standpoint some of the most fruitful days of his Army career. Nate was tireless in his witnessing, which had become as natural to him as breathing.

Lt. Robert A. Malone, a chaplain at Lackland Air Force Base, San Antonio, attributes his conversion to his contact with Nate first at Salinas and then at Merced.

Writing later from Kano, Nigeria, George Hoover, a missionary now working under the Sudan Interior Mission, shed light on the days at Salinas:

"I met Nate for the first time Saturday, July 14, 1945, in Salinas. The next day being Sunday at an invitation from Nate I attended the First Baptist Church of Salinas with him and Rusty Hodges. My heart was moved with the message that morning but I lacked the courage of my convictions.

"Nate spoke to me about accepting Christ then and there and offered to accompany me down the aisle. That was all I needed and that day I became a new creature in Christ Jesus. Nate wasn't one to seek praise. He did what he did because of his love for the Lord. . . . Nate meant a lot to me because it was through him I came to know the Lord. . . . If it weren't for Nate perhaps I wouldn't be on the mission field today."

Since the war effort had subsided, Nate found time for reading.

He had never been too interested in history or literature, but he responded somewhat to his mother's suggestion that he improve his cultural knowledge.

"Took your advice on learning 'living' history via biographies," he told her. "I am enjoying Thomas Jefferson at the moment. . . . Jeff says Patrick Henry was 'about the laziest man of reading' he'd ever met—admitted to the bar after six weeks' cramming of law. . . . His observations of France of the late eighteenth century explains the rotten plight of the country today."

Before Japan had fallen after the blighting scar of Hiroshima Nate wrote Sadie Montgomery:

"How about this new atomic bomb deal? Makes me feel the coming of the King is closer than some of us conservative folks have dared to suspect. The lines of man's moral degeneration seem to indicate an apex or intersection of self-destruction in the not-too-distant future. *'Except those days be shortened, there should no flesh be saved.'* Gabriel Heatter notwithstanding, *'the night cometh when no man can work.'*"

Ike Lanman of Evergreen, Colorado, recalls:

"Saint* took his Bible wherever he went. I remember going to the barber shop and he read his Bible while waiting for a haircut. He had Bible verses stuck on his bunk. He said that when he became a Christian he had written his decision behind a picture in his room. If anything happened to him, he wanted his parents to know where he stood."

---

*During the days at Salinas and Merced, Nate, a man of many nicknames probably because he so disliked his own name, was known just as "Saint." In his childhood he was known as "Than" or "Thanny," the name by which he is still remembered in Huntingdon Valley. Rachel says he was called "Kelley," as Nate always spelled it, from the time he was in the second grade. It seemed that he disobeyed the teacher's instructions about wearing a tie to school, so she placed a huge bow of green crepe paper about his neck. Nate seemed more pleased than chagrined by this punishment and proudly wore the makeshift tie home. There he was greeted by Rachel, who jokingly referred to him as "Kelly with the green necktie." The nickname really stuck when he came home one day wearing a pair of coveralls bearing the name "Kelly" on the back. They had been discarded at the service station where he was employed during his teens. Nate never signed anything but official letters with his own name. Usually it was "Kelley," or "Yardbird," "Schnoz," or "Whitey" because of his blond hair. It was only in the last eight or nine years of his life that he was known as "Nate." Even his wife Marj found it difficult to change from "Kelly" to "Nate."

Transfer to Castle Field at Merced meant the final episodes of his Army days. If his Christian influence had been strong at Salinas, it was increased at Merced. Many of his Army mates were transferred with him and soon the Bible classes were going full tilt again under Nate's dynamic drive. Included in the classes were a major and two lieutenants who found the Christian fellowship so stimulating that rank was forgotten.

Among those in Nate's orbit was skeptical Bob Link, a Yale graduate and son of Dr. Henry C. Link. Bob had many questions about supernatural Christianity, but Nate's buoyant life and his obvious influence on those about him stirred young Link's heart. He loved to sing the old hymns, but his surrender did not come immediately.

8

MOUNTAINTOP ENCOUNTER

Doth the eagle mount up . . . ? JOB 39:27

WHEN the Thanksgiving holidays came around, Nate had a leave, so he decided to visit the Montgomerys who had moved to Shafter, California. While passing through Los Angeles he stopped off to see Joanna their daughter, who was in nurses' training at California Lutheran Hospital.

Joanna had shared some of Nate's letters with her classmate, Marjorie Farris. Marjorie knew that he was her age, a devout Christian and eligible. She examined the letters with more than academic interest, and was particularly impressed with a small snapshot that had been included in one of them.

With thoughts about the possibility of meeting this young man, Marj, who had been shopping earlier in the day in downtown Los Angeles, caught her breath as she entered the nurses' residence on South Hope Street. Talking to Joanna in the lounge was a tall blond soldier in an Air Force uniform. Marj recognized Nate immediately from his picture.

Joanna introduced them. Marj was impressed with his neat appearance and his serious flow of conversation, punctuated with keen humor. As she excused herself to go downstairs to press her nurse's uniform, Nate reached into the air with thumb and forefinger pressed together as though he were about to put a thread through the eye of an imaginary needle. "Now let's see," he said nonchalantly to Joanna. "What was the thread of our conversation?"

"They talked as I ironed in the gloomy basement," Marj recalls, "unhappy with myself for not having ironed that uniform the night before. I kept thinking, 'I excused myself too soon. . . . When will I ever see him again?' Then, like a flash I remembered that he had said that he and a soldier friend (Tom Mitchell) were going out to San Bernardino that weekend.

" 'Strange, isn't it,' I thought. 'I'm going out that way, too. Going to spend my two days off with my aunt and cousins at their cabin in the hills. I'm sure that soldier boy would like to ride out with us.'

"I got excited," Marj admits, "and everything went wrong. The iron struck a place on the uniform where there was too much starch and I had to stop and clean it off. In my haste I had jerked the iron and pulled the cord out of the socket, so I was delayed again. It took ages for that iron to reheat. Once on the elevator, I had to calm down a bit. . . . I was glad that my white shoes and uniform had just been cleaned, and that I had just pleated my stiffly starched white cap.

"As I buttoned my uniform with some effort, I chided myself for not carrying out my frequent resolves to diet. I took care of that little detail by throwing my wool cape over my shoulders, with no regard to the weather.

"All out of breath, I hurried again to the lounge. He was still there!

"He accepted the offer of a lift to San Bernardino but later when we were heading toward the mountains, he declined my cousin's invitation to spend the holiday weekend."

"I'd love to come," Nate declared, "but I promised my buddy that we would give our full attention to his Dad who doesn't know the Lord."

Even in her disappointment, Marj was impressed by his resolution.

Several weeks went by before Marj received a little photograph of Nate wearing snowshoes. Clipped to the picture was a tiny piece of notepaper telling about a trip he had made to the snow country. At the end he wrote, "Thanks for the ride to San Bernardino." Nothing more.

Meanwhile Marj had confessed to her friend Joanna that Nate

was the man she would like to marry. Nate, too, had felt an answering response to that first meeting. He wrote later:

"I was immediately captivated, but tried to hold the fort because I had no idea who she was. After she left us I asked Jo about her—and walked all the way up to the center of town kicking myself every step, the way you would if you had just thrown away a winning ticket, then found it was the winning number."

There are other indications that Nate had conflicting thoughts about Marj in particular and girls in general. In answer to a query about this time from his father, Nate responded somewhat impatiently:

"Dad, you need have no fear. Suffice to say that I, too, am interested in your future daughter-in-law—but I doubt whether the Lord has yet shown me His treasure."

On a trip to Los Angeles a few weeks later when he called at the CAMF offices, he found time to visit Marj again. In advance he had sent a note saying, "Expect to be in L.A. next weekend. Could I drop in to see you?"

Rules at the nurses' home were very strict. Student nurses could leave the building for one reason only—a trip to the library. Marj decided she would obey the letter of the rules so when Nate arrived, off they went to the Los Angeles Main Library, just eight blocks away. They walked *through* the library, they walked *around* the library, and in keeping with the hospital regulations, Marj faithfully checked out *Materia Medica*. She admitted, it was the only book she saw in the whole library. And time slipped by without paying any attention to the desires of two young hearts.

Seeing Marj a second time had more effect on Nate. He confided this to his friend Bob Malone. Somehow the word got out to the disappointment of several young ladies in the Baptist church at Merced.

About the middle of December Nate and two Army friends made a trip to Yosemite. When they arose early the first morning at the park, the weather was foggy and drizzling. In spite of this Nate suggested that they take a hike several miles up to Glacier

Point. "It seemed like a simple deal," Nate wrote later, "to climb a trail that tourists had used all summer. On the other hand, the trail had been closed for the winter, the weather was foul, and I was green. I had been building up steam for several months at the Merced Army Air Base where there wasn't much to do but 'sweat-out the discharge rosters' and I wanted to go." After all, Nate reasoned, it's possible that 3000 feet higher, the sun was probably baking the granite ledges of the canyon rim. His friends decided, however, that they would be content to explore the canyon floor. They were "thumbs down" on the climb. So Nate took off alone, clad in mechanic's coveralls over his O.D.'s and a couple of sweaters, with only a pocketful of peanut chews to eat on the way.

Before he had left, the rangers told him they could not give him their official blessing but offered some helpful pointers and asked him to convey their greetings to Douglas Whiteside, a nature lover and photographer, who was spending the winter at the Inn on Glacier Point, at the top of the trail.

"The trail turned out to be excellent," Nate wrote later. "I was just finishing three years of 'fellowship' with twelve million other people in uniform. This was my party for a change.

"The clouds were low in the valley and soon I was in them, begrudging the loss of the limited view I had been enjoying. . . . The work of the relentless climb kept me warm. My G.I. shoes were only good and damp so far. My coveralls were wet over the shoulders and back, but the wool underneath gave good insulation. I noticed the air getting colder. I hoped the temperature change would be the forerunner of clearing air but instead a little breeze started up showing me how cold the air was really getting. The intermittent drizzle and light rain began to sting a little.

"Visibility was now down to 100 yards. There had been no forks or branch trails so there was no danger yet of getting lost. My legs were beginning to ache and get crampy. That added physical challenge to psychological. I tried changing pace and later walked backward up better portions of the trail. It was getting tough enough to make it almost adventurous but I still felt sure I could make it back down to the floor if for some reason

I decided to return. The question of when to turn back was forcing itself forward in my fatigue—fuzzy thoughts—when an odd shape loomed out of the fog. I had been watching the mysteriously sudden formation of evergreens out of fog for just long enough to get a good jolt out of the straight lines of a cabin roof.

"It turned out to be an emergency shelter with a phone—so a sign said. It was boarded up. I was tempted by the dry interior I could see between the cracks but decided that if I was that far gone I could never justify pushing on. It wouldn't be hard to break into and offered protection this far along the trail. That thought didn't dry my wet feet nor soothe my muscles and the leg cramps got worse as I hesitated. I noted the single wire phone line ducking down the pole, into the cabin, back up the pole and up the mountainside, into the fog.

"By now the project took on the aspect of a real struggle but there seemed no real danger to my life as long as I could reach that cabin in one piece, so I pushed on—munching a peanut bar.

"Shortly after the cabin disappeared behind me, the light rain turned to sleet that stung painfully. Then it turned to softer pellets of half snow and half sleet. By now I had lost track of time and was ready to 'arrive.' I glanced up from time to time, hoping to be frightened by a large squarish evidence of mankind. The pellets of snow changed to heavy snowflakes that quickly covered everything. I began to feel a sensation of blindness as everything turned white and faded into swirling snow and fog or cloud.

"The rate at which the snow deepened under foot was alarming but the trail was well enough defined so that there was little danger of stepping off and hurtling down the precipitous slope. I'm sure I would have turned back at that point except for the recurring presence of the telephone wire. I figured that I could break the wire and that the rangers would find me when they came up looking for the break. I realized that if that didn't work, they probably wouldn't find me until the spring thaw. There were two things I found out afterward: the wire was tough steel, not soft copper; the rangers normally expected snowslides to tear the line down and would not attempt to repair it until spring.

"As the snow continued to deepen, I found new muscles in my legs: the ones that were lifting those heavy, wet G.I. shoes out of their patterned holes in the six-inch deep snow. I had never seen snow deepen so fast. Finally, I realized that at higher altitude it had been snowing while it was raining farther down the trail. . . . I had to stop every five minutes to catch my breath, but when I stopped my feet froze. I was panting so hard in the thin air that it was hard to chew the peanuts I had left. I ate snow for water. I was probably about 7000 feet above sea level at the time.

"I used my hands on my thighs to lend the extra shove needed to get each new footing in the deep snow. My feet were slipping in the hard-packed snow at the bottom of each hole my shoes made.

"It was at about this point that I noticed tracks in the snow. They had to be Doug's. He was the only fellow up there. They were fresh or they would have been completely full of snow. I took courage. Then my foggy head began to register the odd shape of the prints. I could feel the dose of adrenalin the body provides for such emergencies. I dropped to my knees and carefully dug the snow away from one of the prints. It was a bear track. Each print was a good seven inches across, it appeared. It was a long way back now—too far, even if I could make better time. I couldn't wait or I'd freeze to death. Then I guess pushing ahead had become a subconscious habit. I pushed on. I wondered what I'd do if I should meet the owner of those big feet face to face. I recalled Uncle Bill's bear stories and that a bear could claw a man's face right off his skull with one pass. There were no cub prints. That would surely be in my favor. Then there was the chance that if I were only a ranger and knew all the facts I'd maybe know there wasn't any real danger from a friendly old bear. That was a welcome possibility but the 'Don't Feed Bears' signs in the park did not lend credence to it. I tossed glances ahead of me while struggling on. Then, funny thing, it almost seemed nice to have evidence of something living nearby. It seemed a week since I had started up. Then the tracks bounded off the trail and along a ledge . . . I suddenly felt we could have been friends anyway.

"By this time I began to realize that I wasn't reasoning clearly but I couldn't stop to let my head clear. I began to see the real dangers of such a venture. A fellow doesn't ordinarily figure that in a few hours he may be making ridiculously dangerous decisions. Then too, I realized that I had been expecting to 'break out' on top for over an hour. It began to dawn that I might still have hours to go. The heavy overcast could bring early darkness. I tried hard to rationalize but my thoughts seemed like dreams that could never induce my muscles to move. I felt lost.

"I guess I'd been ashamed to pray about my fix. After all I had no business up there. I had deliberately started this climb looking for diversion from the endless routines of the Army. Now I was consciously ashamed. My life wasn't my own. The Lord had called me to be a gospel missionary. It had been a clear, definable Christian experience in which I turned every potentiality of my life over to God for His service. That was a couple of years ago. I remembered the happiness I had felt since that time—looking forward to mustering out of one army and into another. This was the life I had thrown away—deliberately. I wasn't afraid to die. I'd read that freezing was the easiest way out of this life and into the next—especially when fatigue opens the door. And more important, I knew that God loved me like a son. The proof of His love was His *real* Son who suffered in my place on a Roman cross at Calvary.

"As I called aloud to God the snow seemed to swallow the sound. I cried. It was easy. The pain and misery that wracked my body were enough to excuse a few tears before the guilt of foolish stewardship settled over me. At first, there was no desire to plead for deliverance from my circumstances. For some time, *I don't know how long,* as I fought upward, I prayed aloud, thanking God for the shed blood of His dear Son Jesus Christ and for the many assurances of my Savior which His apostles had recorded. I cried for joy as I thanked God for a *sure* salvation. I was afraid to lend more than a fleeting thought to what it would be to die alone—without hope—without Christ. He seemed very near and after a time deep peace settled over my heart. Then quietly I renewed my vows of service. I felt no desire to bargain—just

75

wanted God to know my gratitude for what was already mine and could easily be cashed in during the night.

"I don't remember much more until I was aware that the slope against the trail was disappearing and there was ground visible on the other side of the trail. Then suddenly I realized that the trail disappeared among trees. At first, there were suggestions of it—then absolutely nothing one could trust. I took stock. The last I'd seen of the phone line it was above the trail. I couldn't reason beyond this. The snow was close to fifteen inches deep. In places less—in others more. I had to stop every few minutes to hold off deadly cramps that threatened to tie my legs in knots. Then through the gloom of the heavier forest I spotted the phone line. No wire ever looked so good! I followed it perhaps 200 yards before spotting, through the trees, a single straight line. I was fearful of being deceived and fought closer until I could see clearly it was a roof sticking up beyond a knoll. I stopped and rested, overjoyed but too far gone to express any emotion. From that point to the Inn was not over 100 yards but I had to stop twice before reaching it. I thought, suppose it's locked and no one answers. I'd take a piece of firewood and bash in a window. I had to get inside before the battle was won.

"I banged on the door as hard as I could and called 'Hello!' Seconds later the door opened. 'Hi, you're Doug Whiteside, my name's Saint,' I said, flopping in a chair before my host could get his bearings. He pulled the wet clothes and shoes off and flipped the draft open on his log stove. All I remember after that was the most wonderful bowl of soup I've ever tasted and then I was on a soft, warm bed and he was rubbing my legs with rubbing alcohol.

"Next morning the warm sun on the virgin snow and faraway stretches of the High Sierras made it all seem like a different world. From Glacier Point the canyon floor looked far away and cramped. Doug was swell, a university student and lover of the mountains."

After a day of recovery, Doug allowed Nate to start down on borrowed snowshoes. For an hour and a half Whiteside tramped ahead, telling Nate what to watch for on the way down. He wanted to see Nate past a place in the trail he was sure would have been buried by a slide during the night. Nate talked to him of spiritual things.

"When we came to the anticipated bad spot," Nate's account goes on, "the trail completely disappeared under the slide. Doug began to pick a route across the slide, working up above the probable route of the trail. Looking almost straight down I could see the slide for perhaps fifty feet below and then nothing but misty space for a thousand feet. Doug said that if the slide should let go again—a swimming motion was prescribed—to stay on top if possible. At the far side I took his mail and he took the snowshoes. I watched him work his way back across the slide, called my appreciation for his hospitality and was suddenly alone."

Several hours later Nate was down near the floor. The sun was warm and the trail wide and dry under foot. All of a sudden his solitude was broken by coming upon two girls "decked out in store-bought hiking togs." In their astonishment at seeing him, they asked, "Have you been farther up the trail?"

"I grinned so foolishly as I admitted that I had been, that they probably thought I had a screw loose," Nate said. "If they could only have known, there would have been no doubt."

From the mountaintop of Glacier Point Nate might have looked back figuratively to the earlier spiritual peaks in his life: when he surrendered his life to the Lord in the agonizing pain of the first attack of osteomyelitis; the crushing blow upon his "monster will" in the second attack of the disease at Sioux City; the glorious joy of the New Year's Eve surrender for missionary service. And now on Glacier Point he had "quietly renewed" his vows of service.

Nate had matured in the three Army years. He had learned both to enjoy the Word of God and to use it as an offensive weapon. He had learned to commune with God in heartfelt prayer. Above all he had learned the secret of a life of spontaneous, overflowing witness.

When Nate was discharged from the Army at Camp Beale, California, in mid-February, 1946, he was already as truly a missionary as he was when he later landed on Ecuadorian soil. But just ahead were further lessons to be learned in Mexico and later at Wheaton College.

9

ORDEAL IN MEXICO

If I take the wings of the morning . . . . PSALM 139:9

WHEN a crack-up of their first and only plane in southern Mexico halted the flying operation of the fledgling CAMF, it was more than an embarrassment to its leaders. Fortunately no one had been hurt in the accident, but the situation, at this particular time, appeared to be a blow to the whole cause of missionary aviation.

CAMF had launched its first air operation to serve the Wycliffe Bible Translators. Personnel and supplies were being flown from Tuxtla Gutiérrez, the capital of Chiapas, to the Jungle Camp about one hundred miles inland. Occupants of the plane at the time of the crash were Betty Greene, who had inaugurated the Mexican service, and George Wiggins, a former Navy pilot who was to replace her in Mexico. Before leaving for Peru, Miss Greene was "checking out" her successor in a four-passenger Waco biplane. Everything went well until they came in for a landing at the dog-leg strip at El Real, an auxiliary airport only minutes away from the Wycliffe Jungle Camp. The Waco clipped a small building, damaging both left wings, the propeller, and landing gear. It meant abandonment of the plane on the isolated field until repairs could be made.

Neither Wiggins nor Miss Greene was qualified to make such an extensive repair. Both were expert fliers but neither had had any mechanical training. This posed a real problem.

It was at this time that Jim Truxton of CAMF asked Nate Saint to make a hasty trip to Mexico and undertake the repair operation.

Since Nate's discharge from the Army in mid-February was too late for the second semester of college, he had returned to his family home in Huntingdon Valley. Nate had again bought a second-hand plane and was building up hours at the Flying Dutchman Airport in nearby Somerton.

As a result he had obtained both his commercial pilot and instructor's rating.

With his eyes still on the mission field, Nate expected to enter Westmont College in Santa Barbara, California, the following fall. Betty Greene, of CAMF, had been writing to Nate for several months, urging him to accept the call to serve as a mechanic in the proposed new missionary aviation program that Wycliffe and CAMF expected to launch co-operatively in Peru. Nate considered the invitation prayerfully, but decided he should get at least two years of college training before proceeding with his proposed missionary career.

But now came Jim Truxton's emergency request. What was he to do?

Nate realized that accepting this assignment would probably mean that his college training would have to be postponed further. Briefly he debated the issue, and then responded to the call.

"I'd surely like to go if CAMF thinks I can be of assistance. . . . I'll be ready to leave in a couple of weeks," he wrote Truxton.

But within two days Nate received a letter containing a railroad ticket to the Mexican border and a reservation that left him only three days to clear up all his affairs.

He admitted later that the train reservation turned out to be his introduction to the "fullest, fastest, happiest years" of his life—the beginning of his lifework.

The next few days were a mad scramble. Nate already had an appointment for flight tests the following day with a CAA inspector. Then there were such matters as photographs, obtaining his passport and Mexican visa, selling his plane, "remothballing" his recently reactivated Model-A Ford, and a hundred lesser details.

Nate's parents were a bit bewildered by the sudden change of events but they gave full-hearted approval. Nate wanted to tell them more about what he would be doing. Typically he wrote: "I wasn't selfish with information. I just didn't have any."

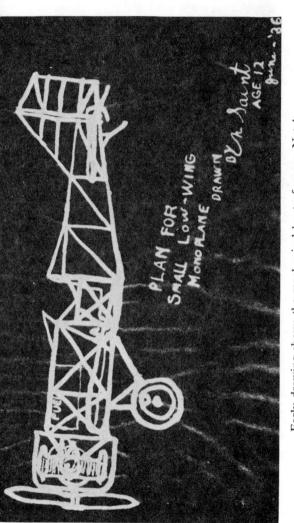

Early drawing shows the mechanical bent of young Nate's inventive mind. "I can't help the gadgets that run in my mind, but I do try to sort out the stuff that might have some value."

Nate's parents, Lawrence and Katherine Saint, carefully taught their eight children from the Bible; three became missionaries, one a preacher.

Nate's father has been one of the leading stained-glass designers of this generation. The great North Transept Rose Window, one of 15 windows Lawrence Saint designed and fabricated for the Washington Cathedral in the nation's capital, is his best-known work.

His army service was the most formative period of Nate's life. Shortly after his induction he wrote: "My shoes don't match—one is a stern-wheeler and the other is a schooner. Bought some after-shave lotion. After you shave with a G.I. razor and cold water, you need something to take the place of your skin." But he was also elated: "The Eagle was about to lay the golden egg—$25,000 worth of pilot training."

Nate's only sister, Rachel, told him missionary stories about John Paton among the cannibals, and about Livingstone, Judson, and others.

Nate nearly lost his life in a snowstorm on Glacier Point in Yosemite. "As I called aloud to God the snow seemed to swallow the sound. ... I felt no desire to bargain—just wanted God to know my gratitude for what was already mine and could easily be cashed in during the night." Nate sent this picture to Marj to express his continuing interest.

To Marj

Marj and Nate were married on Valentine's Day, 1948. Nate's sister-in-law said: "Not many are privileged to see such love and total giving on the faces of two people."

Nate's resourcefulness was tested on his first Missionary Aviation Fellowship assignment, repairing a damaged plane in Mexico. "Some bed sheets finished patching the fuselage. . . . One of the drag-struts on the landing gear was made from a Ford V-8 steering column."

Sam Saint and the early model Stinson in which he first let Nate (age 10) try the controls in the air. The younger brother's eyes shone as he felt the airplane respond to his tug on the wheel.

In a primitive room Nate builds a new wing for the wrecked plane. "Little did I dream that I would [have found] two completely demolished wings in a bushel backet."

The building of the Saint home on the edge of the jungle in Shell Mera, Ecuador, gets under way. "The climate is wonderful. Almost no mosquitoes."

While on a rescue mission Nate communicates with Marj by a hand-cranked radio from a beach on the Pastaza River.

Marj at the short-wave radio. "Marj still keeps everything in order and in hand. Everyone asks how she does it. I don't know, either. The Lord surely knew that in this kind of work I would need a partner with a brain like a filing cabinet and one incapable of saying 'can't.' "

Nate kept track of each pound of cargo and fuel on every flying mission. "I'm concerned about safety, but I don't let it keep me from getting on with God's business."

The unique spiraling-line technique Nate developed for lowering a canvas bucket from an airplane has fascinated aeronautical engineers. "As the bucket dropped earthward it seemed to lose all horizontal motion. Finally it came to rest quietly in the middle of the open field below."

Stevie on the Voice of the Andes radio station HCJB: "I know why Daddy got to heaven before we did—because he loved the Lord more than we did."

Marj wrote in a letter to her children: "Philip, it's easy to tell whose boy you are. You make everything fly like an airplane—everything from a piece of carrot on the end of your fork to the bar of soap in your bath."

"The tape recorder is playing the familiar Christmas carols and hymns, and we feel creeping over us the thrill of that great mystery . . . that God should send His only Son to take on our likeness in a stable."

Nate with the Auca killer "George" on Palm Beach. "Missionaries . . . who know the joy of leading a stranger to Christ, and those who have gone to tribes who have never heard the gospel, gladly count themselves expendable."

Major Nurnberg reporting the death of Nate to Rachel and Marj. Nate's last words to the outside world, sent by short-wave radio from Palm Beach, concerned the Aucas. "It looks like they'll be here for the early afternoon service. Pray for us. This is the day! Will contact you next at four-thirty."

Marj, continuing missionary work after Nate's death, tells inmates of a Quito prison the meaning of forgiveness. "It is hard to convince these women," Marj said. "They can't understand how God can forgive them if civil authorities won't."

Eight-year-old Kathy, who speaks Spanish well, tells the story of Jesus in the yard of the Gospel Missionary Boarding School in Quito.

On the train trip from Philadelphia to St. Louis Nate recuperated somewhat from the hectic days of preparation. The train was late in reaching St. Louis, giving him just three minutes to make his connection.

"Have you ever been in St. Louis on a hot July day?" Nate asked. "I dashed headlong through the crowds with a duffel bag on my shoulder that held all my worldly goods including a toolbox containing forty pounds of tools. Spectators who dodged that duffel didn't realize the favor they were doing themselves.

"Another round of dozing and travel numbness got me down into Kansas. It was time to take stock. They would speak Spanish in Mexico. My vocabulary for the moment would have to be drawn from my childhood acquaintance with the Lone Ranger."

He began to think about the experiences that lay just ahead:

"I tried to imagine the damaged plane. It wouldn't be too bad or they wouldn't have asked me to try to fix it. I could imagine a damaged landing gear and probably a splintered prop. . . . Little did I dream that I would later find two completely demolished wings in a bushel basket.

"I had Jim's letter with what I thought was an address until I found that 'Apartado' means a post office box and not an apartment."

Nate knew that a replacement propeller was waiting for him at the border in a customs warehouse but it didn't strike him until later that it might be somewhat odd for one entering Mexico as a "tourist" to be carrying a seven-foot airplane propeller under his arm!

On the last day of the train ride, four young men of Mexican ancestry got aboard. By this time Nate's interest in Spanish was becoming less and less academic and more and more desperate. They spoke Spanish, so he enlisted them for a few lessons immediately. "They taught me, '*Ayealgringokeykayablaingles*,'" Nate said. "There was no need to learn where one word ended and another began, since they assured me that I would have to say the whole thing to get results. The anticipated result would be that I would be shown someone who could understand English."

From these young men he found out the location of the town

in Mexico where the plane was to be repaired. They were all a bit baffled by the address in his pocket: "Tuxtla Gtz."

"The fellows dug out a map and we searched it high and low," Nate said. "I told them that the town must be somewhere between the Texas border and Mexico City because there wasn't much of Mexico below its capital. While the words were in my mouth I began to notice for the first time in my life that lower Mexico is a suburb of South America and is insulated from the Panama Canal by only a couple of tiny republics. I wonder if my high school geography teacher was aware of that interesting fact? At any rate we found 'Tuxtla Gutiérrez' way down near the border of Guatemala."

Nate described Laredo as "an un-homogenized combination of two vastly different cultures." He raced around the city, trying to cut red tape on permission to take the propeller across the border. Phoning the CAMF office in Los Angeles, he was instructed to ship the propeller by train, and fly to Mexico City.

Betty Greene met Nate when he arrived in Mexico City and helped him prepare for the final lap of his journey. "After getting to know Betty, I got sufficiently open-minded to let the topography share the blame for the plane accident with the 'woman driver,' " he remarked. "Later I found that Betty was a pilot of such caliber that local airline and military pilots regarded her with a great respect. She could handle anything from a fighter-bomber to a Piper Cub." Betty also introduced him to bus travel in Latin America:

"We waited on a corner until the bus bore down upon us," Nate said. "A radiator and a pair of headlights followed by a swaying mass of humanity that made the bus itself almost hard to find. The brakes screeched and the vehicle slowed to twenty miles an hour. A little barefoot boy leaped from a perch on the bus and to my amazement didn't bounce into a high, involuntary cartwheel.

"A half dozen people jammed in the doorway pushed and elbowed until there was room for Señorita Betty but a split-second survey of the situation made it clear there was no room for me. I decided to join the six men on the back of the bus. They were standing on a piece of two-inch pipe that served as both bumper and passenger 'platform.' The bus was starting out by the time I discovered there wasn't room for me on the back either. However, one of the men, seeing my plight, reached out a helping hand and swung out one of his feet, making room for one of mine. At the next corner there was a reshuffling of the fourth-class passengers so I gained another toehold. While still at that stop, the little non-cartwheeling, barefoot boy came around to the back of the bus to beg. I gave him a little something but he seemed insulted and asked for more. Later I learned that he was the official fare collector."

Thoroughly briefed by Betty Greene, Nate completed last-minute shopping in Mexico City, then boarded a plane for Tuxtla in southern Mexico to join Wiggins, who worked with him periodically on the repair job.

Tuxtla was a sleepy provincial town just emerging from the charm of colonialism. It could boast of its position on the Pan American Highway as well as a fairly busy airport. Yet it leaned more to its colonial past than to the busy present. It still clung to some of the older customs such as the Saturday evening ritual in the central plaza. There the young ladies of the town strolled together about the plaza in one direction while the boys circled about in the other. In the distance a marimba played. From time to time a young man would pair off with a girl and they would walk together as lovers always have.

"In Tuxtla my accommodations were modest, but adequate . . . at least some of them were modest," Nate wrote. "The 'bathroom' was a cactus out in the garden that was hardly big enough for one to hide behind. My shower, installed through the kindness of John Kempers, missionary from across town, got whatever modesty it had from two pieces of a packing crate located in such a way that a mud wall made it a three-sided affair, shoulder high. I realized later that this too was quite modest by local standards, but for the first couple of weeks I chose to freeze under a starlit sky rather than bask in the sun while I showered just off the main street. Later on I nonchalantly greeted friends who chanced to pass by while I enjoyed the luxury of a post-siesta shower.

"My room was adobe and tile. It had no windows . . . had two doors, one front and one back. Shortly after I arrived I found out why the doors were built in two halves, top and bottom, like a stable door. A mule walked nonchalantly in the back door and on out the front with an air that said, 'I'm just minding my own business.' He had another air about him but after the pig that lived out back, it wasn't anything to mention."

The rafters and tile roof of the house were infested with scorpions, bats, cockroaches, and rats. "I soon came to regard my mosquito net as wonderful divider between my world and theirs," Nate said. "The first night my heart stopped beating when something that sounded as big as an eagle swooped past my net in the darkness. I was already tense, having lain awake for a couple of hours. . . . The swooping eagle turned out to be a twelve-inch bat. The net seemed to confuse the radar of the bats. . . . A last-minute maneuver permitted them to avoid a collision but ruffled the net with an ominous whoosh. Later I downed a couple of these creatures with a broomstick. They were full of lice and smelled terrible. Needlelike teeth grinned through hideous faces."

At the local airport Nate found the remains of two whole wing panels "in a bushel basket." Pieces of wing struts and landing gear were stacked in the corner, looking like so much junk. Nate knew immediately that he'd have to have help so he employed a Mexican cabinet maker named Santiago.

"He couldn't understand English and I was trying to get back to the third lesson in a Spanish grammar book," Nate wrote. "I could count to thirteen and was pretty apt at drawing little pictures in my notebook to fill the untouched areas of Spanish vocabulary. I have since been told that there are better ways to learn Spanish . . . but it apparently is possible to pick up a language by osmosis."

Back in the shack Nate studied Spanish by reading familiar Bible passages to a Mexican schoolboy. The linguistic prison of the first months was beginning to crumble.

The slow job of rebuilding the Waco wing panels started out in the airport workshop of the operator of a local bush plane service.

Nate decided that he would build the panels at Tuxtla, then take them to the El Real airstrip in the jungle, more than eighty miles to the east, and fit them to the plane. It was to be a long toilsome assignment.

As a missionary worker Nate was promised an allowance of fifty dollars a month, providing the struggling CAMF received sufficient gifts. There was no guarantee and Nate's faith was tested again and again. To his mother he confided:

"These mission oufits run almost 'broke' all the time and the two-bit savings they make really cramp my style."

Charles Mellis, newly appointed secretary of CAMF, wrote regularly to Nate. "Keep a record of your expenses and let us have a copy," he advised Nate, who found keeping books in addition to the arduous repair work an onerous chore.

In his letters home Nate told his parents of his assignment:

"The Waco repair is going to be an uphill operation. Please pray that I'll use the proper tact in the handling of things here. Would like to get the Waco in the air in six weeks, Lord willing."

Nate recognized the responsibility of his job. He told Charlie Mellis:

"I count it a rare privilege to be in on this deal because I believe that CAMF's future depends more than anything else right now on the repair and continued operation of the Waco.

"Please be frank, blunt, with me. This business is the King's and I feel that there should be no room for personal feelings."

Mellis wrote Nate that he was pioneering in more ways than living in a native house and eating poor food. "You are suffering also from pioneering in administration," Mellis said. "Your patience as a 'guinea pig,' will result in a satisfactory policy on these matters in the future."

Nate wrote humorously to his mother of a bout with dysentery:

"The manual I'm going to write on this subject will be entitled, 'The Price of Native Tasties,' or 'How to Save Money and Lose Appetite and Everything in the Digestive Tract That Isn't Nailed Down.' "

When he returned to his lonely room at night, he reported:

"There are rats jumping and skidding around the rafters. From the sound last night, it seemed like a burro had climbed through my roof and was being chased around my cornstalk ceiling by a pack of wild dogs. Falling clods of mud bore witness to the reality of the activity overhead. The comfort of a mosquito net carefully tucked in all around was wonderful."

The native food bothered Nate, too. He wrote to Mellis:

"Chow tonight was blackbeans or frijoles, two hard-boiled eggs, coffee, rolls, and (let me never forget) tortillas. A tortilla looks like it should line a saddle. It would make an excellent potholder or you might use it as a doily. You might saw holes in them and pitch quoits. Oh well, the dogs under the table like them. With rugged determination, I downed three-quarters of one. It tasted like a generous helping of bad cardboard, treated and coated with terra firma—

"—The interruption that just occurred, though unnoticed by you, ended in the capture and elimination of a beastly looking creature almost two inches long. Not a bird, not a beast, not a fish, I trow. Looked like an amphibious, generously armored, highly mobile, semi-oval, allergic-to-light creature."

When Mellis wrote again concerning accounting procedures, he asked Nate to keep the repair expenses separate from his personal allowance. To this Nate sent a classic reply:

"When coping with bugs, no toilet facilities, linguistic prison, malarial climate, tropic heat, bad food, and so forth, forgive me, Charlie. I'm sure you get the point. . . . Today is my first up and around since the all-night-long attack of diarrhea that left me so weak by 5 A.M. that I could only roll on the floor, calling for help. '*Malo! Señor es malo!*' . . . When lying in your own dung, only semi-conscious, linguistically dumb, please forgive me for not being more explicit on the finances."

Yet it was out of these experiences that Nate and the officers of the new missionary aviation organization were learning valuable lessons that would pay off well in the future.

As the wing panels slowly neared completion, a rugged complication came to light. The wing root fitting on the main spar of the upper wing—the most important part—was ready for assembly, but the blueprint brought from the States disagreed with the factory-made spar that had been shipped to Tuxtla. They were two different models.

"The deciding vote seemed to lie in the debris that remained from the old wings," Nate related, "so I pieced splinters together until I was satisfied that I had the right location. Then came the jolt. The plane I was working on was different from either the blueprint or the factory-prepared spar. The only way out was to build the root section in such a way that I could finish the job in the woods where the opposite wing was still intact and would solve the riddle."

Nate worked night and day to complete the job. Fatigue, bad food, and germs ganged up and sent him to bed with a strange malady. Reliable medical help was not available so Nate finally checked his symptoms in a medical book and with mirror in hand found he was suffering from jaundice. While he was bedridden he allowed his beard to grow and then shaped his chin whiskers into a Vandyke that caused him to resemble his bearded father.

The Lord heard Nate's prayers for help and answered them in Phil Baer, a Wycliffe translator among a tribe of jungle Indians in southern Mexico. Passing through Tuxtla, he discovered Nate's plight and left his own work to help the needy CAMF mechanic.

"He asked me what I was eating," Nate said. "I admitted that I was getting along pretty well on tomatoes and bananas and eggs." Baer wanted to know who was helping him on the airplane wings which had been moved to Nate's room because of difficulties that had developed at the airport. The local airplane operator had refused to let Nate use tools in the hangar. In desperation Nate had moved the whole project to his one-room Mexican house. He was working alone most of the time.

Baer, without mechanical experience, took over all the cooking and simple housekeeping. "Before dawn he was out trying to buy a little meat and a few vegetables for our meals," Nate reported. "He also helped where he could on the repairs. I wasn't used to having someone my senior work for me so I suggested jobs that were easiest and most interesting as the wings took shape. But Phil always insisted on the hard jobs—the jobs that made sore

103

muscles and required endless patience."

This experience with Phil left a lifelong impression on Nate. "It was right there that I began to see what the Lord Jesus meant when He said, 'But whosoever will be great among you, let him be your minister; and whosoever will be chief among you, let him be your servant.'"

Finally everything was ready in Tuxtla. The wings had been built up like a model plane kit, piece by piece (without any glue) ready for quick, final assembly out in the woods. Now it would be necessary to charter a commercial bush plane capable of landing on the airstrip where the crippled craft waited.

"For several days we hunted through the town from tavern to tavern trying to find the pilot of the charter plane," Nate wrote. "The guy had a hangover and was so moody that we got a friend of his to conclude a contract with him. The price was annihilating. Phil and I emptied our pockets on the table by lantern light late that night and counted just enough to put the deal over. We thanked God for His faithfulness, weighed up every piece of equipment, took a nap, and trucked the stuff to the waiting Norseman plane by the dawn's gray light.

"When the plane was packed it was solid to the roof of the cabin so that I had to climb in the front end. Yet it was under the weight the pilot had said he could handle easily. Inside the rear door Phil had kept a cubbyhole space for his wife and baby. She couldn't sit up straight because of the spars and some long plywood overhead. Phil would walk the trail, as there was neither weight nor room for all of us. We prayed together, acknowledging our complete dependence on God.

"The Norseman lumbered heavily to the far end of the field and I watched carefully while our pilot, Hank, checked the engine and instruments. Hank was a gifted fellow but good judgment and humility were not among his gifts.

"He was in good shape the morning we left," Nate's account continues. "Halfway down the runway it seemed as though the plane had accelerated all it was going to, though lifting hard it was still hammering its wheels over the ruts. Then we hit a mud puddle and decelerated a bit. My heart sank. Surely he would 'cut the gun' and lighten ship for another try. But no. We struggled on, slowly regaining what we had lost in the mud. I still had an ignorant confidence in Hank. He had flown the bush so much and under such awful circumstances that surely this wasn't anything new to him.

"Phil and Kempers were watching from the edge of the runway. As we raced past them we were still hugging the ground—the trees just ahead. I learned years later that Phil and Kemp were already running toward the spot where we would crash into the trees. But by this time Hank was 'slipping his last cartridge into the chamber' —his flaps. He was furiously cranking them to full down. He hauled back on the control column and we staggered up within a hair of a fatal stall as the trees raced by just under the wheels. Mary Baer, with her baby in her lap, was praying.

"It was here that I subconsciously turned from Hank. He vanished from my thoughts as I suddenly felt myself completely in the arms of Almighty God. I realized that Hank had purchased freedom from those reaching trees by trading the devastating drag of full flaps for one moment of high lift.

"Providentially we were headed down the valley and the slope was downward toward the valley floor. Hank headed down the slope, just over the treetops, while carefully easing back to one-fourth flaps which gave us a 50-50 chance. Then he found a rising air current.

"Twenty-five minutes later we were on a level with a low spot on the valley rim and Hank headed across. It was a grassy, saddle-like knoll with a slight highspot ahead. We weren't going to make it. The airspeed indicator was right on the red line. Hank flattened the prop into take-off pitch and hauled it across so close that Mary told me later she couldn't see anything but a blur underneath.

"Patiently—that's just a figure of speech here—we traded pounds of fuel consumed by the hot, laboring engine for precious feet of hard-gained altitude. The engine had been running wide open since we started the take-off run, almost three-quarters of an hour now—something it wasn't built to stand. I knew that a heat-warped valve or carbon particle on a spark plug could put us on the mountainside. I've heard it said that airplane mechanics don't

105

enjoy flying. There's a large area of truth within that claim and for obvious reasons. Anyhow, we made it. It was one of those experiences where the acid of self-preservation etches your mind unforgettably.

"When we got to the airstrip where the damaged plane was, we found it in worse condition than I had anticipated. But the engine was in good shape. In a cloud of smoke and with a roar sweeter than the angels' songs, it burst into life. The wings fell together easily and were soon ready."

The deadline on Nate's six-month permit was only a week away when he discovered the work of mud wasps in the fuel tank and lines. That lost him a day in the race. Some bed sheets finished patching the fuselage when the supply of fabric ran out. A hardwood strut replaced its hopeless steel predecessor. One of the dragstruts on the landing gear was made from a Ford V-8 steering column. Although it rained the day the wings went on, the men couldn't let up. No rigging data was available so he propped the tail up on a stump and rigged the new wings to match the old ones by eye . . . just as he used to rig models when a boy.

CAMF pilot George Wiggins arrived to fly the plane out. "I tried to dissuade him," Nate said. "I wanted him to understand that I believed the plane was safe enough for a single fellow with no dependents but not for a man with a family."

But Wiggins had firm instructions from the home office to do the flying once Nate okayed it for ferry. Nate, it was decided, would accompany him.

"We agreed that on the take-off run," Nate wrote, "that George would handle the plane in the usual way except that he wouldn't haul it off the ground until I signaled him. I kept an eye on the airspeed indicator and the wooden strut. At 70 MPH the strut looked good so I poked George and we were airborne.

"As soon as the wheels cleared the ground the left wing started down alarmingly. My heart stopped until I noticed that George wasn't using the control wheel yet. I guess he was having a last look at that wooden strut. At any rate a slight adjustment of the controls straightened the plane out. We made an easy circle and swooped back over the landing strip. Our intention was to impose a strain on the plane close to the ground before starting across the mountains. As the plane bounded skyward we were both satisfied with our 'celestial raft' so we headed for Tuxtla. On the way we tried flying hands off. The plane flew as straight as it would with an auto pilot."

Early the next morning Nate awoke long enough in his hotel room in Tuxtla to hear the sound of the Waco engine roaring overhead as George Wiggins soared north to Mexico City. Nate's work was done. He rolled over and slept heavily—skin and bones but happy. Now he could return to the United States.

In this Mexican interlude, Nate had entered into the hard day-to-day problems of missionary effort. He had survived the rats and the bats, the scorpion bites and the dysentery, the bad food and the heat. He had learned firsthand about the hardships and had no illusions of what it could mean to be a missionary. He had learned something about the need for undertaking a difficult, thankless task under unpleasant circumstances. But most of all he had learned something about the discipline of patience.

These were all-important lessons for an Army veteran turned missionary soldier, and this Mexican experience established a new milestone in missionary aviation.

Nate demonstrated in Mexico his unique mechanical ability in making repairs to a plane that would have been difficult enough in a completely equipped hangar in the States. But it was more than a personal victory for Nate.

His experiences pointed up the fact that more than flying ability was needed in missionary aviation. Nate and his CAMF colleagues were convinced that henceforth missionary aviation demanded pilots with mechanical training or qualified mechanics who had learned to fly. Missionary flying was for specialists who would serve missionaries, not for missionaries who could make flying a side line.

The Mexican repair operation also sparked reanalysis of CAMF thinking relating to the most desirable characteristics of a missionary airplane. Nate had pushed hard for the use of light planes and thus helped crystallize the organizational emphasis on this type of equipment.

En route home, Nate stopped in Los Angeles to make a personal report to the CAMF* board, and shared his plans with them for the future.

"It's a God-given privilege to preach the Gospel of Jesus Christ anywhere. He has called me to people who have never heard of His love. That is why I feel led to get additional schooling—so that I might be first a witness of His saving grace and then an airman." He never abandoned this concept.

During his visit to California Nate arranged for Marj to attend a Fellowship dinner. He wanted her to become better acquainted with the CAMF people, he explained. He was polite but avoided sitting with her at the table. He had written Marj from Mexico that he was engaged to Alice and that he did not feel it was right for them to continue corresponding.

While on the West Coast word came that he was accepted at Wheaton College for the second semester in the early part of 1947. He little knew what surprises it would bring.

*The Christian Airmen's Missionary Fellowship was legally changed to the Missionary Aviation Fellowship September 12, 1946, to coincide with a related British organization with similar aims and activities.

10

COLLEGE FOR A YEAR

. . . the time of the singing of birds is come. . . . SONG OF SOLOMON
2:12

To MANY people Wheaton, Illinois, is just a burgeoning suburban
town on the Chicago and Northwestern Railroad, twenty-five
miles west of Chicago. But to Nate Saint it was the town in which
Wheaton College is located.

Although he had applied to at least one other college, Nate
was pleased when he found that he had been accepted at Wheaton.
He began his single year of college January 28, 1947.

The very fact that Nate Saint was enrolled in college was a big
contrast to earlier days when he couldn't wait to finish Lower
Moreland High School in Huntingdon Valley. His change in attitude toward higher education dated back to the New Year's Eve
service, 1944, in Detroit when he responded to the missionary call.
His six-month stint on the field in Mexico had only sharpened his
resolution to spend at least two years in college.

Like many other GIs of the period, Nate plunged into his studies
with vigor. He found the discipline of the classroom challenging—
completely different from the Army regimen or the toil of the
missionary field. Since school was a sort of unknown quantity,
he took no chances on not succeeding. He told a friend that he
"worked like a fiend for the first half of the semester." By the
middle of the term he decided that he was pushing the books too
hard and began to relax a bit, still maintaining a high average
in his studies.

When spring arrived, Nate developed a feeling that he was
hemmed in. Still a lover of the outdoors, he got a job at a nearby
airport, which gave him permission to have his Ford on campus.
That provided him still more freedom.

Yet Nate did not lose what Wheaton officials called his "holy impatience" to cram in as many subjects as he could with a view to getting out to the field as quickly as possible. He took the courses that he felt would enable him to be an effective Christian worker.

His friend Mrs. Montgomery had encouraged Nate to try his hand at writing. She felt, along with others, that Nate had shown an ability to express himself. With this motivation, he enrolled in one of the journalism classes taught by Robert Walker, able editor of *Christian Life*.

Under Walker's instruction, Nate learned by writing and re-writing that "hard" writing makes for easy reading. Little did either instructor or pupil realize that one day Nate Saint would write a diary that would stir the hearts of the entire Christian world.

Nate loved Wheaton campus life but he often expressed righteous contempt for students he thought were wasting their time playing rook. He felt they were showing poor stewardship of the precious time given them by God.

On Sundays he went with other student groups to work among the Negro families of Chicago's crowded South Side. Restless, he sometimes wandered about the city, seeking for an opportunity to talk to someone about Jesus Christ.

"Had the pleasure of leading a sailor to the Lord yesterday in Union Station," he told his mother in a letter. "He made a clean-cut decision that I think is the real thing. He seemed completely blind as I showed him a number of Scripture verses. Then, after I said that God wanted to give him a clean slate and a fresh start, he said, 'Don't see how He could do that. You'd have to be born again.' With that I slid the third chapter of John under his nose. He read the whole chapter straight through. When he looked up, he was a different man. His eye was steady, no longer elusive. He took Christ right on the spot!"

Nate kept in constant contact with the MAF offices and he continued to show his interest in the work to which he felt the Lord had called him. On more than one occasion he carried out important assignments for the Fellowship, such as checking on aircraft they sought to buy. Nate's report on a float Stinson which he inspected in Detroit was a model in its completeness.

The thought came to Nate one day as he sat in class, watching a dangling pencil swing about on a string, that objects could be lowered on a line from a plane.

He also was impressed with the idea—although it was not original with him—of using short-wave radio to maintain regular contact with inaccessible jungle mission stations. He had been approached by a missionary home on furlough regarding the possibility of establishing a missionary aviation program in New Guinea. In a letter to his brother Sam he wrote:

"If the Lord lays the New Guinea project in my lap, one of the immediate prerequisites to safe and sane flying over that rugged terrain will be radio contact. . . . What missionaries need as I see it is something with which they can get through to the outside world in case they come down with acute appendicitis or something of the sort."

In the year Nate was at Wheaton two air crashes endangered the lives of missionaries—one in Mexico which seriously injured Dr. and Mrs. Cameron Townsend, Wycliffe general director, and one in Ecuador in which missionaries George Poole and Robert Hart were involved. Nate carried on a lengthy analysis of these accidents in his correspondence with the MAF office. Like his colleagues, Nate studied the airplane crashes in the hope of working out safer flying standards in missionary aviation.

When school was dismissed in June, 1947, Nate headed for New York, hoping to get a job at Roosevelt Field and, more important, seeking to be near his fiancée Alice Brown, who was pursuing her nurse's training at a New York hospital. Then came the blow.

Alice told Nate that she wanted to be released from her promise to marry him, that she did not feel strongly enough attached to him to consider marriage. Thereupon she returned his engagement ring.

Nate was crushed and turned to Alice's parents, who were very fond of him.

"It was the only time I ever saw Nate with an unsmiling countenance," Alice's father recalls. "Nate and my wife and I all cried, we felt so bad about the matter."

Within a few weeks Nate came to accept this development as

111

God's hand upon him.

At this juncture, Charles Mellis met Nate in New York City during a missionary convention. They had lots to discuss but in the conversation Charlie dropped the name of Marjorie Farris.

"I did a complete flip inside at the mention of her name," Nate admitted a bit later. "Charlie said that she was going with a fellow in California. I guess I turned green with jealousy inside. . . . I'd have to find out what the deal was if I were to get any sleep."

Nate's first step was to write a lengthy letter to his good friend Sadie Montgomery, then living in Santa Monica. Among many other things he told Mrs. Montgomery that his engagement to Alice had been broken. Almost as an afterthought at the end of his letter he wrote, "Please say hello to Marj for me. Thanks."

That did it. Mrs. Montgomery, knowing of Marjorie's interest in Nate ever since they had first met in the nurses' residence in Los Angeles, notified her immediately. At Mr. Montgomery's suggestion Marj and Mrs. Montgomery wrote to Nate.

Things were moving rapidly now. "I was pleasantly surprised, to put it mildly, to find a letter from Marj in tonight's mail," Nate reported to Mrs. Montgomery. Ever cautious, Nate continued: "Charlie Mellis had said that she was going with a fellow out there so it seemed that maybe I ought to take her letter as that of an old friend who was just sympathetic. Marj has been more than just a friend to me. I realized it when I told her that I thought a ring would soon be involved in my relationship with Alice and that I thought it would be better if we didn't write any more. She was so good about it that it was a convicting blessing to me."

Opening his heart to his confidante, Nate described his break with Alice: "I still don't know anything much about real suffering. The Lord filled the big empty place in my heart in a miraculous way. There was a tussle first, but when I gave up, He gave a wonderful peace. . . ."

Spurred on by the success of her match-making, Sadie Montgomery forwarded Nate's latest letter to Marj. "Sounds good, doesn't it?" she added in a note. "This is really getting interesting! I'll have to assure Nate that there's nothing serious about you and this fellow you've been going out with!! After that nature should be allowed to take its course."

The correspondence from California goaded Nate into action. He piled his belongings into his Ford and drove as far as Wheaton and hitchhiked on to California to see Marjorie.

"The little fears were replaced by a peaceful sort of ease and confidence," he wrote Sadie Montgomery, "and have made room for a good deal of happiness and bewilderment that such a wonderful girl should care for me. . . .

"It would be natural that you should worry a little about this being a sort of rebound affair. . . .

"I didn't know Marj very well before," Nate continued in his ecstasy of new-found love. "We didn't have time to really get acquainted. I had no idea what a choice girl I knew—like playing marbles with a diamond. I didn't know that I'd wind up playing for keeps. Glad I won."

He concluded with a final tribute:

"Marj is the most utterly selfless girl I have ever met. I thought that you were saying quite a bit in your letter about her but now I understand why you said all those things. . . . It is incomprehensible to me—such love as hers."

To this letter Sadie Montgomery later added a note to Marj:

"This is the last of the letters he wrote me in my role of 'Mother Confessor'. . . . You took over from here on out and satisfied that lonesome, restless nature. . . . For me it was 'Mission Accomplished.'"

Nate continued to pour out affection in a flood of letters that sped westward from Wheaton. Only once did he falter. The boys of his dormitory analyzed his case as love on the rebound. For a time Nate was upset, fearing that he might be wooing Marj when he wasn't too sure of his own heart. "Let's back off a notch," he wrote to her, "and think of ourselves as hopeful sweethearts . . . at least until I'm absolutely sure."

Marj's understanding letters soon restored his confidence and his realization that this was the girl he would marry. "The fog is thinning out and my heart tells me the story . . . I love you. My heart has been singing that song all along but my head was off

113

pitch for a while. I know now that it is love . . . the realest, deepest kind a fellow can know. It is a wonderful thing, this love. Each day it seems to knock on the door of infinity . . . yet each day it grows." This was the beginning of a deepening love that he never lost again.

While the letters were flying back and forth between Wheaton and California, Nate kept busy in school, worked for the Wheaton Post Office, and continued actively in Christian work.

He passed up the existing channels of Christian activity. Instead, Nate and his roommate Arthur Klem cruised the countryside about Wheaton in an old car seeking new opportunities for service. One particular Sunday the pair drove west about thirteen miles to the town of Bartlett. There they encountered some teenagers playing ball in the park. After conversing with the young people, the two Wheaton students called from door to door in the town, suggesting that a young people's work be started.

It turned out that some of the young people were entering upon a virtual state of rebellion against restrictions that had been placed upon them. In a town of less than one thousand people, there was nothing for the young people to do, except hang around in a confectionery store or the town tavern, Nate was told by representatives of the group.

Some folk criticized the teenagers when they went into the tavern for a hamburger. The little confectionery was also looked upon with some suspicion as their hangout. "But a few of the older folk are on the kids' side and even want a class for themselves," Nate wrote.

Because of the situation the young people had developed a strong group spirit. When one of their number received a real or imagined slight from the woman leader of the young people's group in the local church, they all pulled out. They organized themselves into a group "to get what they wanted." Nate indicated that he felt sure that "underneath they still had a lot of respect for parental authority."

Nate and Arthur soon won the confidence of these teenagers. In the discussion that followed it was decided they would hold a youth club each Sunday night in one of the homes. They asked

Peggy Smith, another Wheatonean, to serve as pianist.

Nate felt that the fellows and girls were most opposed to what they described as "nonsympathetic authority." He agreed to help them arrange for showings of films obtained from the Chicago YMCA, to provide for a forum in which they could discuss problems of interest, and to arrange for various types of social occasions.

When the first meeting was held at Bartlett, twenty teenagers turned out. "Art and I like to think of these meetings," Nate said, "as a candy box loaded with gospel dynamite. God's Word is powerful and we believe that He will honor it with changed lives among these kids. I would certainly not pursue this thing were it not for the fact I'm following the Word of One who wrought such a miracle in my own life."

Nate continued at Bartlett until he completed his college work at Wheaton several months later.

This teenage work opened the door to contact with younger children, and provided Christian service opportunities for an increasing number of Wheaton students. Some of the original Bartlett group later enrolled as students at Wheaton.

When the Christmas recess was approaching, Nate and Marj agreed, in their letters, to meet for the holidays at the home of her parents, Mr. and Mrs. Hubert Farris at Caldwell, Idaho. By this time, Marj had received her bachelor of science degree from the University of Southern California and had completed her nurse's training. Nate presented Marj with an engagement ring, described later as her "left-handed hardware."

Over the objections of Mrs. Farris, Marj agreed to give up her nursing post (then in San Francisco) and to return with Nate to Wheaton where it was planned she would enroll for certain courses and continue her nursing. The wedding was planned for the following June.

Marj quickly obtained employment at the Delnor Hospital in St. Charles, a few miles from Wheaton. Now she would share with Nate in making one of the crucial decisions of his future career.

In November Charlie Mellis had reported to the MAF constituency that Jim Truxton was making a missionary aviation survey in Ecuador. Later the same month Mellis wrote complimenting

Nate on his increasing desire to get out to the foreign field:

"I don't need to tell you how much we need men on the field. At the same time I know how you feel about finishing your year's school work."

Then, even before Nate had left for Christmas holidays, Mellis brought up the subject of Ecuador as a possible field. He wrote:

"Sometime back I mentioned Ecuador to you and didn't get a response. Jim has been both over and through those rugged jungles and he insists the job is ten times as difficult as the one in Mexico. . . . In Ecuador there are just two forced landing areas—the top of the jungle or the raging rapids of a river. . . .

"Jim's recommendation for this work is that if a man must be short on anything, let it be the flying—he must be an absolute expert in mechanics.

"I'm not insinuating anything about your flying ability, Nate, but we don't have a man in the organization whose mechanical ability we're as sure of as we are of yours. . . . As I pointed out before, we must be sure in Ecuador, of all places.

"Pray about all this for awhile, Nate, and then let us know how the Lord is leading," Mellis concluded.

Even before the Ecuador proposal had been suggested, Nate had been approached by Dr. Harold T. Commons, president of the Association of Baptists for World Evangelization, who urged him to consider setting up a missionary aviation program for ABWE in New Guinea. The idea greatly appealed to Nate and for a time he seriously thought of breaking his ties with MAF.

With Marj at his side Nate was able to consider with her the pros and cons of Ecuador versus New Guinea.

To Charles Mellis he wrote of his difficulty in making a choice between the two fields. At great length he spelled out the various elements that ended up in indecision.

"Please forgive me for keeping you circling the field so long, Charlie," Nate continued. "It has been a bit foggy and I wanted to make sure I knew what I was doing before I gave you the light."

In a lengthy reply Mellis discussed the needs of the two areas, admitting that eventually "New Guinea could easily prove to be the very biggest job in the field of missionary aviation."

At the same time he pointed out:

"The purpose of the program in Ecuador is twofold: to provide adequate supply line for the present work and make possible deeper penetration into the jungle to reach souls that have not yet heard of Christ."

Mellis also stated that in Ecuador MAF could substantiate its proposal to use light simple equipment. (In 1948 there were still many conflicting counterclaims of the type of equipment for difficult jungle terrain.)

"If the Lord should lead you to consider Ecuador, I'm wondering if you and Marj would consider making a quick-change act to the Bible Institute of Los Angeles for the coming semester," Mellis wrote. He confided that MAF was promised a gift of a Stinson airplane which could be equipped with a rebuilt engine and flown to Ecuador for the work there.

"How would you like a honeymoon trip flying a Stinson Voyager to Ecuador?" Mellis asked as a parting shot.

By January 8, Nate and Marj, impressed by the needs of the field, felt they should move their wedding date up to some time in the spring and leave Wheaton at the end of the semester.

By the end of January, Nate had received word from Dr. Commons that ABWE could not guarantee when the Dutch government might grant a permit for their mission to enter New Guinea. Then Charles Mellis arrived from Los Angeles early in February to discuss the Ecuador project at length. Together Nate and Marj agreed that Ecuador was the place to which God was calling.

"Perhaps I've gotten into the habit of barging in where angels fear to tread," Nate said, "but I still have the ability to say 'sorry' if it becomes evident that the job is too tough. We know if we humbly seek His face in the matter, crucifying our own desires, we can't go wrong. It seems a pretty safe policy to let little mistakes and failures indicate an overshooting of the Lord's leading, and until they appear, venture by faith. Fear and faith are not fellow travelers."

They decided to get married that month and begin preparations for going to Ecuador as soon as possible.

11

TWOSOME TO ECUADOR

Where the birds make their nests. . . . PSALM 104:17

NATE AND MARJ were married on Valentine's Day, 1948, at a simple ceremony in the Baptist Church in Manhasset, New York, the church the Sam Saint family attended. Sam's wife Jeanne played the piano. "I was able to see their faces during the ceremony," she recalls; "not many are privileged to see such love and total giving on the faces of two people. I will never forget it."

The young couple had driven from Wheaton, without making an overnight stop en route in order to avoid criticism. Neither the winter weather nor a leaking radiator affected their jubilant spirits.

Before they left Wheaton, "Skelp," as Nate always called his brother David, had sent a check, demonstrating the strong family spirit of the Saints.

"I don't know how you intended that big fat check," Nate wrote Dave. "If it was an 'emergency gift,' I think we should return it because the Lord has been wonderfully supplying, step at a time. However, if you want it to go into our equipment for the field, we'll accept it. Either way we're deeply grateful for it as a token of love for Him and consequently for us."

Sam Saint arranged for the newlyweds to fly to Washington, D.C. for their honeymoon.

In March, Nate and Marj visited his evangelist brother Phil in his home at Hawthorne, New Jersey, and discussed at length methods of deputation work.

"We have several sets of slides that can be worked into messages," Nate told his father in a letter requesting that he set up meetings later in the season for the outgoing missionary couple. "We also have a collection of exhibits such as blow guns and poisoned darts, facsimile of a shrunken head, witch doctor's outfit, spears, baskets, pottery, and the like."

It was a case of "Have missionary paraphernalia. Will travel," yet Nate shrank from the fund-raising aspect of missionary preparation. "I am hoping that the Lord will make it unnecessary to mention the matter of support to anyone," Nate confided to Phil. "The Lord said, 'Prove me now' . . . His faithfulness is far greater than our hesitating faltering trust.

"I'm convinced that MAF now has the goods to lay on the counter. It is time to launch out into the deep and see what the Lord will do. We have never done any deputation work to speak of before because we wanted to be sure that we were inviting folks to share in a reliable investment of stewardship. But now we feel confident that the Lord is going to use airplanes and radio to get the work done safely and economically."

Phil had given Nate a used slide projector and mimeograph machine. The latter, Nate figured, could be used "to keep in touch with friends who would otherwise think that we had dropped into an open manhole."

Nate was pleased as support came in quickly. "Without our mentioning it to anyone, Marj's church [Grace Evangelical Free Church, Huntington Park, California] had expressed its interest in sharing in our support. Marj is dear to those folks and the Lord has seen fit to grant me favor with them too."

The newlyweds drove westward in the old Ford, stopping for some sightseeing en route at the Grand Canyon and the Painted Desert before they proceeded to the MAF headquarters in Los Angeles. Southern California was their base for the ensuing five months.

It was beginning to dawn on the young man who had so longed to be an Army pilot that the very thing he had been compelled to sacrifice was being returned to him. He summarized his feelings in a letter home:

"In 1944 the Lord called me from aviation to Himself, and now He has sent me back to aviation for Himself."

Although Nate was convinced that God was going to use him as a missionary flier, he had other interests. When he received word from his sister Rachel that she had been accepted as a missionary with the Wycliffe Bible Translators, he sent warm

119

congratulations, and added this comment:

"My own feelings toward the translation work is such that if the Lord had not definitely called me to aviation, I'm sure I would be in language work. What a priceless privilege, that of leaving something behind you . . . which will enable the Lord to work with new tribes through His own Book. . . ."

Nate then offered encouragement to his sister about financial support:

"We know by experience that His promises are good and that He is abundantly able to supply your needs out of His storehouse where He keeps universes, worlds, moons, stars. In His other storehouse He has grace unbounded, billows of love on oceans of care for His own, mountains of patience, and other good things abundantly above all that we can ask or think. Isn't it a crime that we are so often slow to accept these gifts?"

But there was little time for philosophizing. The Missionary Aviation Fellowship had set August 1 as the deadline for the young couple's departure for South America. The engine of the Stinson was to be replaced and the plane modified for the equatorial conditions under which it would operate. Besides the mechanical work which Nate supervised, he was building up time at a nearby airport for an instrument license and there were important conversations with MAF executives and deputation meetings.

There were personal developments, too. In a letter describing the injections he and Marj were taking to protect them against tropical diseases, Nate told his father: "We started our shots yesterday. Naturally I was on hand to help my helpless little pregnant wife in case the shots made her sick, but we wound up afterward with me stretched out on a bench and Marj mopping my pale and sweating brow." But both of them survived and Marj's doctor said she was making good progress, although there had been some concern over her condition in the early stages of her pregnancy. Both Nate and Marj were thrilled by this development. No child was anticipated with greater love.

Then, because there was much still to be done, MAF set a new and realistic deadline. The Saints were instructed to reach Quito by September 10. They first flew the remodeled Stinson to Idaho, where they stopped to say good-by to Marj's folks, and then on to the East for meetings in the New York and Philadelphia areas and for farewells to Nate's family.

The young couple faced the fact that their first child would be born in South America under conditions that might not be as favorable as the United States. The obstetrician, in his fancy suite of offices in New York City, warned against the move before the baby was born, but Nate just smiled and said, "Dr. C. doesn't know how the Lord takes care of these details. We'll leave on schedule."

As the time approached for departure, it was decided that Nate and Jim Truxton, who was working for good relations with the Ecuadorian government, would fly down to Ecuador in the Stinson and that Marj would proceed by commercial airline to Quito, accompanied by Jim's wife Betty. Their equipment and household furnishings were packed in steel drums and crates to follow by boat.

In a letter sent to his friends, Nate described what lay ahead:

"In Ecuador we'll fly south above the Andes and then duck down the eastern slope to the foothills and the little Shell Oil camp located where the road yields to jungles and missionaries to mules. Beyond lies the vast dank dungeon of the mighty Amazon where thousands are bound in darkness by chains of sin. At Shell Mera we'll meet several other missionaries who will help us raise a house and hangar. This will be the MAF headquarters in Ecuador. Next comes the setting up of the radio-telephone network that will connect the jungle stations to our base. Then, the air penetration program that you pray for and share in so faithfully.

"Our job is not to compete with existing airlines since a commercial company can nearly always do the job more economically.

"Nor are we expecting the airplane to usher in a workless golden age for the missionaries but rather it will be used as a tool that will let them push ahead more effectively.

"We say that God could use even menial things like airplanes if they were dedicated to the reaching of the lost. Our responsibility is to harness aviation to the needs of the mission field."

As the day of actual departure approached, Nate and Marj were still several hundred dollars short of the funds needed. But Nate never showed the slightest doubt that they would leave as planned.

Nate and Jim took off from Brownsville, Texas, September 8. They arrived safely in Quito four days later. The two wives reached Quito September 16 after Nate and Jim had left for Shell Mera to begin constructing the MAF base.

Charles Mellis, Sr., a St. Louis builder and father of MAF's secretary, met them there. He had agreed to supervise the construction of the house Nate and Marj would occupy. They would build on a piece of land opposite the east end of the Shell Oil Company headquarters and airfield.

Shell activities had started in Ecuador in 1938 when geologists began their work. The early operation was extremely difficult since there were no roads into the jungle. A journey of five days was required to go from Ambato to the Oriente, as the eastern jungle is known. An agreement with the Ecuadorian government, eager to see the Oriente opened, gave Shell the right to carry on explorations in the entire virgin jungle area.

The entrance of Shell into the previously inaccessible country had great implications for the missionaries already in Ecuador and the others that would follow them. Hauling in bulldozers and other equipment, Shell personnel performed feats of modern magic. Construction of roads and airfields was made more difficult by the broken nature of the country, the 200-inch annual rainfall, as well as the perils of malarial swamps, poisonous snakes, and hostile Indians.

A road had to be blasted through granite and dug from the miles of mud and loose gravel from Baños to the new Shell base camp at Shell Mera (so called because of the older village of Mera several miles up the pass). The new road became the only entry to the jungle from the western populated portions of Ecuador.

In eleven years the Shell organization reportedly had spent forty million dollars to develop its Ecuador program. They had spared no expense in constructing air fields. Because of the boggy nature of the jungle soil, tons of crushed rock were laid down so that heavy aircraft could land and take off without difficulty.

The first camp to be built was Arajuno, which later was to become a mission station. Then a camp and airstrip was built at

Ayuy in Jivaro country, which gave access to a well drilled at Macuma. The latter point later became an important station of the Gospel Missionary Union. Also a camp was built at nearby Wambimi—also a future mission station. Shell built airstrips and camps at Tiputini and Villano. In a company manual describing these operations, they commented on the indigenous population:

"An ever-present danger, especially in the early days, was an attack on the camp by hostile Indians, the Aushiris, more commonly called the Aucas, who inhabit this part of the country. Some fourteen company workers have been killed by these Indians who are completely uncivilized and ambush their victims, killing them with spears. No serious attempt has been made to contact them and fraternize with them; the present-day location of some of their houses is known and noted from the air; from which it can be seen that the Aucas do a little cultivating on the clearings around their houses. They adopt a warlike attitude, and even throw spears at the planes flying over them."

A number of wells were drilled including the one on the Oglán River which reached a depth of 9435 feet, but no oil worthy of commercial production was discovered.

Nate kept his parents informed of progress on the building of the MAF base:

"I'm in a tent at Shell Mera writing on a cardboard box by lantern light. Jim Truxton is sitting next to me writing a letter. On the cot across from us is George Poole. Frank Drown, Keith Austin, and Morrie Fuller are also helping us build the house. Mr. Mellis, who is seventy years old, works along with us and sparkplugs the project as though he were thirty.

"This corner of Ecuador is a fascinating piece of God's creative handiwork. Mornings, after we've 'washed' in the basin in front of the tent, the sun climbs high enough to show us the snow-coated peak of Sangay, an active volcano about forty miles away. It blows up smoke and ash and at night you can see it shoot red lava fireworks high into the air. When the sun chases the clouds farther up the pass that comes down into Mera we'll be able to see the huge jagged snow-covered crater of El Altar. The climate is wonderful. Almost no mosquitoes. Down behind the base is a small river

123

and the surrounding area is covered with beautiful greenery. We stopped along the road near here the other day and picked a half dozen beautiful lavender orchids. The country is so beautiful that it is hard to get yourself accused of exaggeration.

"It is fun roughing it, washing in a pail, using tent ropes for clothes lines, cooking on a camp stove. We eat our evening meals at the Shell Camp because about all we can buy to cook for ourselves is rice, potatoes, and navy beans."

Nate was in Shell Mera only a few days before he was flying supplies and equipment as well as personnel into the jungle stations. In one of his early letters to friends back home, Nate described the stations he was serving. These included Pano, where the Henry Millers worked; Dos Rios, where the David Coopers carried on work among seventy Indian children; Ahjuana, a new station on the banks of the Napo River to be manned by the Morris Fullers; Macuma, where the Frank Drowns and Keith Austins served the Jivaros; Sucua, also a Jivaro station served by the Mike Fickes; Chupientsa, a mule-day away from the Sucua strip.

The missionary plane performed two mercy flights also during these first days. Missionaries at Macuma reported that they had been without fresh foods and medical supplies for five months. In thirty-seven minutes this need was cared for, contrasting with a five- to seven-day trip on foot.

Mrs. Grace Cooper of the Christian and Missionary Alliance had been carried from her jungle home at Dos Rios three weeks earlier on an Indian's back. She had suffered a severe attack of malaria. Partially recovered from her illness, but too weak to return to her home on foot, Mrs. Cooper was flown to her station, along with her husband and two children, in a thirty-two-minute trip. It had taken three days for the same journey before the airplane arrived.

"I want to share these stories that are unfolding all around us," Nate wrote to Mellis at the MAF office. "Mine would only be attempts, to be sure, but attempts plus helpful criticism may allow me eventually to be able to tell stories with flavor that can only come from an eye-witness. Your comments on journalism are all well taken, Charlie. Naturally it would be hard to sit down and write 'Difficulties of Missionary Life' when I know so little about the subject. Maybe mine is a one-track mind. When I take pictures, they are of the work the Lord has laid close to my heart—Indians and airplanes. When I lie awake at night (I seldom do) my mind is on safety devices and methods for the airplane to help reach the Indians. When it's a letter home it's airplane—Indian—Christ. You can see, can't you, that when I try to write a story, I like to write about airplanes and Indians. The Indian is the motive. But all I know about him is that he's lost unless I keep the airplane going and get the news to him. The airplane is my job. I don't want to be a great writer but I long to express myself just as I've often longed to be able to sit down at a big pipe organ and express myself. Nuff said."

Marj meanwhile had stayed in Quito with Betty Truxton. Writing to friends in the States, she relayed word from Nate that he had acquired a hen called Gertrude and a rooster. "The hen laid her egg for today next to yesterday's in a box of nails at Gertie's egg depot. Nate added some straw to encourage her domestic instincts. Come down in a few months," Marj concluded, "and we'll serve you scrambled eggs or fried chicken."

On October 30 Nate reported to MAF headquarters:

"Our crew assaulted the bush with tents, rice, and machetes. First, it was necessary to clear the land and make the foundation (cement pillars with canals for oil—keep ants out of the house). The house is just across the road from the Shell Company landing strip which you see in the immediate foreground in the enclosed picture. Tonight we opened the gates and taxied the ship across the road right up to the house. It wouldn't go through the kitchen door so we are hoping to get the hangar under way next week. The sides will be boarded in to make a storehouse and workshop. We feel much better now that the plane is just outside our back door with Skipper, Poole's dog, sleeping in it."

It was while the missionary construction crew sat about their campfire or sprawled in their tents that Nate first learned from David Cooper, who was passing through Shell Mera, about the savage tribe of Indians who were dreaded by everyone in Ecuador . . . the naked Aucas. Both Dr. Tidmarsh, Plymouth Brethren missionary, and Cooper had made efforts to reach them but their advances were repulsed. For nearly three centuries, the Aucas had refused friendship with white men and neighboring tribes of Indians.

The standard Auca reply to overtures of friendship was an ambush that left the bodies of victims pierced with nine-foot chonta spears. When the Spanish explorers entered South America, they were followed by Roman Catholic priests, and one Jesuit missionary reportedly succeeded in establishing friendly relations with the Aucas. But ill health forced him to leave the jungle. Later rubber hunters and gold prospectors sought for easy gains and ruthlessly raided the Indian settlements. This only caused the Aucas to retreat deeper into the jungle and become more wary than ever of strangers.

The name Auca, Quichua word meaning "savage," for generations has been a synonym for terror in Ecuador. The tales of Auca savagery are a part of the country's folklore. The stories Dave Cooper told about the Aucas made a deep impression on Nate, and he was never able to shake it. He thought of them not as savages, but as a people for whom Christ died. The seed of compassion was planted in Nate's heart, and as time went on this seed grew into a real passion for the souls of these men of the forest.

Writing to his parents in October, 1948, he mentioned the Aucas for the first time in a letter:

"Not long ago we talked to another missionary who is longing to contact a tribe of killers. Neighboring tribes live in mortal fear of them. We expect the airplane will somehow play an essential part in the reaching of these people one day with the Gospel.

"We're watching and praying for that day."

While the construction work was in progress, two little girls, children of Shell Oil Company executives, visited Shell Mera and asked when a Sunday school would be started. It was one channel of immediate service. "I'm planning to use object lessons and stick pretty much to the practical side of every day being a Christian," Nate wrote. "The first Sunday I'll remodel one of Dr. Rimmer's sermons on the 'Flying Worm'—caterpillar to butterfly —and illustrate it comic-strip style with colored chalk. I can use a roll-up blackboard we brought made of a window shade painted with some sort of flexible paint. The idea is simply that the worm wanted to fly but didn't believe God's way would work. So he made some wooden wings and tried this and that. Finally when everything else had failed he decided to do what the 'worm's Bible' said and . . . 'be born again.' "

Nate took a walk one Sunday afternoon to the neighboring town of Puyo, terminus of the road heading toward the jungle. "The Lord burdened me heavily for that town," he told his parents. "It will be within reach on my motor-scooter or I can ride one of the trucks that pass frequently. I prayed a lot about it and what do you think happened? Within a week I ran into the mayor of Puyo marooned at an isolated airstrip in the jungle. While giving him a lift, we got acquainted. I found out later he was sympathetic to the evangelical cause."

Finally came the day in October when Marj traveled by car from Quito to Ambato to meet Nate and together they flew to Shell Mera.

At last they were in their own home together. Shell Merita—an affectionate term for the rambling house—was built of rough-planed lumber from native trees, stained a warm friendly brown on the outside and varnished on the inside. The roof was made of corrugated aluminum with wide overhanging eaves. There was an opening between the top of the wall and the roof all around to let the breezes of Shell Mera's perfect climate blow through the house.

"We figure that if a thing is both useful and practical it will have a good look about it so we have devoted outselves, of necessity as well as of philosophy, to making everything about the house simple, easy to take care of and useful," Nate said.

"In between flights and airplane maintenance, I continued to make improvements about the base.

"The bathroom is taking shape now. The sink is in place with a cabinet around it. One side of the cabinet is for the photo-developing supplies. Soon we're going to make a stall-shower. It's hard to describe the way we have enjoyed opening up the crates of equipment. Some of them were packed so long ago we had forgotten what was in them . . . guess we were like kids under a Christmas tree. Item by item we thought of the different folks who gave us this and that. The thing that has perhaps impressed us most is the utility of the things we have been unpacking. Everything seems to have a useful nitch. For the past few days it has been hard to walk around the house. We have had to use the lumber that the crates were made of in order to have cupboards and closets to put things in. Even the crates seem made to order. The refrigerator box, turned inside out, makes an excellent closet. The water system hasn't materialized yet so we store water in wash tubs. The rain water from the aluminum roof is sparkling clear and very soft. When we uncrated a new washing machine the other day we read in the instructions that if we used water softener it would make our water as soft as rainwater. We smiled at each other . . . poor people in civilization. Did we tell you about the mystery box that arrived from the States? We had no idea what was in it. Well we opened it as soon as it came and there was a beautiful Thor electric dishwasher instead of the Maytag gasoline-powered washing machine we had originally ordered while in New York. We shipped the Thor back, canceled the order for the Maytag, and bought a washer in Quito.

"We have a little meat closet so that the smoked meats don't have to hang from the rafters of our unfinished kitchen ceiling any more. The side door on our house leads into the living-dining-radio-Sunday-school room. From the kitchen window, we can watch the planes taking off and landing, at the same time enjoying the mountain scenery and jungle growth in the foreground. Just the kind of setup that makes you hang your chin on the window sill and philosophize yourself to sleep.

"We're expecting half a dozen missionary children in from the Quito school en route to the jungle stations for vacation with their folks. Also we received a note from Dos Rios calling for an ampule of antitetanus serum. The note just said, 'Nancy Gail sustained bad gash.' Nancy is the little Cooper girl. As soon as the radio equipment is set up we'll be able to have information of this sort twice a day and get right on the job with the plane to meet serious emergencies. The equipment for the radio net is here at last, though still crated. One of the head technicians from HCJB is coming down to set the whole works up for us. The outfits operate from auto-type batteries which are charged by gasoline-driven generators so that an engine failure will not cut off communication."

The house with the tiny hangar became the MAF Air Station at the gateway to the jungle. To Nate and Marj it was to be a habitation of love and a strategic base for service.

12

CRASH AT QUITO

. . . hide me under the shadow of thy wings. PSALM 17:8

"DECEMBER 30, 1948. QUITO, ECUADOR TO MAF HEADQUARTERS, CALIFORNIA: VIOLENT, TURBULENT AIR CAUSED CRASH AT QUITO AIRPORT. NATE AND TWO PASSENGERS NOT CRITICALLY INJURED. PLANE WASHED OUT. DETAILS FOLLOWING.

TRUXTON"

With this brief cable Jim Truxton told the home office that Nate had crashed during a take-off from the airport in Quito.

From early December, Marj had been in the capital city awaiting the arrival of their first child. A weekend visit was Nate's first occasion for a flight back up to Quito with its 9300-foot elevation airstrip. On the return flight to the jungle, Nate had as passengers, Mrs. Tidmarsh and her twelve year old son Robert. During the take-off the yellow Stinson was caught in tricky air currents from the surrounding mountains and fell back to earth. As with other critical events in Nate's life, he wrote the story himself better than others could write it for him. Seven days after the accident, with Marj taking dictation by his bedside, he wrote his parents, who had been waiting anxiously for details they feared were being withheld:

Quito, January 6, 1949

Dear folks:

About time we let you in on the recent happenings. We know it has been harder on you than on us because you were too far away to help. The folks here have been knocking themselves out to take care of us the way you would if you were here.

In the providence of God, neither Marj nor Dr. Tidmarsh were at the airport when we took off for Shell Mera—Mrs. Tidmarsh, and her son Bob and I. The take-off was perfectly normal until we were about 200 feet above the rather large Quito airfield. Then a sudden and violent down-draft caught us and we started dropping like a stone. In an attempt to break our fall somewhat I turned left into the wind but we crashed, almost completely without control, in a plowed field. The initial impact broke the engine and landing gear right off the plane and the momentum bounced the wreckage fifteen yards through the air, catapulting it in such a way that it came to rest upside down.

I can't remember a thing after seeing the ground right in front of us—coming fast. I don't recall any particular fear at that moment, nor since, as we've talked and hashed over the whole business. This, I believe, is the result of the deep assurance we have in our hearts that Satan himself cannot stop us, nor sign our death certificate, without the permission of Almighty God. In this experience I have not felt particularly close to eternity because I am deeply convinced that we live moment by moment by His tender mercies because He has a job for us to do ere we see Him face to face. I see no reason to expect that our homegoing should be dramatic, since it is not determined by dangerous nor dramatic circumstances but by the will of God. When God calls us home, certainly we shall have no regrets. Mrs. Tidmarsh did not lose consciousness at all during the crash. She told us the story of what had happened. Robert was free and screaming with fear— pretty well cut up on the forehead and foot. Mrs. Tidmarsh herself was hanging by her safety belt and was unable to get it loose. Her nose had a mean gash across it, her forehead was cut and bleeding and both ankles were pinned.

She said that I was very animate the whole time, asking her if she could get loose and talking about this and that. She says that I did get my belt loose but that my body was pinned between baggage and the control wheel and my left foot was securely pinned. Also my forehead was needing some stitches and the right side of my jaw was swelling. The wreckage on impact had scooped up buckets of dry dusty dirt which coated us all heavily and when mixed with blood made a beastly mess. The rudder pedals were all the way up where the instrument panel belonged. The control wheel was bent as though it were putty—one end broken off. The fuselage was not just buckled; it was broken in two, hanging on one bent longeron.

In about ten minutes some Ecuadorian army boys got to us. They're swell fellows and mean well but Mrs. Tidmarsh related that when they saw the mess, they got excited and just yanked us out. At that, maybe it was better than fiddling around while we made fruitless donations of blood. She says that I jabbered constantly with the fellows in Spanish. This interests me because I know so little Spanish up to now and speak it with such difficulty.

An Ecuadorian air-force truck rushed us to the Ayora Clinic at the direction of Mrs. Tidmarsh.

Marj says that when she walked in I was a horrible sight—my teeth were so black with dirt she thought at first they had all been knocked out. What worried her most was the big dent she saw in my back as the doctors worked on me.

At first, I thought I was blind. I had always thought blindness would be the most terrible affliction a man could suffer, but now I didn't mind—I knew the Lord could still use me.

I see I haven't given you the actual report on physical damage. Mrs. Tidmarsh is five months pregnant. The baby is okay! Praise the Lord! In addition to the cuts and so on it was found that she had broken the small bones of both lower legs. Bob escaped with minor injuries. As for me, I turned out to have, besides cuts and bruises, a compression fracture of the fourth lumbar vertebrae in my back and badly pulled ligaments in the left ankle. In the operating room they shot me with a dose of "happy juice" called morphine and proceeded to arch my back smartly. Then they built a plaster cast around my body. Another cast on my foot completed the uniform.

You are probably wondering how the shock of this has affected me. Frankly, as nearly as I can detect, it has left no fears or qualms. An answer to your prayers is reflected in the strength and courage Marj has shown these days. Our baby is due any day now, yet she has been constantly making me comfortable, reading to me, taking dictation, helping me eat. Her cheerfulness and faith have been a real blessing and have made my burden unusually light. One could easily forget whether her tentative appointment is with the baby clinic or the dentist.

We'll appreciate your continued intercession. Pray with us that God will, out of the debris of this battle, challenge the hearts of many who still don't know the blessing of all-out abandonment to the Lord Jesus Christ and to the job He wants us to do in simple obedience. The world is dying for want of a Savior—yet so many who profess to love Him are still living "business as usual" lives, cheating themselves of the "high calling of God in Christ Jesus."

Your kids,
Nate and Marj

Almost before the plaster was hard in Nate's cast, he and the officers of MAF began a series of long letters and interviews, studying into the cause of the accident. MAF pilots Jim Truxton and Hobey Lowrance agreed with Nate that a downdraft or windshift had been the underlying cause. During the co-operative discussions that followed, Jim and Hobey expressed the opinion that better recovery techniques would probably have minimized injuries, while Nate maintained that the unusual wind condition had to be experienced to be fully understood. His pilot brother Sam wrote:

"It seems clear to me that a gust petered out and left you sitting there with a stalled airplane on your hands. You did the only thing you could have done from that altitude—make it as soft as possible."

Later Nate granted that had he anticipated what was coming, he would have had more speed even though less altitude and the accident might have been avoided. He also resolved, "If I should ever fly around these hills again I'd give myself about three times as much margin." Nate summed up the matter in a characteristic letter to headquarters:

"God only knows how often I've had occasion to hate my old cocky nature. I hate it . . . but I'm grateful that when sanctified it can be a somewhat useful sort of nature. It seems to me that rather than let this thing focus my attention on one small point, I should carefully restudy all my flying practices in search of flaws in technique. The accident is in my file under: Risks Matured and Collected."

Out of this crucible of testing came MAF's growing emphasis on flight orientation of its missionary airmen. Also, MAF began equipping all its planes with shoulder harnesses to minimize injuries in future accidents. Significantly, there have been no injuries since that date.

Nate was flown to Panama nine days after the accident to have his back checked further by the United States military doctors there. The following day, January 10, 1949, Kathy Joan was born in Quito. Marj wired this good news to Panama.

"Thank God for the wonderful news in the telegram," Nate replied by letter. "I didn't realize how much concern for you I had suppressed until the telegraph messenger boy walked into the ward. It took all the courage I had to hold steady while I opened the envelope. Honey, don't be afraid to give that little gal lots of loving. She'll need the practice for when her daddy gets home.

133

"God has been so good to us—even counting us able to suffer a little. It's been tough in spots but He has always supplied the needed grace, hasn't He?

"I love you two more than you can possibly imagine and always will. Only death can separate us and then even that will be temporary. I can hardly wait to see our precious baby.

"May the Lord guide our steps until we are making footprints side by side again."

Back with Marj and the baby in Quito, Nate adjusted to the new circumstances. Nate wrote to Marj's parents and his own again on January 30:

Dear Moms and Dads:

This morning Marj squeezed me into my clothes (they barely make it around the cast) and I went to church with the Clarks. When we got home, Marj and Kathy were at the gate waiting for me. They had been soaking up some nice warm high altitude sunshine. We're hoping to be getting down to the jungles within a couple of weeks. After being in the mountains for a while, the air down at Shell will be good enough to eat. The air up here (9000 feet above sea level) is plenty good, but there just isn't enough of it to go around.

The cast hits me just below the Adam's apple in front so that I can't hang my head forward, but it is lower across my shoulders and back—kind of has a wasp waist with a highly arched back that gives a bustle effect where it quits about half way down my posterior. It takes in my hips but is cut out in front so that I can sit down—makes me sit and stand very erect. Marj says I look like a Singer dress model. The cast isn't too bad now. I get the itch once in a while so we put a piece of gauze through between the cast and me, make a loop of it outside and tie a knot. Now when I get an unbearable itch, Marj pulls the gauze loop around until the knot is over the itch. It is a stupendously wonderful feeling. There's nothing like it after you've unconsciously reached around to scratch and have run into plaster. When I first tried to walk after they took the cast off my leg, I waddled like a duck and had to use a cane. Now you'd hardly know anything was wrong. A visitor tonight didn't even realize that I was in a cast. I'd like to have the chesty posture that he thought I had.

We've been concerned about what the accident might do to discourage people about missionary aviation, but the many wonderful letters from our friends in the jungle have assured us they are eagerly awaiting the day when we will be flying again.

You know safety is a relative thing. Since our plane service has been interrupted, the trail has nearly claimed a missionary life. Three men struggled ten to twelve hours a day for six days from isolated Macuma. Crossing a turbulent river on a raft, they lost part of their equipment, and an Indian carrier, whom they gave up for dead at first. Then, one of the missionaries became violently ill from fatigue. Because their food rations were dwindling, he struggled on with the others, reaching Shell Mera with feet and legs so swollen he could hardly walk.

A letter from MAF in Los Angeles tells us another plane will soon be on its way down. It looks as though Hobey Lowrance, a former captain on American Airlines, who joined MAF not long ago, will do the flying until I get out of the cast.

Everyone around here makes a big fuss over the baby. We can't understand why they should get so excited—just because she's the cutest thing in the world. They should have expected it, knowing her *mamasita*. Isn't it remarkable how prejudiced parents are? Guess it's just that we love the little pumpkin so much.

Until the next time I can get propped up in front of this printing press, please convey our gratitude to all those there who have stormed the throne on our behalf.

Your kids

Before leaving Quito with his family for Shell Mera, Nate gave a brief talk over the HCJB radio station, and the talk was recorded. His subject was: EXPENDABILITY.

"A fact that is mixed in a very important way with our work is the thing that became commonly known during the last war as 'expendability.'

"The flying business is full of illustrations of this basic principle. God has seen fit to make a vehicle that is expendable essential to progress. There is always a price that must be paid.

"During the last war we were taught that, in order to obtain our objective, *we had to be willing to be expendable*, and many lives were spent paying the price of our redemption from the bonds of political slavery.

"This very afternoon thousands of soldiers are known by their serial numbers as men who are expendable. During the last war we saw big bombers on the assembly line, row after row, powerful, costly implements of war! Yet we all knew—we actually *knew*

135

that many of those bombers would not accomplish even five missions over enemy territory. We also knew that young fellows, many of them volunteers, would ride in those airborne machine-gun turrets, and their life expectancy behind those guns was, with the trigger down, only *four minutes*. Tremendous expendability!

"We know that there is only one answer when our country demands that we share in the price of freedom—yet when the Lord Jesus asks us to pay the price for world evangelization, we often answer without a word. We cannot go. We say it costs too much.

"God Himself laid down the law when He built the universe. He knew when He made it what the price was going to be. And the lamb of God was slain in the counsels of God from before the foundation of the world. If God didn't hold back His only Son, but gave Him up to pay the price for our failure and sin, then how can we Christians hold back our lives—the lives He really owns?

"The Lord tells us that He that loveth his life—we might say that he that is selfish with his life—shall lose it. It's inescapable.

"Missionaries constantly face expendability. And people who do not know the Lord ask why in the world we waste our lives as missionaries. They forget that they too are expending their lives. They forget that when their lives are spent and the bubble has burst they will have nothing of eternal significance to show for the years they have wasted.

"Some might say, isn't it too great a price to pay? When missionaries consider themselves—their lives before God—they consider themselves expendable. And in our personal lives as Christians isn't the same thing true? Isn't the price small in the light of God's infinite love? Those who know the joy of leading a stranger to Christ and those who have gone to tribes who have never heard the gospel, gladly count themselves expendable. And they count it all joy.

" 'Except a corn of wheat fall into the ground and die, it abideth alone,' the apostle Paul said. 'I die daily. I beseech you therefore, brethren, by the mercies of God, that ye present your bodies a living sacrifice, holy, acceptable unto God, which is your reasonable service.'

"And Jesus said, 'There is no man that hath left house, or brethren, or sisters, or father, or mother, or wife, or children, or lands, for my sake, and the gospel's, but he shall receive an hundredfold now in this time . . . and in the world to come eternal life.' "

13

CRUSADE FOR SAFETY

. . . His wings shall fill the breadth of thy land. . . . Isaiah 8:8

"The best news of all: Another plane, a newer model, has been bought and is being specially equipped in Los Angeles for its ferry trip down and its work here," Nate wrote. "Looks like Grady Parrott of MAF will fly it down and Hobey Lowrance will fly it here on the field until I'm out of the cast and have all my joints properly oiled and working again. The Lord has been good.

"When we got here to Shell Merita, the house was about the same as when we left it except that the hangar looked sadly empty, but we trusted that to the Lord who has proved His exceeding abundant ability. The grounds were in better shape than we had ever seen them before. The national Christian who lives in the little tile and bamboo house on the rear of the compound kept it that way.

"This is the only home we've had together since we've been married and the Lord has seen fit to let us fall in love with the place and the work.

"MAF shipped equipment for a short-wave radio-telephone network to cover the air operation as well as provide isolated stations with 'telephone' service. Technicians from HCJB will install the equipment as fast as palm trees can be made into antenna poles."

Nate and Marj had resumed their Sunday school on the Shell property as well as the Spanish Sunday school at Shell Merita that grew bigger each Sunday.

One of the jungle missionaries loaned an old portable organ to Nate and Marj as an adjunct to the Sunday school work. When Mrs. Reuben Larson, of Radio Station HCJB, saw the organ she recognized it as one she had used. It had been given to her by Dr. V. Raymond Edman, president of Nate's alma mater, when he and his wife had to leave their missionary work in Ecuador because of illness.

Nate, though still wearing a body cast, continued work on the house and hangar, digging post holes on his knees, grading the driveway for the plane.

"When your back is stiff you have to be double jointed everywhere else," he said.

The Quito crash intensified Nate's preoccupation with safety measures. He dwelt so much on the subject that some felt that safety was almost an obsession with him. But it was an understandable attitude and it served as motivation for Nate's later inventions that have made all bush flying safer.

Nate's penchant for safety was given further bolstering on May 9 when a new Grumman plane, under test by an experienced Shell Company pilot, crashed and took the lives of two men. "These experiences are going to make me the safest pilot in the business, and I'm saying that solemnly," Nate reported to Los Angeles. "May the Lord grant wisdom and steer us around mistakes, may He hear our prayer for the removal of the nerve-gnawing characteristics of our work so that we may serve Him longer and more effectively."

Then an Ecuadorian transport plane crashed in the mountains, thirty-five miles from Shell Mera, with eleven killed and no survivors.

Thus the dangers of flying in the mountains and in the jungle were constantly impressed upon the man who so recently had miraculously escaped death in a crash.

But the MAF plane was proving itself to be a constant boon to the missionaries. On a day in July, word came over the newly installed radio that Robert Fuller, ten-year-old son of Morrie Fuller, of Ahjuana station, had fallen against a circular saw. It had ripped open his arm. Nate, still grounded by his injuries, talked by radio to Hobey Lowrance, who was flying to another station when the word came through. Lowrance flew immediately to Ahjuana. Meanwhile Nate turned the microphone over to Marj, and rode off on his motor bike to notify the Shell Company doctor.

Within a matter of minutes, the Fullers were talking by radio to a nurse, the plane had been dispatched, and the doctor consulted. A few hours later, Morrie and his injured son, formerly trapped behind four days of jungle trail, had been transported to a doctor's office. "We're thrilled to be a part of this jungle missionary work," Nate wrote jubilantly.

Then came the day when Nate discarded his heavy body cast, took his check-out flight with Lowrance, and was permitted to fly again. The eagle had been restored to his element.

"Sorry that you felt it necessary to ask me to take Hobey's check-out kindly," Nate wrote MAF. "I realize that too often I act as though all wisdom and skill will perish when I lie moldering in the grave, but the Lord is patient wherein there's hope, I think."

In the summer of 1949, an earthquake struck the town of Pelileo, a town of 3500, in the mountains about sixty miles above Shell Mera. It was necessary for the authorities to pour gasoline on the ruins to destroy the decaying bodies that threatened to precipitate an epidemic. One tiny nearby village reportedly was swallowed by a huge crack in the mountain.

The tragedy occurred within the shadow of Tunguragua, the volcano that wiped out the town of Baños with lava and Ambato with ash one hundred and fifty years previously.

"Cars on the roads were buried and towns wiped out," Nate wrote. "Hundreds of people leaped into eternity with the quake. A Shell Company plane crashed the very next day. It was flying up to Ambato to take relatives of people living or dead in the little town near there. All thirty-eight passengers were killed.

"A Shell man asked me the other day how we feel about being trapped back here, by the road that is no more. We don't feel at all trapped. Other missionaries have our problem plus the long jungle trails.

"Absolutely nothing resulted from the quake here in our vicinity. Indirectly we see results; people trudging up the road with their little bundles, anxious to see if their relatives in Pelileo survived. The news hitting here has come mostly by foot and mouth and has been so distorted that we would pay a buck for a

140

Los Angeles daily so that we could find out what happened in Ecuador."

Both before and after the Quito accident Nate's letters to the MAF office and to his brother Sam contained his thoughts about devising an alternate fuel system, which, like the already accepted dual ignition, would reduce the peril of a single engine halting in mid-air.

"As I sit above the jungle listening for the symptoms of trouble that I never want to hear," Nate wrote to Sam, "I have in the back of my mind little things like the fuel line that fell off in my hand in Mexico a few years back. The flare had broken on one end of the tubing, but natural spring tension had kept it in place. I think of the quick work of the mud wasps when they decide to plug up a fuel vent. I also think of lying gauges, of water in the fuel, of cracks opening up in the fuel tanks, of obstructed screens, blocked jets, and dirt under a float valve seat. We think too of the temptation to make a short hop on the few gallons still in the tank. To be sure, I am impressed by the 'long end' of statistics but I am also impressed by the dire consequence to my passengers, not to mention my own bones, if we should come out on the short end somewhere over those tall trees."

Missionaries in Ecuador well knew that Nate's concern about an engine "conking out" in mid-air was more than a supercautious view.

Before the MAF operation was launched in Ecuador the Gospel Missionary Union had pioneered in missionary aviation.

Bob Hart, the missionary pilot of the GMU plane, was flying one day at about 1500 feet when his engine missed a little. It wasn't one of those "mental misses" that are common where there is no place to "sit down." Bob was not looking down on an alfalfa patch or a golf course, but on several hundred square miles of almost impenetrable jungle. The nearest landing strip was about twenty-five miles away. Bob was taking stock of the situation when, abruptly, it got quiet and the tachometer unwound to 1500 rpm before the engine caught hold again. In spite of all his valiant efforts with the gadgets in the cockpit, the engine cut out again. Between cuts it built back up to full power. An open river bed

141

where the wreckage could be spotted seemed the best possibility so he set a direct course for the Pastaza River. Each burst of power brought new hope but the altimeter was steadily telling the unhappy truth. Down near the treetops Bob offered the controls to George Poole, a pilot friend who had gone along that trip. George had no special tricks he wanted to try and Bob was doing a good job so he declined. They settled on down into a sort of trough between higher treetops. A jungle giant sprawled dead ahead. One last burst of power lifted them over the top of the giant tree, almost stalled, and then dropped them into a palm tree that flipped the left wing back and over. They dropped through the green curtain upside down to the floor of the jungle.

Both men survived the crash, but Hart's ankle and knee were broken, making it impossible for him to walk to civilization. By agreement, Poole, whose injuries were not quite so severe, struck out to reach a jungle path or a river. They separated for what they thought would be a short interval, but when Poole tried to return later that same day he was unable to find his partner. After wandering about for nine days, he made his way to Shell Mera. Hart, however, could not be located when rescuers came to find him. He had limped away, desperately in need of food. Soaked by torrential rains, he wandered about until, on the eleventh day, missionary Dave Cooper and a group of Indians found him.

It was another grim experience that underlined the dangers of jungle flying and the need for the safety measures.

While he was working in the MAF hangar at Shell Mera one day, Nate saw a truck passing by on the road in the direction of Ambato, high in the Andes.

"A boy was sitting on the roof of the cab with a five-gallon can of gas and a syphon," Nate wrote. "At the lower end of the syphon there was another boy riding the front fender. One arm and the syphon disappeared under the partly open hood in the direction of the air cleaner. You and I have started our cars that way after running out of gas, but these fellows were headed out on a five-hour trip, a good part of which called for second and third gear and lots of shifting. Yet they 'steamed' by our house. Everyone, including some twenty-five passengers, seemed happy."

To perform this stunt did not require much equipment . . . just a can, a hose, and a boy to meter the gas by pinching the end of the hose.

The wheels in Nate's inventive mind began to turn rapidly. Why not feed gasoline to an airplane engine in similar fashion?

He quickly lifted the cowl of his plane and squirted gas into the manifold through the carburetor air temp gauge fitting. Each squeeze on the gas-loaded tube produced a burst of power.

Next, a couple of his wife's cooking oil cans took on the shape of a three-gallon tank.

Nate shaped a piece of balsa wood, which grows abundantly in the jungle, to streamline the improvised tank, and the tank, thus fitted, was strapped to the struts under the left wing. A piece of brass tubing in which Nate fitted a valve connected the auxiliary tank to a fitting on the intake manifold. Then he extended a control rod from the valve to the instrument panel and was able to control the flow of fuel from the special tank to the engine. "That night I thought of a dozen reasons why it wouldn't be practical or wouldn't work at all," Nate wrote. "But at my lowest ebb, I remembered the old truck racing for Ambato in second gear without a carburetor. I could see Bob Hart helplessly working the throttle back and forth while the plane settled toward the woods."

Next morning he tested out his new Rube Goldberg apparatus while the airplane was on the ground. It worked without a hitch. Now it was time for tests in the air.

"Two thousand feet above the landing strip," Nate wrote, "I pulled the mixture control to idle-cut-off. It was quite a novel experience for a fellow who had listened so long, hoping never to hear it happen. But a turn of the new little T-handle on the instrument panel brought with it a wonderful feeling as the engine wound back up to smooth full-power. For the next twenty minutes the normal fuel source was shut off tight. The engine never missed. It picked up from a slow windmill without so much as a single cough.

"I put the plane into every imaginable attitude at various power settings. It never faltered. 'Feeling' for the best mixture setting with the emergency T-handle was no more difficult than 'leaning' the engine with the regular mixture control. Same thing.

"The whole rig, tank and all, weighs only four pounds. The only thing it has in common with the ship's fuel system is the engine. It takes care of common troubles such as clogged vents and broken lines and water in the gas, and faulty gauges. With the simplicity and low cost of a deal like this, why do we fly along with our only source of fuel supply in jeopardy at several points between tank and engine, and no alternative? We are all sold on dual ignition; why not an alternate fuel system for emergencies."

In time the cautious Civil Aeronautics Authority approved the installation of the new system and a patent was obtained from the U. S. Government. Now every MAF plane carries the alternate fuel system—a permanent mark Nate left on missionary and other hazardous aviation. Perhaps the alternate fuel system has even greater significance in long-term values than the bucket-drop which performed more dramatically in Nate's subsequent experiences.

Jungle flying often presents the problem of supplying a missionary stationed or marooned in a spot far from a landing field. Nate had experimented with parachuting supplies under such circumstances. Shifting wind currents sometimes carried the loaded chutes to a high tree or to an inaccessible part of the jungle. Other times the chute failed to open. There was the problem, too, of communicating with the person on the ground. Hand and body signals could not always be understood.

Nate remembered the day he was very close—yet very far away from some people needing help. "I flew over a small jungle town and noticed that everyone was in the clearing in the center of the village waving pieces of white cloth. When I circled one person stretched himself on the ground, face up and arms out straight and the others gathered around him. How would you read such a crude message? About all I could do at the time was to drop a supply of aspirin, probably a feeble answer to the real need of that desperate village. At best a runner might bring the plane back again in a week."

Then he thought back to the day at Wheaton when he sat daydreaming as he watched his pencil swinging from a string.

"The idea struck me like the silver lining under a hunk of cumulus," Nate said. "I wondered if the same principle would not work if an object were to swing on a line from a plane. Why not give it a try now.

"We began by taking about 1500 feet of cord and a little canvas bucket," Nate said. "A helper went along to manage the items of equipment. We took off for our first tests. The bucket was tied securely on one end of the cord and lowered from the door of the plane. One end of the line was tied to the plane so that there would be no unanticipated complications if the line should become snagged. It would simply break."

When Nate returned to the United States for his first furlough, he carried on further tests of the bucket-drop at an airfield in the Los Angeles area.

"While Henry Walton, a friend, was letting out the line," he said, "I circled at about 1000 feet. The circles had to be large ones, but now with the bucket some 1500 feet behind us, we were ready for the test. It is like fly casting with a 2000-foot pole.

"I banked and turned more sharply, gradually making the circle smaller while we watched the bucket. Like an obedient caboose on the end of an invisible train, it followed in our wake. Finally, strange as it seemed, the bucket was directly opposite us, though a little lower, traveling in the opposite direction! It seemed completely independent, just mimicking our pattern of flight.

"As I turned still more sharply, a curious thing began to happen. Up till that time the bucket had traveled about sixty miles an hour. Now it began to move more slowly. The large arc of cord behind it was finally bending in toward the center of our circle permitting the bucket to settle downward toward the point of a huge invisible cone.

"As the bucket dropped earthward it seemed to lose all horizontal motion. Finally it came to rest quietly in the middle of the open field below.

"Then we climbed a little, still circling," Nate continued. "The bucket obediently lifted from the ground and hovered."

Back at the airport the men examined blades of grass in the bucket that came from a field where they could not have landed and to which they had never been nearer than 800 feet.

During the next tests, MAF pilot Dan Derr was stationed on the ground to receive the bucket and send it back with simulated mail packets.

Nate soon came to feel that the technique should not be regarded as a toy for the curious nor a stunt for the novice pilot—it was not inherently dangerous, but like anything aeronautical, it was very unforgiving of any carelessness.

Back in Ecuador Nate soon had an opportunity to try out the bucket-drop in a jungle situation. He tells it in his own words:

"Frank Mathis of Wycliffe Bible Translators had received a call for help from the huge village of Arapicos. He had already headed out on the trail when we received word that the area was contaminated with a highly contagious disease. A twenty-two-year-old victim had already died.

"We were now equipped with more than the old canvas bucket, having acquired a pair of field telephones and 1500 feet of wire. . . . with fellow missionary Bob Hart in the plane to help, we took off, and in due time arrived over the village. Frank had already arrived on foot. We circled and saw him waving at us.

"We proceeded to unreel the wire at the end of which was the phone nestled in the bucket. It dropped right into the clearing in the center of the village."

"Hello, Frank," Nate's passenger spoke into the phone in the plane, "this is Bob Hart."

While Hart talked for several minutes to Mathis, Nate relayed over the plane's short-wave radio to a doctor in Quito, nearly two hundred miles away, the symptoms of stomachache, headache, leg cramps, cold extremities, and clenched teeth. They learned that Mathis was not in danger, so flew back to Shell Mera for the medicine the doctor had prescribed for the sick Indians.

Shortly after this proof that the bucket-drop had practical implications Nate and Bob Hart had an opportunity to demonstrate the aerial phone to the president of Ecuador. Both of the missionaries talked to the president himself as the Ecuadorian flag floated overhead "without a flagpole."

"We have been wondering," Nate said, "about the possibility of an amplification of the rig being capable of rescuing a human being. I think that it is altogether possible, but should be approached rather seriously with responsible engineering help. It is a fascinating subject and although I haven't consulted our dog yet, I believe he is going to 'volunteer' to demonstrate how useful the technique could be."

Nate continued to make drawings and wrote letters to experts in the aviation industry concerning a plane better adapted to jungle flying. "There is no market for the type plane we need and consequently it isn't built," he said. "So, we just bite our lips and go ahead with what is available, knowing that the job has just got to be done somehow."

Though he received practically no encouragement from engineer friends, Nate tenaciously refused to give up the idea. He even explored the possibility of equipping a light plane with parachutes that would check the plane's momentum in case of engine failure and a forced landing.

"I've written to a fellow in California for some information and will continue to look for snags that anyone might be able to point out," Nate said, "but if nothing turns up to discourage me I'd like to get hold of an old forty horsepower Cub somewhere and hook a couple of standard seat pack chutes to it and run some tests. Starting out using them simply as landing brakes on the ground and working back up 'til we're popping them as far off the ground as the ship will stand without folding up.

"Weight of the parachutes was my conjectured objection. Two twenty-four-foot chutes weigh thirty pounds! For a landing of twenty-five miles per hour instead of sixty into trees or a river I would diet off thirty pounds if necessary."

Because of his persistent efforts to design a small tri-motored biplane, Nate was called a genius by some and, by others, a visionary challenging the laws of aerodynamics.

Friends smiled at his constant concern for safety. "After all," they said, "a missionary is supposed to trust the Lord."

"We can't miss, Dave—we must not," Nate wrote to his brother. "Check over your little Sammy once and imagine his Daddy as having to saddle up a single man-made high output gasoline engine whose continuous operation or single failure could leave him fatherless or with an invalid father.

"Perhaps my reasoning *is* pagan, as I've been told, but none of these things move me, neither is it possible to listen to the voice of men now. I feel desperately in need of wisdom of the sort that comes from Him who 'giveth to all men freely and upbraideth not'! I do believe in miracles. They are nothing to God, surely. But the question is one of finding the pattern that the Lord has chosen us to conform to. I wouldn't be here if I weren't trusting the Lord. Chances are that those who shrug it off by saying, 'The Lord will take care of you,' are the same ones who would hardly expose themselves to the bacteriological risks of working in a downtown rescue mission. Forgive me if I feel a little strongly at this point. I'm concerned about safety, but I don't let it keep me from getting on with God's business. Every time I take off, I am ready to deliver up the life I owe to God. I feel we should be quick to take advantage of every possible improvement in carrying out the job before us. I know people who fly as though those little engines never quit. They figure they are statistically safe. That sounds good in Kansas, but somehow that good, 'statistically-safe' feeling stays behind when you climb up over the Andes and lower into the jungle region on the far side. You too would see it differently if your design-meditation-parlor were a cockpit located behind a single engine droning along above big old trees. Well, anyway, we plan to investigate the whole thing thoroughly and prayerfully. Then as long as the green light is reflected down the rails we'll bend the throttle wide open. Now that I've tooted the whistle for the big crossing I haven't steam enough to drag my freight out of the way so that traffic can be resumed."

To the men at MAF he wrote:

"A lot of ideas that have been in the 'deep freeze' have started to thaw out. I am trying to steer clear of gimmicking for the sake of gimmicking. Nevertheless I can't help the gadgets that run in my head, but I do try to sort out the stuff that might have some value.

"The only discouragement on the tri-motor so far has been my own brother's 'Sounds impossible to me.' He's figuring I'd have to get a degree in engineering first, and so forth. I'm not dreaming of myself as an engineer but just as a third-grade mathematician. My first aim is to show that a machine can be flown (if only a foot off the runway) on two of three engines and still be economical enough to be practical for highly specialized needs such as this in Ecuador, and still be small enough and light enough to fill our bill. We shall see. If a fellow's useful existence is worth anything at all in this business, then I feel that this investment is little enough to make it all safer. Now, I don't aspire to convince you that I will surely come out with THE ANSWER.

"It involves more than Marj and the kiddies. It involves all the other fellows' wives and kiddies who watch for a speck and listen for the sound of that single engine. Believe me, I've spared you reams and reams. It's like being in jail to have the gloves on and a sweat up without being able to find a sparring partner."

At the same time Nate was concerned about unnecessary equipment. The austerity of his thinking is revealed in a letter directed to a class of young people in the States.

"We make sure that we don't carry anything in the airplane that isn't necessary. When our mission bought the plane, it had nice, soft seats in it. But we found that these seats weighed almost eight pounds each. So we decided to use harder seats that weighed only one pound, and take seven pounds of extra food and cargo.

"On the wheels of the plane there were nice streamlined fenders—or pants as they call them. They looked very nice but inside they were full of heavy mud. We decided to take them off too.

"You know, lots of things are like that—they feel nice, or they look nice but they don't help us to get the job done. They hold us back, so we need to get rid of them. The job that the Lord Jesus Christ has for you and me is not an easy one. If you want to serve Him, if you want to help win others to Christ, you will have to choose one thing or another. It may be something you like very much but something that will hold you back." Characteristically, Nate turned this to spiritual illustration: "When life's flight is over, and we unload our cargo at the other end, the fellow who got rid of unnecessary weight will have the most valuable cargo to present to the Lord. Not only that. There's another secret.

149

Two airplanes may look alike, but one may be able to lift twice the load into the air. The difference is the horsepower of the engine. Bible reading is the power of the Christian life. Dead weight doesn't do you any good and a big plane with little horsepower doesn't go anywhere."

Nate's evaluation in this area was correct. Personally he was concerned more about safety than he was about outward show. He was overconscientious about having unnecessary equipment. "I've decided that for myself, God helping me, I'm going to develop a nose for smelling out the 'time-traps' that make me a captive of technological progress."

Some of the officials of MAF had thought it would provide better communication between the home office and the field if short-wave radio could be employed. Nate had been a strong advocate of the radio network on the field but he took a stand against short-wave communication with the homeland.

"I have come to feel," he wrote the home office, "that to maintain a ham station here demands more time and effort than is available. . . ." At the same time Nate readily admitted that some of the things he did could be placed in the same category.

Besides his flying responsibilities Nate spent many hours to make Shell Merita more habitable.

Because electric power was not available in the primitive village of Shell Mera, he dammed the stream at the back of the MAF property and installed a hydroelectric plant. A diesel engine and generator served as a standby. A constant supply of power was needed to operate the short-wave communication radio as well as other household equipment that enabled Marj to handle the huge "hotel" operation that developed at Shell Merita. "What has been a hope and a hobby is now pumping electricity into the house twenty-four hours a day for free," Nate said. "We call it the 'Shell Mera Power Company, Ltd.'—limited to 200 watts. I've been very self-conscious about the time I've put into the thing so far, because it closely resembles the sort of thing that gets so many of the Lord's servants doing 'something else.' I think that the cost of the whole project was only about $150 and probably has about a month of my time in it. HCJB gave us the generator and most of the other material we have been gathering bit at a time over the past year and a half. I've tried to keep it to 'hobby level,' putting time in on it as I've had it, a day this week and another next week, or maybe two."

The house as originally built at the MAF base soon proved to be too small for the numbers of people who came to Shell Mera on the way into or out of the jungle. Missionaries at the various jungle stations stopped at Shell Mera on their way to Quito or Guayaquil for periodic shopping trips, visits to doctors and dentists, or to attend missionary field conferences. Missionary executives from the United States came through on survey trips.

Visitors from the States made life interesting for the Saints. Marj wrote home that Paul Robinson, director of the Moody Bible Institute Missionary Technical Training program, and "another fellow from Moody," were coming to visit them. The other "fellow" proved to be H. Coleman Crowell, executive vice president and board member of the Moody Bible Institute. Crowell had been an early exponent of practical missionary aviation and other methods that would make the extension of the gospel more efficient.

"Mr. Crowell was quite reserved when he first arrived not to mention being fairly well scared to death by a rather thrilling ride down through Baños pass by car," Nate wrote his parents.

"The road is even worse at times. Sometimes they use a thing they call a *taravita*. I'm not sure what the word means but in view of the contrivance it represents, I'm sure it's not adequate. The gadget consists of a cable stretched across a chasm where the road or a bridge used to be. Under the cable they sling a two-foot by four-foot sideless wooden platform suspended by two home-made iron pulleys. You are offered a beggar's choice of a steep ledge trail down to a footbridge consisting of two eight-inch wood poles laid between boulders that straddle a churning cascade, prelude to a 150-foot waterfall or the cable crossing—a wingless version of primitive aviation. Passengers dangle across the canyon nearly a quarter of a mile while about six men haul on a too-worn-out rope, pulling them to the other cliff.

"We have had the pleasure of frequent surprise visits. But to

151

top them all, who should drive up yesterday but Jimmy Doolittle. When Mr. Humphries of the Shell Company introduced him, I thought he was joking because of a resemblance so I almost replied 'Glad to know you, I'm George Washington.' (Me and my big mouth), but it was General Jimmy Doolittle in plain dress with the usual baseball cap. He asked about the work of the mission and of our 'little Air Force.' He talked about Jake DeShazer who had been in his outfit during the hazardous first bombing raids on Japan. DeShazer was captured and imprisoned by the Japanese, but later returned to Japan as a Free Methodist missionary."

Actually the missionary plane caused a step-up in missionary operations. When Nate and Marj went to the jungle in 1948 some twelve missionaries were served at six stations. By the end of 1954 there were twenty-five missionaries on nine stations.

The brown-stained house had to be expanded until it became a sizable building that provided sleeping quarters for twenty or more.

"Let me say here that we do not plan this house expansion to take the place of another house for MAF personnel," Nate wrote headquarters. "The expansion will only take care of handling what is now only the usual guest traffic. Our family has occupied only one bedroom. Kathy is now sleeping on a cot in a closet under the new stairway that cuts through a corner of our room. We recently had nineteen guests overnight . . . foreign missionaries, national workers, a school teacher and family, and some Indians! I sincerely believe that you could count the days that we've been alone as a family recently on the fingers of two hands." Marj and Nate took great pride in the rambling home that looked much like a Swiss chalet, with wide eaves that protected against the constant jungle rainfall and gutters that caught the water for household use. Nate connected the eaves troughs that caught the water from the aluminum roof to a solidly constructed concrete cistern. He had ingeniously built a two-foot rim around the top of the cistern so that it served as a safe wading pool for children.

It was a big day when Nate installed the first shower bath at Shell Merita, just in time for a visit from his sister Rachel, who was passing through Ecuador en route to her linguistic assignment in Peru.

Nate described the new device:

"We fastened a regular brass faucet to a five-gallon drum and soldered the shower head right on to the faucet. This whole works fastens to a rope over a pulley on the ceiling and slides up and down on a wooden track. We simply heat a pan of water on the kitchen stove; lower the drum, pour in the hot water and add a pan of cold to adjust the temperature; then raise it to the desired height to enjoy a real treat for five minutes. A warm shower has had such a drastic and good effect on us that we feel that it should be written into the by-laws of the MAF corp."

In front of Shell Merita Marj and Nate lovingly planted bougain-villaea vines that added to the beauty of this Christian way-station to the jungle.

"Thanks for your letters," he wrote to Jim Truxton. "Sorry we're so long answering. My pigeonhole looks like a dinosaur nest and probably contains official correspondence from George Washington but I'm determined to put first things first and not succumb to the easy pitfall of fatigue. If I don't get a short note off to you right now it would seem possible that it might carry a millennial postmark.

"I surely wish you could see 'Shanty town' now. Vines are climbing around the new bodega. Flowers are blooming in two front-yard plots and the grass is in such a state that we're on the lookout for a lawn mower. To some, it may seem too much luxury but we enjoy it. I can think more clearly and am easier to live with when I can feed our nice little squadron of chickens in the evening without feeling the weight of sixteen emergencies over my head.

"But if anyone ever suggests raising ducks to me again—I will know the answer in advance. They like mud as much as pigs and make plenty of it everywhere they go. If you would care to join us in a duck dinner—we'll furnish the ducklings, all sixteen of them for one meal.

"Things are getting fairly well under control now. We see little patches of blue breaking through the solid schedule of urgent jobs. Today we hope to lick one of the remaining items by moving the boards on the side of the house. The siding was all green lumber when we put it on so it has now shrunk till the tongues are out of the grooves. We didn't drive the nails home when we put the sides on for this reason so it won't be too hard to move them . . . we hope. . . . We had a visitor the other night in the storehouse room. Whoever it was must have known the dogs. The poor rascal had tough luck. The first bag he picked up was loosely tied and a couple of cooking pans fell to the floor with what must have sounded to him like a clap of thunder. Anyhow, he took off on the double and only got a bedspread, a pillow, and a few little personal things . . . cheap lesson. I'll have to get me a muzzle loader and buy a keg'a blastin' powder. Probably the best medicine for unwanted intruders would be one of those Jivaro toted flint lock antiques rammed full of TNT and rock salt. They say it makes a fellow's hide feel like a cactus growing inside out.

"A carpenter is outside building our shop right now and aluminum roofing is coming up from Guayaquil. Things are looking up. A little more rock and mortar will finish the septic tank and soon after that we'll have an indoor 'John.' We'll miss the fun of slithering down the little hill through the mud and using our three-sided 'John with the northern exposure.' We've got a little welding shop too in operation now. Oxygen costs nine dollars a charge and is available in Ambato. Acetylene generators cost too much down here so we made one for a material cost of thirty dollars and six hours' labor. It is safe and has all the features of the commercial jobs." For this Spartan quality, Jim and Betty Elliot later jokingly dubbed Nate "Make-it-rustic, Make-it-functional-Saint." Nate built a kitchen that was comparable to one in the States. He insisted that construction of the house be simple so none of the rooms were ceiled and only single board walls divided the rooms. This was done in order that there would be no place for bats, rats, or other jungle fauna to hide out.

Because of the constant humidity at Shell Mera, it was difficult to get the washings dry. Nate installed a kerosene-operated refrigerator so that it opened into the kitchen and backed into the storeroom. The exhaust of warm air turned the storeroom into an excellent drying quarters.

He also employed the warm lower compartment of the refrigerator as an incubator and reared several broods of chickens in the warmth of the kerosene burner.

His handiwork and ability to use the materials at hand were a help to all the jungle stations. To practical Nate Saint this was a part of his Christian stewardship and a means of making missionary enterprise in Ecuador more efficient.

14

LOG OF A JUNGLE PILOT

. . . And he was seen upon the wings of the wind. II
SAMUEL 22:11

OPERATING the MAF base at Shell Mera was more involved than
an outsider might realize. "This radio communications time, plus
buying for so many jungle stations, handling mail, running errands,
moving hundreds of gallons of gas and kerosene each month, plus
the flying and airplane maintenance . . . means that running a
home and raising one's family here is something like running an
orphanage in connection with an orange drink and hot dog stand
at Broadway and 42nd street in New York City," Nate said.

Aviation gasoline in metal drums had to be stored. Nate devised
an efficient method of piping the gasoline right to the hangar so
that it would not be necessary to lift the heavy drums when
gassing the plane. He mounted a drum on top of a pole over
twenty feet high. A small hand pump raised the gasoline to the
drum on the pole, and then by gravity it was fed to the hangar
tap.

Likewise Marj had a full-time job to perform in addition to
rearing her family which eventually included Kathy, Stevie, and
Phil. Whenever the MAF plane was in the air, Marj stood by at
the short-wave radio set and checked its progress. To keep her
hands free for an enormous bookkeeping job, as well as the other
paper work, Nate devised a foot pedal that would open and close
the transmitter microphone.

The radio network connecting the jungle stations with Shell
Mera had revolutionized life in the Oriente as much as the missionary airplane. More recently the technicians had set up two
more network stations in Ecuador's principal cities of Quito and
Guayaquil. These facilitated faster handling of urgent matters. Still

more important, they produced a sort of radio-medico clinic in which physicians of the HCJB medical staff diagnose treatment for distant tribesmen, who then get the prescribed medicines from their "drugstore-in-the-bush" at Shell Mera.

In addition to her radio and bookkeeping chores and the supervision of the operation of the household, Marj conducted the "jungle super-market."

"At 7:00 in the morning," Nate explained, "while I'm getting the plane ready for the day's flying, Marj is on the radio calling all the stations. Missionaries give their orders for fruit and vegetables, meat and all the staples, kerosene, and medicine. 'Good morning, Carol, good morning, Carol; HC7NS is standing by for you . . . over.' We say 'over' when we listen for the other fellow. Out in the north jungle they say that all the Indians are saying 'Okay, over . . . Okay, over.' They hear it quite often as they crowd around the missionaries' houses, peeking in at the windows to hear them get voices out of the box, 'Over to Frank,' then Morrie, Mike, Jerry, and Henry, and so on around the circuit. We use the first names of the missionaries rather than call letters. Missionaries up in the mountains listen in to us even though they don't have transmitters. They say that the 'junglers' are their favorite radio program—never the same twice. Either Frank announces that he ran over a four-foot alligator with his dugout canoe, or, as just today, Mike tells of a man who fell on a pole and punctured his abdomen and might have to be flown out to save his life."

After taking the orders, Marj would buy the supplies of staple goods, vegetables, and fruits which were trucked to Shell Mera from the nearest city, Ambato. Then lists would be prepared for the various stations and she would help Nate weigh the load for the plane including the mail that means so much to isolated missionaries.

Everything was flown in—food, people, stoves, light plants, aluminum, refrigerators; things that change jungle life. On several occasions, calves, pigs, rabbits, goats, turkeys, and burros were tied down in the plane and flown to a jungle station.

Because of the large numbers of visitors Marj also had to see that ample foodstuff was on hand at Shell Merita and that meals were prepared for the guests who "always eat like harvest hands."

Nate's days were filled to capacity. One day in May he kept a log that demonstrates most clearly "a slice of his life":

It's a clear sunrise. Feels like a good day coming up.

6:30 A.M.—Gassing the plane and making inspections while Marj goes over the priority lists of missionary cargo.

7:00 A.M.—Marj is on the radio checking with the jungle stations while I am stowing away some breakfast. The plane is loaded and ready. Dos Rios reports ground fog. Pano station has no fog. I could land there in case the fog at Dos Rios doesn't clear by the time I get there. First destination: Dos Rios, 45 miles.

7:21 A.M.—Off the runway at Shell Mera.

7:44 A.M.—The fog has risen and somewhat broken. I am preparing to land at Dos Rios.

8:00 A.M.—The Dos Rios mail has been sorted and remaining cargo rearranged. Off the runway and bound for Pano station, 4 miles away.

8:03 A.M.—Preparing to land at Pano.

8:10 A.M.—Weekly food supply. Fresh vegetables and mail are unloaded and off to Shandia, 6 miles from Pano. This is the north jungle "milk run."

8:15 A.M.—On the ground at Shandia. Mail and food supplies unloaded.

8:18 A.M.—Off the runway for return to Pano. A missionary has to be flown out for dental work. The Pano strip is short so the plane had to be emptied before taking off from Pano with a passenger.

8:26 A.M.—Off Pano for Shell Mera. As I radio in the position reports I hear Marj handling the morning radio traffic for all parts of the eastern jungle as well as Quito and Guayaquil. We get word that permits have come through for the importation of the new engine we will need next month. That is cause for rejoicing. We've been trying to get the permits since the end of January.

8:33 A.M.—Report position: Ila, 4500 feet altitude.

8:45 A.M.—Landing at Shell Mera.

9:00 A.M.—Marj is still handling radio traffic. Kathy and Stevie are out of their Pj's and into play clothes. They seem to have had breakfast. Ralph Stuck, a fellow missionary outbound on this next flight, has his load all ready and is securing it in the plane while I pump gas and check oil.

9:15 A.M.—Off Shell Mera for Sucua, 75 miles deep in the south jungle. Passengers are Ralph Stuck; a national worker;

and a seven-year-old Jivaro boy who had been flown out a week ago with a broken arm. He returns with a cast and a barrelful of wild tales about the 'big city' to share with tribal playmates.

9:54 A.M.—Planning to land at Sucua.

10:08 A.M.—Off Sucua to Shell. Passengers: G. Christian Weiss, mission executive, who last visited the field on foot in 1946. He is thrilled with the implications of missionary aviation; Señor Carlos Malordo, Ecuadorian soldier left stranded when a military plane pulled out without him yesterday.

10:47 A.M.—Preparing to land at Shell Mera.

11:00 A.M.—While servicing the plane, we try to decide which flight should have next priority. Frank Mathis is waiting for the plane at Montalvo, 85 miles east. He's surveying for Wycliffe Bible Translators; has no radio; expects the plane today. Decide that that must come next but we can go by way of Macuma and leave a load there to economize. It is 53 miles southeast so it will be a triangle flight.

11:15 A.M.—We are about ready to leave when the military commander for the eastern jungles arrives. He explains that they dropped supplies to the military post at Montalvo but that a good share of them burst open on impact with the ground and were lost. They urgently need 200 pounds of rice and our plane is the only one in the region small enough to land on the small landing strip that the soldiers have finished recently.

11:17 A.M.—Off Shell Mera for Macuma. Miss Dorothy Walker, missionary to the Jivaro tribe, and Linda Drown, daughter of Frank Drown, are passengers.

11:48 A.M.—Out of Macuma for Montalvo with 200 pounds of rice and a good map. Area over which I will be flying is almost uninhabited and relatively unexplored except along rivers.

12:17 P.M.—Sight Bobanaza River and start letting down from 8000 feet. Finishing cheese sandwich Marj sent along. Thermos of cold milk hits the spot. The sun is clear and hot through the windshield even though the air outside is cold at this altitude.

12:30 P.M.—Planning to land at Montalvo. On the approach I spot Frank. He has made it in from his overland survey on schedule. I was a little worried about this. The strip seems clear. I go in for the landing.

12:35 P.M.—About 50 Ecuadorian soldiers have jammed around the plane. The captain explains that their radio is dead because their light plant is broken down. He has the broken parts for us to take out to be fixed. Capt. Jacome is a good friend. He used to be at Shell Mera. He consents to my giving out tracts and gospel literature to the men. I have opportunity to speak to the men a minute. Give them a word of personal testimony.

12:50 P.M.—Off Montalvo for Shell Mera. Establish radio contact with Marj. Frank is grinning behind a battered half cheese sandwich. Weather seems to be holding off okay in spite of scattered showers. We follow the Bobanaza River northwest for half an hour, then decide that we'll detour a little to be able to drop Frank off at his mission station on the way to Shell Mera. His strip is a small one but we are light on gas now and find a favorable wind blowing.

1:31 P.M.—Preparing to land at Llushin. Frank's family is tickled to have him back safe and sound. Miss Kathy Peeke, on the strength of Frank's survey findings, decides to go out to Quito to get ready for moving into Montalvo. She climbs aboard and we take off for Shell Mera where she will catch a bus for Quito.

1:49 P.M.—Preparing to land at Shell Mera.

2:00 P.M.—Weather report from Macuma is still good. A rain is building up near here. Frank Drown and Roger Youderian help us gas and load the plane for Macuma. They have been out to the city doing their annual heavy buying. Mrs. Stuck is only passenger except for her baby. She will take care of some loose ends at Macuma and then fly over to Sucua tomorrow to join her husband on that station—a new assignment for them.

2:23 P.M.—Off for Macuma. Rain is near when we take off but radio tells us Macuma and points east are okay.

2:52 P.M.—Preparing to land at Macuma.

3:10 P.M.—Off Macuma for Shell via Llushin. Marj tells me by radio that Mary Sergeant, Kathy Peeke's tribal work partner, also wants to go out to Quito before heading for the tribe. Llushin is right on the route and the plane is empty so it is okay.

3:28 P.M.—Landing at Llushin.

3:40 P.M.—Off Llushin for Shell.

3:46 P.M.—Landing at Shell Mera.

Weather is still holding up fine, but I'm not. We call it a day.

We have dragged you through today—May 21—with us. Not every day involves so much flight work—but every day is full. There is the maintenance of a dozen radio transmitters and receivers for the stations, plane maintenance, and the building program that moves ahead under the capable persuasion of a faithful Indian helper.

The ground Nate had covered by air in less than a day would have required forty hard days of ground travel.

15

CORRIDOR BETWEEN THE CLOUDS

He made him ride on the high places of the earth. . . .
DEUTERONOMY 32:13

WHILE Hobey Lowrance, the pilot substitute during Nate's convalescence, was still in Ecuador, it was decided that they should go together to make a survey of a new airstrip site at Chupientsa, where two Christian and Missionary Alliance workers, Mr. and Mrs. George Moffat, had labored for twenty-three years under unbelievable hardships.

Accompanied by Marj, the two fliers saddled horses at Sucua station and hit the trail for Chupientsa. The Moffats had been forced to consider retirement because they no longer felt up to the long trip on horseback to reach civilization. Before the days of air travel it had taken as much as two to three weeks over hazardous slippery mountains and jungle trails.

The three found that riding hour after hour on horseback was no picnic. The horses struggled through mud up to their knees and sometimes to their bellies, forded rivers, climbed steep embankments where they hesitated to pick up a hoof. Nate figured that an hour of this kind of travel was equivalent to one minute in the air over the same territory!

After six and a half hours they reached Chupientsa, a beautiful compound hacked out of the jungles on the edge of a cliff that drops seven hundred feet to the Upano River below. The Moffats had worked among the Jivaros and brought some of them from raw paganism to a knowledge of Jesus Christ. Yet there were many Indians who had not responded to the Gospel message.

One Jivaro in particular had been charged with killing fifty men in the course of his life. He had often been jailed but always managed to get out again. The murderer's son became a fine Christian under the influence of the Moffats' teaching.

Although the Jivaros were constantly murdering one another in typical revenge tradition, some of their jungle mores offered strange contrasts to the touted safety of civilization. The Moffats in all their years in the jungle had never locked the door of their house and never had lost anything by thievery.

Even though Nate, Hobey, and Marj were exhausted by their long horseback ride they pumped the Moffats for stories of the early years of missionary work. Mrs. Moffat told of an incident that graphically illustrated the perils of jungle work.

"We were on our way out of the jungle on foot for our annual missionary conference," she said. "The first four days, an Indian carried our six-month-old baby girl in a basket strapped to his back. When we reached the place where we could rent mules, we couldn't get another carrier. So George strapped our daughter to the mattress and carried her on his animal.

"When we got to one rickety bridge, we sent the pack animals across—then George started across without dismounting. The mule took fright and his hind legs went off the bridge. The muleteer quickly grabbed the bridle, enabling the mule to regain his foothold. But George and the baby were thrown right over the precipice.

"I screamed. All I could see was a sheer drop of several hundred feet with a raging torrent below. I realized that only God could save my husband and baby, so my heart cried out to Him. I was shaking so much I couldn't dismount. It seemed like an eternity. Then suddenly I saw George's head appear. My first thought was, 'He's alive, but surely the baby must be gone.' I couldn't conceive how he could get up that rocky precipice and hold a baby.

"The next second George called the muleteer to take the baby. I could hardly believe my eyes and ears, but I dismounted in time to receive her, wondering if she were still alive. When I took her in my arms, she heaved a big sigh.

"We went across the bridge and then stopped to examine her

more carefully. She had dirt in her eyes, ears and nose, but otherwise she seemed to have suffered nothing from the fall. I wiped the dirt from her face and we went on. . . . What about George? Oh, he was all right, but it hurt his Scotch soul to lose his hat."

The MAF team found that land which had already been cleared years earlier was adaptable to an airstrip. Then they headed back over the long trail to Sucua, leaving the Moffats buoyed in heart over the prospect of plane service.

During the return journey Nate and his companions discussed the differences that the missionary plane had made in the lives of missionaries. "Missionaries had tried to impress me with the tremendous difference between travel over the old back-breaking trails and the new air transportation," Nate said. "Now at last I was getting a painful personal understanding of the difference."

At last they sighted the yellow plane at Sucua. Mike Ficke quickly greeted them, then said, "We've been watching for you. Henry Miller's waiting on the radio. Their baby is seriously ill."

Inside the house Nate sat down by the short-wave radio and called Pano station, 120 miles to the north. Soon Henry's voice crackled back through the static:

"It's little Donnie, Nate. We've tried everything but it looks like we'll have to get him to a doctor quickly."

All gathered about the radio knew what that would have meant a few years before. The baby would have been carried three days on an Indian's back to the nearest doctor or five days to the nearest hospital.

Perhaps weeks would have been lost from the gospel ministry among primitive Indians before they could have returned from such an expedition. The baby's life would have been in grave danger.

It was already two-thirty in the afternoon. Nate knew that he would have to refuel the plane at Shell Mera. Since Henry Miller would have to take the baby five miles to the nearest airstrip, it would take him about two hours. That meant Nate could make a side trip to take another missionary and Marj to Macuma station, fifty miles out of the way.

"We took off immediately and climbed up to 8000 feet," Nate

reported. "Thirty minutes later we turned through the Macuma pass and started the descent toward the eastern jungle's most isolated station, deep in 'head-hunter' country.

"At Macuma my missionary passengers were exchanged for a native Christian schoolteacher who was bound for our base, fifty-three miles northwest. The mountains were unusually clear, promising good flying weather right up to our sundown deadline."

At the base Nate unloaded the airplane and refueled. Minutes later he was in the air again, bound for Tena airstrip. Flying northward Nate studied the occasional Indian clearings below, looking like "tiny corks floating in an endless sea of tangled green." On some of them he could make out bits of the northern trail. It had been two years, he mused, since a missionary had been required to use that trail.

In twenty-five minutes he was circling for a landing at Tena. He saw Henry and Vera Miller emerging from the trail at the edge of the strip.

"Later that evening the baby and his mother were in a doctor's office," Nate said, "and Henry was back at work on his mission station. While he had traveled two hours overland I had traveled nearly the equivalent of a three-week expedition, and I met him right on time."

Mercy flights that challenged his flying skill became routine to Nate Saint. Even though he constantly worked for flying safety, he was obliged again and again to take the "calculated risks."

Missionary Morrie Fuller had moved to a new location at Ahjuana on the banks of the Napo River, north and east of Shell Mera. Nate had flown the Fullers' first loads of equipment to the abandoned Arajuno airstrip. From there the supplies were floated down the treacherous Arajuno River in dugout canoes to Ahjuana.

A smallpox epidemic had broken out at Ahjuana . . . this time a faster means of transportation had to be found. The witch doctors would blame the missionaries for the deaths. There was only one thing to do: Take vaccine to Ahjuana immediately.

"The cold steel propeller blades felt good as I cranked the engine to check the compression offered by each cylinder," Nate wrote. "Every piston registered my tug on the prop blades, promising to respond faithfully to a touch of the throttle."

"The Andes Mountains in the west were a ghost of dark masses piled up into the lightening sky. In the south I could see the flowing lava of the volcano. Whenever the glow of Sangay was visible we were assured of good weather.

"Twenty minutes later," Nate continued, "I eased back the throttle and the engine quieted to a low drone. The altimeter unwound to 1200 feet and we were slipping into a tiny slot between the tall trees. The floor of the slot was the Arajuno landing strip.

"While unloading the cargo at the edge of the deserted airstrip, I recalled stories about the Aucas whose general location was now only fifteen miles away.

"Temporarily unburdened of her cargo, the monoplane sprang lightly off the airstrip and soon I could see the wide silver ribbon of the Napo winding its way toward the east where it joins the mighty Amazon. As I approached I could see light-brown patches along the river . . . sandbars? Yes they were. So I throttled back and lowered the flaps. Dugout canoes scurried for the edges of the river. We banked a little left, then right, easily following the curves of the broad river. The longest sand bar in the area was right across the river from the mission. A close look showed that it was covered with stones. A cut tire here would mean that not only the Fullers, but the other missionaries as well would be without supplies for a while. As I flew low over the bar again I could see Morrie frantically waving his shirt and running toward a dugout canoe. I was sure he caught the idea that I would try to land there.

"As I gained altitude again the challenge of the situation plagued my mind. The decision could not wait because the engine was burning precious fuel every minute, so I scribbled on a piece of notebook paper, 'Need 200 x 10 meters. Remove all largest stones possible within an hour.'"

As the plane passed over the heads of the crowd of Indians waiting with Fuller, Nate dropped the note, then pulled his plane's nose skyward. He returned to Arajuno and reloaded. An hour later he was again skimming over the water toward the sand bar which the Indians had cleared of the largest stones.

"As I got close I handled the plane more carefully than ever before," Nate wrote. "I glanced at the airspeed indicator and eased the throttle back a shade. I was only a few feet above the water—up a little and over several boulders. The engine silenced and the wheels grabbed the rocky surface. Indians surrounded the plane immediately and seconds later I saw Fuller pushing through the crowd of excited Indians. 'Vaccine?' he shouted. I handed over the precious medicine."

A few miles away in the key jungle town of Tena, the missionaries had planned an evangelistic campaign. They arranged for a tent, colored slides, and special music. They had invited Jim Savage, a visiting missionary from Venezuela, to speak. Nate was to fly him in.

That same day a workman in Tena had suffered severe body burns and a mangled hand when a stick of dynamite he was holding exploded. Most of the townspeople were at the airstrip when Jim and Nate arrived. Nate immediately flew out the seriously injured Ecuadorian and took him to a doctor. The incident opened hearts in Tena to Savage's message.

Because MAF operated in Ecuador with the blessing of the government, a contract had been granted the noncommercial airline. It proved to be a mutually profitable arrangement, as the plane often carried government officials and Army personnel.

On February 18, 1950, Nate was notified that a plane flown by Col. Edmundo Carbajal, Commander of the Ecuadorian Air Force, had crashed at a tiny airstrip 165 miles from Shell Mera in the southern jungle. The details were sketchy concerning the seriousness of the accident. Nate knew the importance of his going to the rescue both from a diplomatic and a spiritual standpoint.

He took along three bundles of Scripture portions to drop to little villages along the way that had no Gospel witness. He flew over hazardous terrain to the area. Somewhere in that valley there was supposed to be a tiny airstrip cut out of the jungle. He spotted the clearing when a flash of sunlight reflected the twisted aluminum wreckage. As Nate started to circle down, he saw a military

167

transport plane overhead at 6000 feet. The larger plane was unable to make tight enough turns to get down into the boxlike valley. Nate was not familiar with the tiny strip. For twenty minutes he circled and swooped over the clearing, studying the local air currents and obstructions. On the last few runs across the strip he touched his wheels lightly to the surface. He radioed the transport that he was going in. The landing wasn't especially exciting. But then a crowd of people converged on the plane from the brush at the edge of the strip. Nate finally got a coherent report of the colonel's condition. He was told they would bring him to the airstrip. So he radioed the transport that he would fly the injured man to Sucua about seventy miles to the north where he could be transferred to an Ecuadorian Air Force plane.

The local community was making the most of the occasion. They were having a feast. Nate graciously declined the invitation to leave his plane to go into the village, so food was brought to him. He "dined royally" in the shade of his plane's wing. He wondered about the weather and how long it would be before he could get off the airstrip with the wounded officer. As he waited, Nate testified to the throng about his plane, of his faith in Christ. The crowd listened quietly and respectfully. He presented Spanish New Testaments to the local officials and the police helped him distribute gospel tracts. Then the whole population pitched in to help Nate inspect the airstrip to clear it of stones, fill the ruts, and tamp the soft spots.

A singing, shouting crowd of two hundred finally escorted the injured officer on horseback to the airstrip. They looked as though they might go on for hours. Nate noticed the weather was closing in fast. Only a mile away it was raining.

He explained the situation to the commander, who responded to Nate's request that the flight be made at once. As the engine turned up full power several horses stampeded and headed off into the forest, wild with fright . . . never having heard a plane's engine before.

Nate removed his cap and prayed for a moment, released the brakes of the plane and raced down the strip between the cheering crowds, and bounced into the air.

"A minute later I contacted home base by radio," Nate said. "The weather there was still okay. The big question that still remained lay up in the nearby granite ridges. We couldn't risk getting trapped. At 8000 feet we had black cumulus storm clouds behind us and on both sides, but straight ahead we broke into a river valley that harbored our destination.

"The whole valley was like a narrow sunlit corridor between dark and foreboding clouds. Visibility ahead was about twenty-five miles. It was no accident—that trip. It was another missionary flight, ordered of the Lord."

16

SHELL MERITA

. . . in the shadow of thy wings will I rejoice. PSALM 63:7

EVEN though the increasing tempo of life in the jungle sapped the strength of both Nate and Marj, they took time to spend with their children. Nate was strictly a family man. His injuries kept him from being present when Kathy was born, but he more than made up for it when the family was reunited and the three returned to Shell Merita.

As soon as Kathy was able to toddle, she followed her father about like a puppy. While Nate ate his breakfast—which took a long time since he was a slow eater—Kathy was in the high chair by his side.

Her laughter and friendly disposition made Shell Merita a joyful haven. Even after being spanked, Kathy was always ready to love her Daddy.

Two years later when Stephen Farris Saint was born on January 30, 1951, Nate was right on hand at the HCJB Clinic in Quito. Everett Fuller, the doctor on duty, okayed the proposition that Nate watch the delivery, making the obviously necessary provision that he would have to watch from the outside through the window since the delivery room wasn't very large.

"The doc gave me a briefing on all that would be going on, using an obstetrics book with photographs for the personal lecture," Nate wrote to the four grandparents. "When I got outside it had started to rain. It was about nine o'clock at night, I guess. I donned raincoat and umbrella and fixed a chair to stand on under the window. . . . I prayed aloud out in the dark and rain . . . and thanked God that I was privileged to be there watching.

"It was a rather long vigil, but a couple of deft moves and the doc was holding him up by his heels. Now Mother and Dad—only now after this experience am I beginning to own the capacity for gratitude that I know should be mine."

From the very start Nate and Marj impressed upon their children the importance of letting Jesus Christ come into their hearts and direct their lives. Family devotions were held usually after the evening meal. Nate would often put the children to bed, telling them a story and praying with them before they were tucked in for the night.

"Sitting or lying on the bed with the children, he would talk to them simply, about the Shepherd, Heaven, or what it means to be good," Betty Elliot recalls. "He would ask them questions then, too, and pray and sing hymns with them. Sometimes they would talk about the sins the children· had committed that day, and what they should do about them."

When Nate read the King James Version of the Scriptures to his children, even if adults were present, he "translated" into colloquial English. He would stop occasionally and ask a question, such as, "Why did Jesus take the little boy's lunch away, Kathy?"

The children were taught to respect the people about them; there was no place for racial or other types of prejudice.

"Kathy has already made fast friends with her playmates who are the children of the Institute's staff workers," Nate told friends in a letter. "It's a lesson and a challenge to watch them play with some of the Indian children, mixing up baby talk in three languages. They aren't the least worried about the war. Why then should we be, children of the coming Prince of Peace?"

In another letter he wrote to his aged grandmother:

"The kids are growing and getting more interesting every day. We enjoy Kathy's familiar talk about Jesus and heaven. You'd think she had already been there. She would rather have me repeat the 'Crown of Thorns' a dozen times than to hear of 'Peter Rabbit's difficulties' once."

In earlier years Nate had been critical of his father's way of life which contrasted so sharply with his own practical approach to life.

But on other occasions Nate had expressed admiration and fondness for his father. This was especially true when Nate had grown older and had children of his own. He tried to make up for his wrong attitudes toward his father after a vivid dream awakened him one night at Shell Mera.

"The other night, in a dream," he wrote his father, "I was in the old Huntingdon Valley kitchen when you came in out of the pouring rain. As you brushed past me, you leaned down and whispered in my ear ever so kindly, 'I'm in a hurry now. I've got to go get my new body.' I thought you were dying and I woke up.

"Immediately I attributed it to an article I had read in *Reader's Digest* about people being 'advised' of a loved one's death in a far-away place. The quotation about the new body is one that we hear frequently from Kathy. She repeatedly asks when we'll get our new bodies.

"When I awoke . . . I was sure that the Lord had told me of your home-going. As I became wider awake I realized that you must be in your seventieth year. . . . The blessing of the dream is the surfacing of the deep, heartfelt appreciation I have always had for you and Mother, and the haunting fact of my ill behavior and lack of respect as a lad. I regret it without brooding because I realized at the time that it was wrong and I realized, too, that you had forgiven me even though I hadn't yet begged your forgiveness.

"Perhaps, yea, doubtless, your patience and the grace of God manifested in your spirits has been my spiritual schooling. I believe He has used those childhood experiences of witnessing a mature faith and a natural outflowing of the realities of Christian grace and experience.

"The other night as tears soaked my pillow, I thought how awful it would be if you should be called home without my ever having told you how grateful I am for your sincere concern for my soul. May God keep me faithful to the trust as we train up Kathy to carry on Mom's ministry and a Stephen who may, two millennia after his namesake's death, also have the joy of witnessing for his Lord 'by life, or by death.' "

Nate had consistently displayed a love for his mother. When he was in the Army, he had written to Sadie Montgomery about his mother's attributes:

"Mother has given her last ounce of strength for us kids with the

172

most energetic, almost fanatical unselfishness and self-sacrifice. Her modesty has been so successful that it is only recently that I have begun to see what she has given for us—always pushing the credit to someone else."

In the letter, writing to his father from Ecuador, Nate proceeded again to eulogize his mother:

"I hope Mom is feeling better. My what a debt we all owe her. And how much her present ministry of intercession means in these days when the battle is not won by might or human strength. We certainly believe the coming of the Lord must be near.

"Thanks, Mom, for continuing to hold the fort. Thanks for thousands of pots of soup on the back of the old stove, thousands of mendings of shirts and socks, tens of thousands of washings, and thanks, Mom, for the many tears shed in secret that brought divine intervention into the lives of your brood. We shall never fail for lack of understanding, of sacrifice, or perseverance . . . more important, we shall never fail to recognize the worth of a human soul for we have been pointed to Calvary since the days before we could walk."

Nate likewise showed appreciation and love for his wife in a very intimate letter to her after they were married. He wrote:

"Your love has sustained me through heartbreaking crisis and heartening little successes. If I had known you before as I know you now I would have answered the preacher with a shout instead of a quiet 'I do.' How glad I am to have you working at my side always. I have felt that I had sufficient 'snort' and drive for the sprints, but God knew I would need a 'flywheel' to steady me for the long haul."

Nate told his parents that "Marj still keeps everything in order and in hand. Everyone asks how she does it. I don't know, either. The Lord surely knew that in this kind of work I would need a partner with a brain like a filing cabinet and one incapable of saying 'can't.'

"Marj shares the burden of the work as much as though she were right in the plane with me with a steering wheel of her own. Her job is even tougher than mine."

Letters home frequently described in detail the little things the children did or said:

"Kathy is carrying her doll on her back in a shawl that Marj and I brought back from Quito.

"The other night Kathy was with me when I took a load of believers home after church Sunday evening. Out of the clear blue, when we were returning home alone, she asked, 'Why did God make us two arms?' I was caught off balance for a better answer so I said I guessed that He thought we'd need them. With the authoritative tone of a theologian, she said, 'He didn't *think* we'd need them. He *knew* we'd need them. He knows everything.'

"Guess she's not unusual or a prodigy but . . . we love her to pieces, always a smile for everyone and special ones for the Indians. We trust that her liking for people will be the gentle wedge that will open up their hearts to listen to the gospel of hope and love and assurance in Christ. Really it would break your heart to see the empty sad faces of some of these people. Life means little to them. Death means demons and torment.

"One day Kathy found a 'wordless book' such as is used by children's workers in making the gospel intelligible. We overheard her explaining it to Stevie and his friend, Randy Wittig. Standing up before the boys like a teacher, Kathy said:

" 'What is black for?'

"Stevie was silent, thinking hard.

" 'Well, what do you call it when Satan tells us to do something?' Kathy pursued.

" 'Sin!'

" 'That's right.' She then proceeded to explain that red was for the blood of Christ, white for sins forgiven, and gold for heaven.

" 'Now Randy can sing. Stevie, you go out and tell people about Jesus. It's very important because we don't want people to go to hell. Even the rich people we want to go to heaven!'

"The children have taken to putting little verse cards under our plates at mealtime. Then after eating we all read them. Stevie holds his up proudly, studies it, and then no matter what is on the card, right side up or down, he seriously goes through John 3:16. 'For God so loved the world, that he gave his only begotten

Son, that whosoever believeth in him should not perish, but have everlasting Life.' "

One evening when Kathy was still quite small she carried the piece of canvas belting used for punishment to the supper table with her, laying it by her father's plate with a big smile. Nate was unable to account for her actions but decided "she must have felt mischief coming on."

Sam Saint earlier had expressed the fear that Nate would be too strict with his children. Nate insisted that this had not developed.

"We give them just enough punishment to keep them sweet," Nate reported, "but not enough to remove the twinkle that soon returns after a few tears have been shed. Nor do I think we can love them too much as long as the 'antidote' is kept handy for the quick remedy of any developing symptoms."

Whenever the children were hurt during the course of a disobedient act, Nate believed that it was important to show concern for the injury first and to withhold discussion of the naughtiness until later. He explained . . . he spanked . . . and then he showed them love afterwards.

Nate wanted to give his children the same set of spiritual values that he had been taught as a boy. Thus he instituted a program of Bible memory work in which the children repeated a new verse for two weeks at breakfast and dinner. The program also included Bible stories in the evening. Sometimes he turned off the living-room lights so the children would not be distracted.

Nate's tenderness was evidenced on more than one occasion. Marj recalls that Kathy was ill and Nate was concerned about her condition. Worn out with the heavy duties at Shell Merita, Marj fell asleep. Waking in the night, she found that Nate was praying quietly over his little daughter.

When Nate noticed that Stevie's little soapbox racer had a bent axle, he asked how it happened. Stevie said he had not done it. Did he know who did?

"Then Stevie's face screwed up with the forced sincerity that precedes a lie like clouds do rain," Nate said. "Seeing that I was loosening up my belt, one of his playmates confessed. Stevie had

175

lied to cover for the other boy. Actually the axle didn't matter but we're trying to teach the kids to tell the truth habitually without even considering the circumstances or what it might cost them. Well, Stevie and I went to the storehouse. . . . within five minutes he was skipping around in his cowboy boots as happy as ever. I always ask whose fault it is that he is being punished and he always answers, 'It's my fault, Daddy.'"

One night at bedtime it was discovered that Kathy had no clean nightgown. In such emergencies she wore whatever was handy—this time it was one of Nate's soiled T-shirts.

"Ummm," she said, "this smells good—just like my sweet Daddy. Now when I wake up in the night I'll think you're right in bed with me."

Nate's happy family life undoubtedly stemmed from the loving atmosphere that had surrounded him as he was growing up in Huntingdon Valley. Marj proved to be an ideal mate and their affection for each other flowed out to their children and was warmly returned. Nate's attitude on love and marriage was graphically expressed in a letter to Ben, his younger brother who was then at the marriageable age:

"You recall the acute infatuation I suffered for several years. As I see it now, it was the result of suggestion. I was teased about Alice before I even knew who she was. One notes, too, the fascination one experiences with the unknown, or rather for the unknown. We meet a girl, exchange a few pleasantries and then go our way, free to imagine all sorts of wonderful things about the lovely creature we have just met. The phantom belle of our imagination can become so real that it excludes from our observation the basic facts of married life and of daily and lifelong compatibility.

"While convinced that I loved Alice, I met Marj. And because of the conviction that our friendship was only 'brother and sister' in nature, I was not blinded to Marj as a capable, sensible, likable girl. Nor would I have been blind to her faults. I was free to appreciate her in a sound and sensible way. I grew to *admire* Marj greatly. It wasn't the light, fluttery feeling in the upper chamber of the stomach . . . it was solid head-to-toe assurance that the fellow who married her would be a fortunate man. I found I wanted to see her get married . . . felt that it would be a tremendous loss to some needy man if she ever remained single.

"Time came when Alice and I became informally engaged by mail while I was in lower Mexico. On my way home from Mexico, I had to pass through Los Angeles and elected to tell Marj *personally*—although I had written to her earlier—of my engagement and to suggest again that it would be more proper that we continue not to correspond.

"When I told her she understood, smiled, and wished me God's blessing through a few tears. When I left her, we just said good-by. She turned and walked toward the nurses' residence, and I headed toward downtown Los Angeles and thence to Philadelphia. But I'll tell you, Ben, I had a lump in my throat like a football. I wanted to bawl like a baby. I even talked to myself, at moments audibly. I said, 'Son, you've just said good-by to a wonderful girl.' I repeated it in a way that was incongruous with my supposed exclusive love for Alice.

"I was like a lad suddenly leaving the security of mother earth, headed for an unknown life in an unknown atmosphere on the moon. I had thrown the switch and was on my bewildered way. There was no proper turning back. I had made my decision and I must stick by it. I was not exactly sorry, not consciously anyway. I guess I just felt that it was a shame to have to terminate such a wonderful, mature friendship just because I was going to get married. . . .

"Looking back on it now, Ben, I recognize the *flutter* as more associated with sex than anything else. It should be said here that sex has a God-ordained place in love clearly. But sex is the *flower*, not the *root*. Love is the root that sustains and supports the stem and the leaf, and blossoms out to the flower. The divine order is love first, then sex. The human order is sex first (even in the limited plane of natural attractiveness without any abuse of propriety), and then true love. And for the Christian, if it doesn't turn into true love, woe, woe to that condemned soul. The modern tendency is to plant the flower. We should be more concerned with the root. . . .

"Don't get me wrong. I'm not condemning sex. God made it and it is sanctified to sincere believers. . . .

"Few young fellows contemplating marriage realize the extent to which sex drives a man. The fellow who has no other reason for living with a woman for the succeeding twenty years finds himself condemned 'until death do us part.' They should enjoy fellowship, friendship, help, support, sacrifice, collaboration, etc. It is in terms of these factors that love must be measured."

Nate never ceased to marvel at God's goodness to him in giving him the right mate: "What the Lord has done for us in bringing our lives together when the odds were so slim in the natural realm is one of the big blessings that will constantly be a shot in the arm to my faith. You are very precious to me, Marj."

On one occasion Marj planned a surprise party for Nate on his birthday. Children enrolled in the English Sunday school at the Shell property joined with the Saints to play games and eat a three-layer cake. Nate was thoroughly surprised, he admitted. "If you ever want to have a surprise party for your husband, just have it on a day that isn't his birthday." Marj had mixed up her parents' wedding anniversary with Nate's birthday.

There were all sorts of experiences in the life at Shell Mera. Not only were there errands of mercy on behalf of missionaries and Indians, but even the animals around the base required attention.

The Dave Coopers had loaned the Saints a female police dog named Dolorina to guard the airplane. Nate thought that the roar of the engine and the spinning of the propeller would be sufficient to keep Dolorina away from the plane but he figured wrong. As he cut the engine one day after taxiing up to the hangar, Dolorina got too close to the plane before the propeller had stopped turning. One of the blades struck her in the head. Nate, in the cockpit, could not see the dog but he knew immediately what had happened.

The dog lay crouched and stunned from an enormous gash that exposed the bone just in front of her eyes. "It looked like the front end of her head was going to drop off," Nate graphically described it. "I decided to get the .38 and end her misery."

Marj came running out and said, "Oh, no, maybe we can save her!" So they sutured the wound shut. By the next day the dog was romping around again.

Hardy Dolorina shortly after the incident gave birth to a litter of puppies. One night Nate heard the puppies raising an awful fuss. When he examined Dolorina he found that a huge hole had been torn in her udder. Again jungle surgery saved the patient's life. A needle and thread remedied the trouble but the puppies had to be fed from eyedroppers after that.

Nate often expressed regret for his own lack of patience. It was true that he had misunderstandings with some of those with whom he worked. At times he spoke bluntly but he constantly strove to overcome his faults. After one such misunderstanding he wrote to the person involved:

"Money is safe carried 'on account' but I don't want our differences carried that way. I believe all of us would get along better if we could only bring ourselves to handle our feelings like cash on the counter in front of the Lord and the 'client.' What do you say?

"The Word says that if a brother trespass against you, rebuke him. And if he repent, forgive him. I've found that the quickest way to distinguish between trespasses and misunderstandings is to speak to the person then and there. 'Let not the sun go down on thy wrath' . . . 'when thou comest to the altar, if thou rememberest that thy brother hath aught against thee, leave thy gift at the altar and go and be reconciled to thy brother.'

"Our first concern is that we please the Lord, but in weak moments we also like to think that maybe those we serve are pleased too. The present schedule keeps a fellow close to business . . . excludes the many little niceties and overtures that go to cultivate mutual esteem and appreciation, but we trust that you won't receive our efforts as cold business. We think the world of you people.

"If you have any ill feelings toward us or the way we do things, you owe it to us as a favor to tell us. 'Faithful are the wounds of a friend.' We're just youngsters and we realize that our mistakes and incapacities are legion."

Because he faced his own sins and shortcomings, Nate was

realistic about the role of a missionary. He felt that the Christians at home made too much over missionaries. "It's too bad there has to be so much band-playing and bugle-blowing to get so little accomplished," he confided to his mother. "I wonder if one reason people tend to make a missionary a hero isn't that if they can make themselves feel somehow that he is doing the impossible, they themselves are not directly indicted with responsibility for not going. . . . If there is anything worse than someone staying home for nebulous psychological or theological reasons, it is someone who *goes* on that basis."

Nate often pondered upon the ways in which the Lord had been working. He wrote his friends at home:

"Have you noticed that when a man finds the will of the Lord for his life, there always seems to be an evident relationship between the talents or gifts or preparation the Lord has given him and the job the Lord has called him to do? Has that been your experience? When Marj and I first dedicated our lives for missionary service, we felt that our foregoing efforts and pursuits were entirely in the wrong direction. We were ready and counted all those things lost for Christ and the gospel. But as soon as we began serious preparation for the field, God called our attention to the heartbreaking lack of transportation in pioneer fields—fields where penetration is nearly impossible because of the physical barriers. Now we rejoice in God's gracious care for our lives even before they were entirely His—preparing us specifically and without any wasted motion for the job He had for us to do!"

17

CHUPIENTSA

. . . the stretching out of his wings. . . . Isaiah 8:8

In 1949 Nate learned of the Shell Company's plan to terminate their eleven-year project in the Oriente. He quickly responded to the opportunities to acquire land and equipment from the company for the missions.

"Marj and I have been having a running business meeting," he wrote the MAF office. "Now while the thing hasn't had time to do much maturing in our minds it seems that the thing to do is buy this little plot where we are now and the surrounding land. It just gives natural boundaries, access to the river, the property that the antennas stand on, and a bit more elbow room . . . about two hectares in all. Up the road a bit there are another two hectares that would seem to us to be a good investment.

"Secondly we can see the possibility of a missionary doctor locating here. When Shell leaves, the only doctors in the entire Oriente will go too. A doctor could have a tremendous ministry working out of Shell Mera by air for clinics. I am convinced that medicine is a means of getting Indians in to the stations even from a distance.

"We are constantly amazed at the tremendous medical work being carried on daily at the jungle stations by the missionaries with no medical training. They can't stand by and watch people die so they do what they can. Here in Shell Mera there has been lots of medical work too. Right now we have an Indian boy with a broken leg outside the kitchen door in a little tent we rigged because there isn't even space for him in the storage room. My shop is occupied too. Just the other night Marj and the missionary nurse up at the Bible Institute delivered a baby about midnight. Earlier that evening they were called out on a heart attack case."

Demonstrating his usual acumen, Nate bought huge quantities of lumber, shop equipment, and supplies of all sorts for a negligible amount from the departing oil company officials.

He encouraged the Gospel Missionary Union officials to buy several buildings of the Shell property for a Bible institute. The mission had been discussing the importance of establishing a school for nationals in a center removed from the distractions of urban areas.

For $5750 GMU was able to buy a property that had cost the Shell Company $60,000 to build. Nate and Marj wrote home:

"We are so thrilled . . . not just because we'll get nice neighbors as delightful as that is, but because the facilities for a Bible Institute that Ecuador needs is here with 'a red cellophane ribbon around it.'"

Keith and Doris Austin, who had been working with the Frank Drowns at Macuma, were put in charge of the new Berean Bible Institute and before long a staff of teachers had been assembled and a small student body was enrolled.

The Shell Company on which Nate had so greatly depended in launching the aviation work was soon to be out of the picture. Shell Mera was to become an evangelical training center instead of an oil town. Nate often remarked that the Lord had permitted the Shell engineers and workers to be the advance men for the evangelical missionary cause in the Oriente. Certainly, the airstrip at Shell Mera made it possible for MAF to begin its operations in eastern Ecuador much sooner than would otherwise have been possible.

The cessation of Shell activity closed the English Sunday school attended by children of the oil company employees. It also meant that many good friends the Saints had made were soon to be reassigned to other countries. Both Nate and Marj had witnessed faithfully to the company workers and their families and some came to know Jesus Christ.

Marj described a used kerosene stove they bought from the Shell Company:

"I just can't tell you how much we appreciate the stove and

182

oven. We had our first oven-cooked meat today. Pork, potatoes, and dressing all cooked in the oven; green beans seasoned with a piece of bacon rind and applesauce made from apples that one of the missionaries dried for me last year.

"Oh, incidentally, a hot water tank came with the new stove. What a difference it makes to have hot water on tap!"

Nate continued to visit the neighboring town of Puyo. He attracted attention by means of a loudspeaker. Nate would read from the Spanish Bible, commenting extemporaneously as he went along even though his Spanish wasn't as fluent as he wanted it to be.

For many months Nate had carefully refrained from making a flight to Quito in deference to those who since his accident questioned the wisdom of it. Some folks were just superstitiously afraid that if Nate, Stinson, and Quito ever got together there would be trouble again. However, when his plane radio went out of commission, he was faced with the choice of flying the plane to Quito, or asking a technician to drive down to Shell Mera. The radio set was so built that it could not readily be taken from the plane. Nate discussed the matter with Marj, who said she would not worry but was concerned about the attitude of others, if anything, however slight, were to happen to the airplane. That is an important consideration in public-service work. On the other hand they agreed that the work had to go on despite the fears of people who didn't know anything about the technical part of it. Nate finally decided to make the trip.

He described the return flight from Quito:

"It was really wonderful to be up there at 15,000 feet among the snow-clad peaks, free as a bird at last. At any rate it was good to have the flight out of the way and people breathing easier again. . . . Pfew! Was it ever cold! Yet where the sun hit, it almost burned. On this side of the Quito pass, which runs from the valley floor up to 12,000 feet, the overcast thickened somewhat at around 14,000 and finally I decided to go down through a hole and finish the trip underneath. In the thirty seconds or so that it took to get down through the hole, there was a change that was as profound as that of going from sunny Florida or California to the Arctic in a half a minute. Underneath it was all grisly gray winter and really cold. Just a half hour later I was down in balmy Shell Merita eating a second breakfast with Marj. We're glad that in this very legitimate and important trip to Quito a lot of the stigma has been removed."

In the same letter he told his mother and father about the battle waged with ants:

"Outside the roses are getting back into business after an attack by the ants. Our ants work at night. They can strip a small tree of everything green in one night. They can't get into the house because we have oil canals around all the support bases. Out at Dos Rios station not long ago the ants carried out a hundred pounds of shelled corn in one night, one kernel at a time. . . . Henry Miller says he has seen the soldier ants . . . on encountering a stream, roll up into a big ball and then roll themselves into the water to float down stream to a fresh start in new territory. When they come to the difficult low-mown grass of our yard they go to the trouble of cutting a roadway smooth to the ground about three inches wide for their heavy traffic. I tried arsenic on them and lost half a dozen chickens that ate contaminated ants. There is an ant mound about 12 feet in diameter within 150 feet of our house."

Always ending his communications on a spiritual note, Nate added:

"The Lord has been very good. When I fell at Quito I didn't suspect until the last moments what I was in for. Although God granted me this one whopping reminder of our dependence on Him at the very outset of our labors in Ecuador—He has not allowed me even a minor accident since then. So time and again I wonder how often I have been only a moment away from the pitfall of the enemy while flying and carrying out other duties that come our way. The same is obviously just as true of your use of the kitchen stool to reach something on a high shelf. The Lord is our sufficiency in any case."

Then he told his parents about a tense time involving an encounter with a religious procession of another faith.

We were about to start an open-air meeting when we were

interrupted by the clanging of a bell. It made an ear-rasping thud like a tire-rim fire gong. They hammered it as though there were a fire. It continued to clang incessantly until the procession was abreast of our truck. Then it was silent until they got past me and finally started up again and continued as they went down the street.

"When they first started out I was ready to leave. . . . My first reaction was, 'Why invite trouble?' Why not just quietly shove off? While I turned this over in my mind, I noticed that the men in the plaza had taken off their hats, almost to a man. They were glancing at me with looks that told me all this was for my benefit. . . . I climbed up on the truck body. There was the problem of my sun helmet too. As a visitor in a synagogue I would have respectfully left my hat on as the Jewish people do, and when I have visited Roman Catholic cathedrals as a guest, I have always removed my hat, as I would expect anyone to do in my home or church. But I was in no man's land this morning. That hat had to stay on.

"I have listened to veteran missionaries tell about similar experiences, except a hundred times worse, with stonings and bloodshed. I have wondered what I'd do under similar circumstances. Should a fellow just stand by and risk his life? Where would he get the courage to do it? I thought of the martyrs I had read about. I thought of the children and Marj. As soon as I had decided that I wouldn't leave . . . as mute witness to the truth of the Gospel, the Lord gave me a perfect calm. There was no fear. I knew assuredly that Marj would have stood by me if she had been there. The Lord made it a rich blessing to me."

Whether Nate's danger was as great as he thought, there was courage in his heart. He had no "martyr complex" but he had faced in his heart the thought of being a martyr. Another letter about the same time indicates that Nate contemplated the possibility that he might be killed in the course of his duties. He was writing to his parents after he had received word that he was one of the beneficiaries of his grandfather's estate.

"First, *gracias a Dios* for the faith and industry of Grand-dad Proctor. Then, may we be wise and faithful stewards. In praying what we should do with what has fallen to us, we think of three needs. First of all, I want to set aside a fund to tide-over Marj in case I should be killed. She is a good business woman and would keep her feet well on the ground until she could get settled again. Then if the Lord should tarry His return, and we should get a furlough we want to do a bit of development of some safety gadgets which will require a bit of cash. For this sort of investment we'd rather not have to solicit funds. . . . Marj is enthusiastically behind me in investing these funds this way. She sits by the radio day after day when I fly and notes my position reports for one reason . . . to know just where to send a rescue party if I should call in saying the engine has quit. Third, we'd like to get the rest of the cash busy getting the gospel out. . . . We'd ten times rather look to the Lord to supply through interceding friends than to lean on the bruised reed of a deaf and prayerless bankbook. We have invested everything He has sent so far and He has always sent as fast as we could turn it into a producing gospel investment."

Thus "Get-a-Penny Than" had come to realize that money was a trust from God. It was not to be wasted or spent on selfish interests.

The local commercial plane that shuttled between Quito and Shell Mera crashed in the mountains. Four and a half days later the pilot and two passengers walked out of the jungle. There had been no loss of life but it again pointed up the need for aviation safety. Nate assisted in the search for the plane but finally gave up, without finding the wreckage.

"The accident didn't give me the creeps as some people thought it would," he wrote to the MAF office, "but it did give me cause for some philosophizing. . . . The thought has been sneaking up on me . . . that I am tired. Marj hates the word 'tired'—she just gets 'sleepy' but will never admit tiredness this side of the grave. . . . It is imperative that we start figuring on relief. I hate to admit it. I don't have it tough here now but the past three years have told their story, and I feel like I want to back off a notch and drag in a long, relaxed, and unburdening breath of air. I want to get in shape for the next round. . . .

"After a good meal and a little time, I feel, well, foo, I've got lots left yet, but I know it doesn't last any more . . . Anyhoo, here it is at last: Nate is poooing out.

"I've pried into my innermost motives for all the answers to see if perchance it might be spiritual lack or something else but the spirit and the desire are all there. It's just that when I push the accelerator, the response is mushy. Kinda like my old Ford. It wouldn't idle so I'd just have to jazz the accelerator to keep it going at all. Marj and I don't want to go home. We are not homesick. Shell Merita is home to us and we thank God for it.

"For us the years have flown so fast that it all seems like a fantastic dream. When we recall driving across the States in that old Model-A Ford, flying back to New York in the Stinson, on to Ecuador, the accident, living in tents in the mud and dampness while building the house, preaching in the streets in Puyo, seeing the Shell Company leave the jungles, purchasing land from them in faith believing God would some day have use for it—land that now embraces an expanded MAF headquarters, and we hope some day a hospital and missionary children's school—when we see all these fantastic dreams parade before us we blush with shame and wonder why we ever hesitate to believe God. I'm taking vitamins and the doctor has been supplying me with a special protein preparation that is supposed to help guys that have their hides draped loose over bones."

Nate told the MAF officers that since it was nearly time for an engine change, "we're looking to the Lord to make it possible for a furlough replacement couple to be here for the installation. We are getting along okay although constantly confronted by little mole-hill mountains . . . as seen through tired eyes. It is not so bad when everything is routine but the danger comes at the end of the day when there is a decision on a short field. As a matter of fact I'd even venture the guess that eventually MAF will arrive at a shorter term. Even a vacation doesn't do the trick. A fellow periodically needs to wash his mental hands of the whole works. In our organization success depends (first on help from above) on a keyed-up existence and any slackening in the suspenders, as Grady put it, can mean loosening up on decisions . . . weather and landing strip conditions, or finding out whether it's a valve or a primer system that's making the engine act up."

He reported that he had not taken as many movies of the operation as he would have liked. He did succeed in getting some excellent shots of El Sangay erupting, some sequences of Jivaro life, including a woman suckling a baby pig. He had rigged up a mirror on the camera viewer to catch the latter shot.

During the years of jungle flying Nate had exercised stiff self-discipline on flying regulations.

"Yesterday while taxiing at Macuma near the end of the run-way," he reported, "I hit a soft spot of fill and nosed up a bit. If I had been taxiing a bit faster, I'd have gotten acquainted with the Macuma trail while toting in the new prop. Answer: Always taxi slowly and stay on the beaten track.

"Another such draining experience occurred last week. A big police dog decided to attack the big yellow bird at the front end on take-off. Guess I had gotten 15 or 20 mph. He was out to lend himself to our $255 jiffy-'n'-thin meat slicer, when I hit the brakes. The tail came up so I had to ease off to keep from going on up. The thump, thump never came out front, for which we praise the Lord. On the landing made just before that incident, both sides of the 20-meter-wide strip had spectators along them! It wears a guy out. Recently an Indian woman on her first time up grabbed my right arm on landing approach to a short field where I was working it down with the throttle. She didn't pull it, but the lesson was very much there. Now, when possible, I keep first-timers out of the front seat and when there's any question, I just 'use' the throttle, rather than hold it as usual."

Nate's analysis of these and other near accidents or safety violations—no matter how slight—contributed to a standard MAF practice. Today such information is exchanged regularly between fields.

Meanwhile George Moffat and a crew of Jivaros had worked for months clearing the ground for the airstrip at Chupientsa. Finally word arrived at Shell Mera that the new field was ready.

D. Stuart Clark, veteran missionary and co-director of HCJB, was notified that the Chupientsa strip was about to be opened.

Mr. Clark had expressed a deep interest in this development because many years before he had surveyed the area. Now he wanted to see what the plane would mean to the missionary operation.

Nate wanted to go in alone first to check the new strip, so he dropped off Clark at Sucua. He soared south to Chupientsa. Circling above, he watched the Moffats waving excitedly. Nate dragged the strip but did not land. Instead he dropped a note, saying, "Sorry but this plane has wings. Maybe you'd better fell those two trees off the edge of the runway. Signal me how soon you can finish the job." It was to be the next morning.

Returning the next day, Nate went into Chupientsa for another check. "It is hard to describe the mingled feelings that swam through me as I circled the Jivaro outpost," he said. "I knew that Marj shared many of my own sensations as she heard me report, 'Zero Mike preparing to land.' At the end of the airstrip I saw where Mr. Moffat had dug away a mound of pottery fragments from the days of the Incan empire . . . an entire empire that slipped into the pages of archaeological history without one entry on the pages of the Lamb's book of Life, as far as we know. The air was quiet and heavy . . . ideal for test landing. Reeling in the trailing radio antenna and getting the flaps down for the landing helped break into the sanctum of meditation and reset the mental stage for the job of getting landed. I wish there had been more time to let the challenge of those moments carve themselves deeper into my heart. . . . Intentionally the new airstrip had been kept narrow." When Nate felt his way in for the first landing he said, "It was like parking your car in the garage at seventy miles per hour." This landing inaugurated air service at another jungle mission station.

Nate returned to Sucua for Mr. Clark.

The Moffats were delirious with joy and excitement as the plane reappeared with the first passenger.

"I can tell you're not used to airplanes back in these woods—you're so un-airporty," Nate told the Moffats. Smiling, he pointed to Mrs. Moffat and said, "It's not customary to stand right in the middle of the runway to take a picture of an airplane landing . . . besides it's non-habit-forming."

189

"D. S. Clark kicked up his heels and showed the other missionaries his white socks. 'Look', he said, 'and they're not even wet!' But happiest of those present were the Moffats. Mr. Moffat led in a prayer of gratitude that I wish I could send to you fresh from his lips."

"I had the privilege of attending the first baptism among the Jivaros at Chupientsa," Nate wrote a bit later. "It gave me a real spine-tingling thrill to see (not hear) five Jivaros testify to their faith in Jesus Christ there at the edge of a roaring rapids that drowned out every sound to those who weren't up close."

There were other flights to the Jivaria in which Nate provided the transportation key.

When Dr. Glenn Curtis of the Inter-American Co-operative Service on Public Health indicated he would like to study the medical needs of the jungle, it was Nate who for three days ferried him about in the MAF plane to Chupientsa, Sucua, and Macuma.

In the course of his inspection trip, Dr. Curtis treated Jivaro Indians from morning until night while missionaries, with handy notebooks, jotted down directions.

One of the highlights of 1951 was the visit of Rachel Saint to Shell Merita.

Rachel told of the trials and joys of carrying on her linguistic work in Peru. She shared her desire of working with an unreached primitive tribe. Nate and Marj extended themselves to make her visit a happy one.

The high point was reached when Nate flew her out over the jungle. He pointed out the location of Auca territory . . . the tribe which had never heard of Christ: "There's your tribe, Sis, just beyond that ridge."

Acting on Nate's request for a replacement couple, MAF announced that Robert Wittig and his wife Keitha were to replace Nate and Marj during their furlough period. Nate felt that this had been a veritable provision of the Lord. "We're grateful for such a highly qualified couple to help in the work." It took some remaining weeks to make arrangements for leaving but in February, 1952, the four Saints left for their native land.

18

ODYSSEY BY AIR

. . . who walketh upon the wings of the wind. PSALM 104:3

ORIGINALLY Nate and Marj thought that it would be better for them to rent a house trailer for living quarters during their furlough so that they could keep their family together. However, this plan was abandoned when they obtained a pleasant cottage in the missionary colony operated at Glendale, California, by Mrs. Jennie Suppes. Thus Glendale became their headquarters during their stay in the United States. Marj's parents moved to a nearby house and helped care for the children while Nate and Marj were engaged in deputation work.

There was a happy time of reunion with Grady Parrott, Jim Truxton, and Charlie Mellis of MAF. In addition, there was at least one evening of fellowship with other MAF members and fliers, including Clarence Soderberg, working with the Sudan Interior Mission in Nigeria; Jim Buyers, with the Presbyterian Foreign Board in Brazil; Larry Montgomery, with Wycliffe in Peru; and Jim Lomheim, who had been assigned to work in Mexico. It was one of those once-in-a-lifetime gatherings of friends from afar that never could be duplicated.

After discussions with these MAF officers and comrades, Nate immediately devoted his time principally to the safety projects close to his heart—the spiraling-line technique, referred to as the bucket-drop, and plans for a plane with two or three motors.

Nate sought the help of three able Christian engineers at North American Aviation Corp., active advisers of MAF. Henry Carlisle, Charlie White, and Windsor Vick listened to Nate's concept of a safer airplane. In time the project was launched and near the end of his furlough, drawings had been made of an experimental model. Nate's MAF superiors granted him permission to work on the development program and to extend his furlough for that purpose. But Nate finally decided that it was more important for him to return to the field than to continue as the project's sparkplug.

"It was very hard to decide what we should do," he wrote to a friend. "MAF okayed our tentative plans to stay over and work on it but I didn't feel at peace in my heart knowing the strain of the needs for personnel on the field.

"Now, however, the Lord has given us the assurance of continued pursuit of this project inasmuch as the engineers who have done most of the work on it so far have volunteered to carry on if we should go back to Ecuador."

An attack of pneumonia in February, 1953, gave Nate pause. "The Lord used it to help me 'let go' of the plane project," he said. "So easy for one to get to feeling essential."

But in the fourteen months they were in the United States, Nate and Marj traveled extensively, telling Christians about their jungle experiences and urging them to pray. One trip carried them to the Pacific Northwest. Another to the East where Nate was fondly greeted by his father and mother and other relatives. He spoke in churches in the New York and Philadelphia area, and over Dr. George Palmer's "Morning Cheer" radio program. A few years later Palmer visited Ecuador and Nate and Marj served as his hosts at Shell Mera.

The time in the United States raced by. By spring of 1953 both Marj and Nate were eager to get back to their real home in Ecuador. Because of the increased air operation in Ecuador, MAF officers decided Nate would ferry back a second plane, a Piper Family Cruiser. Marj and the children were to return on a commercial line.

Modifications were made on the Cruiser and both Nate and Marj, assisted by a number of volunteers, helped with the enormous job of packing the extra paraphernalia they had gathered for shipping. This extra stuff amounted to eight wooden crates and nine steel drums!

On May 29, accompanied by Henry Carlisle, Nate took off

from the Hawthorne Airfield and headed south and east to Calexico. Marj packed Nate's fifteen-pound ration of clothing and a *twenty-three-pound lunch!* After crossing the border, they cleared Mexican customs and headed for Punto Penasco.

Typical of Nate's far-sightedness he rigged up a fifteen-gallon auxiliary tank in the rear cabin of the Cruiser. A bicycle pump provided air pressure to lift the extra gasoline to the main tanks while in flight. Cost of this device: seven dollars.

"The flight is over sage-sprinkled desert all the way," Nate wrote in his diary. "At worst we might spend the night on the desert, but the margin seemed safe. The desert is monotonous. Our sense of proportion lacks anchorage. Distances are vaguely defined. Visibility fifty miles . . . we hit Punto Penasco in time to circle a time or two before landing. We, and the sun 'set' together. No gas available here. We are glad for the ferry tank. Our main tanks are still full."

After a gas stop at Obregon, the pair pushed southward. In the afternoon Nate observed that the sun was getting low and realized they had forgotten to change their watches as they crossed time zones. They found the town they had planned to reach, but there wasn't an airstrip as the map indicated.

They looked about for a landing place in the rapidly diminishing light. Nate decided it would be the deserted highway, even though the road was lined on either side by a six- to fifteen-foot embankment. Nate wondered how they would get the plane off the highway once they landed, but the important thing now was to get the plane on the ground.

"We let down and flew about twenty feet above the road to check for signs or other obstructions," Nate continued. "As we pulled up to circle back for the landing, a car passed by in the direction of our landing approach. As we slowed down with flaps and let down to land, the car, evidently chasing us, pulled over to the side of the road and stopped. There was no other traffic and we still had room enough to complete the landing.

"We taxied up and saw that the car had stopped by the only turn-off in miles! It was driven by a Mexican rancher who helped us cut back the brush and move the plane about 150 feet off the road, out of sight. He then sent for a hired man to guard the plane all night, and took us to his rancho. Henry experienced perfect peace during the landing but found his knees noticeably weak on disembarking. I was concerned about the circumstances until we dragged the road. I realized we were going to land on a better landing strip than many of our jungle mission stations enjoy. The Lord surely prepared the way for us.

"The rancho boasted a chime clock that advertised the time very 'adequately' every fifteen minutes. It was a hot sticky night. We hit the hay (no figure of speech) at a little after nine. I heard Henry's breathing 'shift gears' a time or two which indicated that he was getting snatches of sleep. I missed the clock at ten and eleven but heard twelve, one, two, and three and most of the quarter hours. We had drunk about a quart of black, black coffee each in an effort to take on sterile moisture before going to bed."

The two men were up at 4:00 A.M. and en route to Ixtapa, MAF base near the Guatemalan border. Nate recorded the next day's main event—finding a place to land:

"Late afternoon: Same old stunt in new location. The landing strip indicated on the map was not on the physical topography below us. We finally located the 'airfield' . . . a cleared section of mule trail complete with scattered pigs and burros, five miles from the precise spot marked on the map. Henry and I were taking a dim view of the map by this time. During the afternoon we flew past a hill marked one thousand feet on the map. At three thousand feet we were just opposite the top of it! At the landing strip we found 'guest accommodations' with a three-quarter size bed made of tight ropes stretched over a wooden frame. This hemp grill was protected by a single-layer woven grass mat . . . I suppose this was to keep our hard old backs from damaging those nice ropes! Fortunately??? there was a mosquito net. It was about as porous as canvas. Outside the net the air was laden with the presence of pigs. After fifteen minutes within the protection of that canvas bag we decided it would be suicide to stick it out so we poked our heads out, carefully retucking the net around our necks. The people of the house wandered freely to and fro. I don't know whether they ever did go to bed. I guess we already occupied the family bed. Seeing our heads poking out and knowing our fear of malarial mosquitoes, our hosts very kindly shared their protection with us . . . a smouldering beehive whose smoke repulses the most famished aspirants for transfusion. Its effect on Henry was about the same. We thanked them kindly and went back to feeding the mosquitoes.

"I finally saw the sky clearly visible through cracks in the beanpole stockade wall that supported the thatched roof. I didn't need much encouragement to believe that daybreak might be nearing. I rolled out, dressed, and by the faint light found my watch somewhere between three and four oclock. Neither Henry nor I entertained any thought of going back to bed for the remainder of the night. Our hotel bill for accommodations and a pot of boiling water to which we added wild lemon juice, was fifty cents.

"Our lunch weighed fifteen pounds by then," Nate's log continued. "We jettisoned the lettuce before eating our sandwiches. Henry finally weakened and declined the ham. I capitulated also. The tuna salad was holding up pretty well. We discovered that our box had a false bottom under the sandwiches. Underneath were candy bars and Velveeta cheese. I remembered Marj had said she was going to send some things with us for the missionaries we visited en route.

"As we flew along about two hundred feet above the breakers I was fascinated by curious clumps of seaweed floating just outside the breakers. As the morning sun cleared the water, they took on better shape. I tipped the plane up to give Henry a look. He informed me they were broad-mouthed sharks! We eased our course a few feet closer to the beach!"

Finally the fliers sighted the MAF base at Ixtapa about 10:30 A.M. They landed and were met by Selma Brown and Ruth Weir, MAF workers there. To the weary, travel-stained men it was like heaven. They decided while in the area to make a quick detour in order to visit the Tseltal Indians where so many had been converted to Christ in a revival that had swept the tribe.

"We saw the landing strip," Nate wrote, "tucked among a cluster of hills at five thousand feet elevation. Henry realized, I'm sure, why I had not been too concerned about the road landing a few evenings earlier. We were greeted by scores of Indians that ran up from all directions. They extended their hands in welcome and poured out smiling paragraphs of greeting and inquiry in their own language. The only word we caught was 'brother.' They wanted to know right off the bat if we were their brothers in Christ. We enjoyed a never-to-be-forgotten visit with the Indians and their spiritual shepherds, Marianna Slocum and Florence Gerdel of the Wycliffe Bible Translators.

"We were on the trail to the landing strip by dawn. Calculating the probable performance with Henry's 180 pounds aboard, we decided to send the remaining ten pounds of lunch over the hill to Marianna and Florence. We took off, throttled back to an economical power setting, and slowly circled for altitude. At 10,000 feet the bunched-up clouds were below us and we got through to Wycliff's jungle camp. After greeting old friends there we took off for a quick look at Phil Baer's Lacandon Indian station. It was in this same area that Phil and I had worked on the plane repair about seven years before. I wanted most urgently to greet him and visit his station. Rain set in . . . we took it that the Lord would have us learn something about the work there. We did.

"All evening, all night, and into the following morning we listened to a weird chant coming from a Lacandon god-house. We were even permitted to stand under the eaves of the consecrated house and watch them chant and wet the open mouths of stone images with samples of their native foodstuffs. Oh, the depths and gross darkness of heathenism, and what a tremendous contrast after the radiant, joyful experience of the Tseltal tribe!"

The pair returned to the base at Ixtapa, where they prepared the plane for the next day's push. They hoped to fly over Guatemala and make the MAF base in Siguatepeque, Honduras, nonstop.

"On this flight, the landmarks were not so good and our navigation suffered considerably," Nate admitted. "We weren't exactly lost. We just didn't know quite where we were for awhile. Once across the Guatemalan mountains the landmarks began to make sense again.

"It was good to see Don and Phyllis Berry and the children. Their MAF base is another beautiful island of fellowship and refreshment," Nate wrote. The fliers visited the Central American Mission's hospital which works closely with MAF in Honduras and continued their journey the next morning. It proved to be nonstop across Nicaragua to Costa Rica. Thunderstorms kept them from landing in the mountainous capital city of San José, so they spent the night at a coastal airstrip fighting mosquitoes. Next morning they flew above a little electric narrow gauge railroad through the mountain pass to San José and made it into the airport ten minutes ahead of a storm. After visiting friends at the Latin American Mission, Nate and Henry proceeded to Panama.

"We headed offshore in order to comply with flight prohibitions over the Panama Canal," Nate said. "We kidded each other about what kind of impression our tiny flying machine might be making on the radar screens below. We decided that we would probably look more like a celestial or electronic defect than an airplane. We landed at Paitilla Field. The Joe Christopher family were our hosts in Panama. They treated us royally."

When the pair started out the next morning, they found the gas pump broken at Paitilla Field so they hopped over to Tocumen, filling all the fuel tanks and two jeep cans. They planned to make it all the way to Ecuador in one hop, thus avoiding the heavy landing fees usually imposed in Colombia. They took off.

"About fifteen minutes from Tocumen," Nate wrote, "we were climbing over the mountains toward the Gulf coast. We had about five thousand feet of altitude. Henry was flying while I studied a map. We were headed into the roughest stretch of the trip, when the engine cut out. Henry jumped six inches off his seat like a human cannonball. I don't know how far he might have gone if his safety belt had not been fastened. The only reason I did not share his reaction was that I had just finished looking over an emergency landing field below us. Strange as it may seem, it was almost a good feeling to have the experience. It was one I had dreaded for some five hundred hours of flying over dense jungles. I often wondered what my reaction would be. Of course, the experience was graciously cushioned by my awareness of the field below."

They made a one hundred and eighty degree turn, conserving altitude while working with the controls. Nate decided it was a sticking valve, caused by the heavily leaded fuels of the area. When the engine cooled, it ran smoothly but refused to take full power. They returned to the field at Panama. After careful check, they found their earlier diagnosis of valve trouble to be right.

Faced with removing the cylinder and losing another day, they decided to give a try to an alternative. "We dropped the intake pipe," Nate wrote, "which gave us access to the ailing valve stem, opened the valve and scraped the stem with a hunting knife. Henry and I then held a committee meeting and decided the stem was as clean as it could be made on a top overhaul. I took up the plane for forty-five minutes, and subjected it to every imaginable abuse. It ran smooth as a kitten. Again we stayed overnight with the Christophers."

The next morning Nate and Henry flew first over the San Blas Islands, then ran into foul weather in Colombia. "We thought we were stymied," Nate wrote, "until we found the only road that breaks the jungle vastness of that region. We followed it, knowing that we could always make it back to Turbo on the coast if necessary. After a half hour we broke out into better weather in the foothills of the Andes. We landed at a rubber plantation which had a private airstrip, and put some of the reserve gas supply in the main tanks and oil in the engine . . . then took off again.

"The road began following a river whose gorge got steadily deeper. An hour later we were flying seven thousand feet above the river, yet within a quarter of a mile off either wing tip were beautiful little mountainside farms. They seemed so close we could almost touch them. The slopes were so steep we marveled that human beings could cling to them, not to mention farming there. For the next several hours we had a speechless, illustrated demonstration of the etymology of our word GORGEOUS. We flew at ten to twelve thousand feet the rest of the day.

"Some time after noon Henry located a 'Babe Ruth' candy

bar. I wasn't hungry. I muttered something about having heard that peanuts and altitude don't mix well. About half an hour later Henry had contributed everything that was inside him and was trying for more. I don't know when I have seen anyone so sick. Sundown forced us to give it up for the day on a little emergency field the airlines use in Colombia, not far from the border of Ecuador. With another hour we could have made it to Quito the same day."

The emergency field proved to be the same one that Nate and Jim Truxton had visited five years earlier. The radio operator remembered Grady Parrott and Larry Montgomery.

"He fixed up Henry with a cot and a hot drink," Nate said. "It's a good thing he still didn't have any appetite. If he had eaten the soup they very kindly served me, in the condition he was in I'm sure his tour of duty this side of Jordan would have ended on the spot. Once the gas was aboard, I went to sleep under the wing. An hour later I woke up, wet with dew and eaten alive by the bugs. After a fresh sousing with insect repellent, I went to sleep sitting up inside the plane . . . surprising how well I slept."

With Henry feeling better, they took off next morning as soon as the early fog opened up. In an hour they had reached Quito, stopping off at the HCJB compound until the next morning when they headed for Shell Mera. Nate continued in his journal:

"The pass to Ambato was open and we got through at just under twelve thousand feet . . . it occurs to me now that I never once thought about the crash on take-off from the Quito strip that almost took my life five years ago. We got as far as Baños but the pass was choked with clouds and rain. We landed at Ambato and later made two attempts to get through without success. We stayed overnight with George and Naomi Dokter, missionaries among the Salasaca Indians. Next morning the pass was still closed so we decided Henry would have to go to Guayaquil in order to make connections with the airline for the States. It was a keen disappointment not to have the privilege of showing him the part of the vineyard the Lord has set before us but the purpose of his coming was fundamentally completed. We thanked the Lord for his care and parted company."

Meanwhile Marj had flown from Los Angeles to Mexico City. There she was told by Pan American officials that since she did not have visas for Kathy and Stevie, she could not proceed. The Ecuadorian consul in California had told her that the children were so small, visas were not necessary, but Pan American refused to hear this explanation. She made the rounds of the consular offices without success. Finally, after much discussion, a high official of the company permitted her to continue her journey to Panama. After an overnight visit with the Christopher family in the Canal Zone, Marj left the following day for Guayaquil.

While with the Dokters, Nate had a close-up view of a Salasaca fiesta:

"Early this morning I woke up hearing drums pounding out an Indian dance rhythm. The Indians were already gathering for an early service in a nearby chapel. I ambled over there. Two women excitedly herded a few Indians inside the building. I was permitted to stand in the doorway. There were several reasons for standing near the door, not the least of which was the fact that these people carry their water up steep mountain slopes and never waste any of it on such foolishness as bathing. Then, in addition, there was diffused into the already pungent atmosphere the strong aroma of native whisky, made from freshly cut corn . . . their staff of life and exit into alcoholic oblivion. Many Indians started celebrating early and some were already drunk. When the service ended the drums and firecrackers began again.

"Back at the mission station I found the Dokters together with four Salasaca tribesmen, singing, 'O, si yo quiero andar con Cristo' (Oh, yes I want to walk with Jesus)."

Communications between Marj at Guayaquil and Nate at Ambato were difficult, but Nate finally conveyed word that he would meet his family in the coastal city. But first he flew down to Shell Mera. He arrived just thirty minutes before a drenching rain . . . a junior cloudburst.

"I never expect to see anything more like paradise this side of the millennium," Nate declared. "Bob and Keitha have done a wonderful job of carrying on the work there and the Lord has crowned their consecration with good results."

Later Bob Wittig flew him to Ambato, and Nate proceeded to Guayaquil via Quito. While on the coast Nate and Marj spoke in several meetings with GMU missionaries while waiting for the freighter bringing their baggage. When the ship arrived, the customs men told them that the baggage had come through as "freight" and therefore would require a huge duty, instead of the light fees imposed for "unaccompanied baggage." Eventually the red tape was unsnarled but it took much time and effort. Just another of the complications of serving as a missionary to another land!

Back at Shell Mera, Nate learned of an accident that had imperiled Bob Wittig's life and put the Pacer out of commission. Bob was taking off from Shell Mera for Dos Rios with materials for Henry Miller's new house. He had almost reached flying speed when a large dog tore out from TAO hangar. Bob saw the dog coming and tried to pull the plane up, but he wasn't able to get it up quick enough. The left landing gear struck the dog with such force that it was torn off and the dog was killed.

Wittig jettisoned the cargo, consisting of a kitchen sink, two sacks of cement, groceries, and fifteen gallons of kerosene. Surprisingly enough a bottle of vanilla and a bag of cocoa landed intact. With his wife and some of the people from the Bible Institute praying and with most of the population of Shell Mera and the Army post watching, Bob approached cautiously for a landing on the undamaged right wheel. The plane settled slowly on one wing and came to a halt in a turn. The propeller was bent and the end of the wing was torn, but the MAF pilot was unharmed.

Later the same year Nate was headed home from Macuma about five minutes behind his deadline schedule—a deadline set to avoid encroaching darkness. About ten minutes out of Macuma, Nate's flight developed into a race with a rainstorm at Shell Mera but the weather was still good at Macuma. Radio interference was bad. Within three minutes of landing, forty-mile-an-hour winds struck and the field was obliterated by a blinding cloudburst. Nate wheeled the plane around and used all the power he dared racing the darkness back to Macuma. The moon was mixing its rays with the fading daylight as he "felt" his way onto the Macuma strip. Nate reported his violation—impressed again with the need for not pushing a deadline.

Since several new jungle stations were being opened, there was need for dropping supplies from the plane. Through experience, Nate had learned to respect the dangers of dividing his attention while flying near the ground, risking fouling of lines in the tail wires, chute opening inside the airplane, and depending on manual manipulation on a tight target. He remembered some experiments he had made several years before back at the Somerton Airport near his home in Pennsylvania. He had written about these earlier experiments:

"All day today Ben and I have been experimenting with a rig that we've made to drop canned goods from a cub. Up until this afternoon we hadn't had a drop in which some of the cans were not damaged. Then this afternoon I cut up my old sailboat sail and made a larger chute. The tape that I used for shroud lines was pretty light but it was the only thing I could get my hands on easily so we tried it. You've guessed it. The lines broke when the chute popped open and we had a free fall and three more cans of beans that had to be eaten up. It wasn't all lost because the evolution that came with repeated attempts has given us a very practical and easy method of attaching, releasing, avoiding fouling with the stabilizer, etc. I'm hoping that tomorrow will see some successful drops."

Applying this earlier experience at Shell, Nate made a pod out of a fifteen-gallon oil drum with hinged "bomb bay" doors released by pulling a pin. The only thing associated with the chute or cargo that was fastened to the plane was a light string static line . . . twenty-pound test. The pod clamped to the lift struts. It worked like a top. The pilot needed only to yank the release line when over the target—and could hit a plot about 100-foot square.

So this earlier experience was put to work in the jungle. The Puyupungu airstrip being built by the Elliots was to be ready for service within a month. Meanwhile, Nate kept the Elliots supplied by parachute.

"Yesterday," Nate said, "I rigged a 100-pound bag of beans with a 12-foot Gibson girl chute, and headed for Puyupungu where Jim Elliot had a bunch of workers but nothing to feed them. The beans were too heavy for the chute or something for they broke loose when the chute popped open. The beans were in a double sack so were recovered okay. A few days before we had used one of the big orange parachutes and dropped them a supply of fresh food including potatoes, green beans, frozen meat, peas, cucumbers, lettuce, and butter . . . it landed in good condition. Immodest of me to say so, but I get a big bang out of these 'bombing runs.' I enjoy my work to the full."

Aluminum seemed to be the ideal roofing for jungle stations, so Nate devised a harness for slinging seven-foot lengths under the plane. "The sling," as Nate described it, "is made in such a way that if any of the four corners break loose, the whole thing drops free. As an added precaution, I take a rope loosely under the whole works from strut fittings on one side over to the strut fittings on the other side. To protect the underside of the fuselage, we slip in an air mattress between the aluminum and the belly of the plane and partially inflate it. The aluminum rides snug and adds very little drag since it conforms to the shape of the underside of the plane.

"So far there has been no hint of trouble. But I am constantly aware of the fact that we are playing with fire when we leave the straight and narrow. I feel that we fellows on the field should be required to explain and seek permission on such stuff from the home office. Passengers are never carried when hauling aluminum."

Bob and Keitha Wittig remained at the base for a time until both planes were in good shape, but Bob eventually was loaned to HCJB to care for diesel engines powering the transmitters at Pifo. Thus Nate was obliged to carry on the mounting flying load alone. When he had first come to the field, his schedule had been full because of the building requirements at the base. Now the activity which had been made possible by the airplane had created the need for more flying. He also at this time launched the expansion of the Shell Merita base which continued over a period of months. Along with other correspondence about this time Nate received a letter from the home office involving a "little friendly chewing out," to which he replied:

"Your points are well taken, Hobey, regarding the adventurous nature of the trip from Los Angeles to Quito in the Cruiser with Henry. Yes, I fully concur: the handbook we have all been talking about will help me measure myself too. After introspection, it seems to me that with all the talk of my 'perhaps being a little overcautious,' I kind of decided maybe I had better 'be one of the boys.' The pendulum has swung though and is proceeding once more toward the conservative end of the oscillation—perhaps a little to the right of center again.

"Not too long ago I helped Henry Miller and Jerry Conn pull out a V-8 Ford engine for a sawmill they hoped to put up. The job required staying overnight. I slept??? in the plane while the fellows finished the job. Before going to sleep, I took mental stock of the situation. Different stories of Auca killings at Arajuno crossed my mind. The .38 seemed a wonderful bedfellow. I wondered what I'd do if I woke up and saw a dark face peering in the open window. It would require a book to contain all the mental 'committee meetings' I had that night. Now, I know Los Angeles isn't the safest place to live. Dad always told us kids that if a thief breaks in at night, we should sleep like mad—maybe even snore a bit. Somehow or other that rule doesn't seem adequate now, although the basic principles are still excellent.—Back to Arajuno. If I heard any suspicious noises, would I have let fly a slug into the air? It would have scared me to death, but that would be a slight sacrifice on my part as long as the effect might be mutual!"

Nate was testing out the bucket-drop one day at the Shell Mera airstrip, when an Indian runner handed Marj a note:

"Looks like my leg is broken. The fellows have cleared 250 yards of sandbar. Do you think you can make it? Hurriedly, Bob Schneider."

Schneider, working on the Wycliffe base at Llushin, had suffered a broken leg when a tree fell on it. Several ligaments were torn from the bone.

This note altered Nate's plans for the day:

"I lightened the plane to a minimum gas load, removed unnecessary seats and equipment, and took off the cabin door," he said. "Then I softened the tires to 8 pounds to keep it on top of the unco-operative sand, ballasted the cabin with 165 pounds, Schneider's estimated weight, and began a series of tests in a measured length of the Shell strip. Under the least favorable conditions, i.e., uphill and down-wind, I consistently broke ground with ballast at 250 yards. On the favorable run in 110 yards and less. I decided the attempt was warranted.

"We committed the project to the Lord. If we should fail, Bob would face a tortuous eight-hour trail trip on an improvised stretcher. If we should succeed, he would be in Shell Mera in ten minutes. Marj followed me by radio. Bob's wife listened in Quito.

"Frank Mathis and Ralph Eichenberger had marked off with palm leaves, the 250 yards of usable sand. After a couple of test runs over the sandbar, the plane snuggled into the tiny strip without incident. The take-off was consistent with the indications of the trial runs in Shell Mera. Ten minutes later, we landed at our base, gassed the plane, and continued as far as Ambato where Harvey Bostrom met us in his car and took Bob on to Quito for an operation."

As soon as the rescue flight had been made Nate and Marj began a 400-mile overland trip through the Andes to Ipiales, Colombia. The journey was necessary because they had overstayed their time in the States and had lost their Ecuadorian residence visas. By traveling to Ipiales, they could re-enter Ecuador as permanent residents. The long journey was tiring but having their papers in order again lifted a load from their minds.

Up to this time Nate had depended on HCJB technicians to maintain the jungle radio network. However, HCJB activities were stepped up and it was no longer possible for the radio station to render this service, so Nate took on a new role as radio repairman:

"When our stuff arrived we dug out the tube tester, a gimmick with enough toggles and buttons to make a radio man out of anyone. . . . I tucked tongue in cheek and waded in. The first day the receiver I worked on succumbed to my mutterings and starings and the sound of fluttering technical manual pages. It was a condenser. It works! I felt like a butterfly that had left the cocoon with the aid of a cartridge seat injector. You have no idea how I dread hauling those radio receivers up to Quito only to have something else jog loose on the way down—especially now with no road."

He also told the home office that the hydroelectric plant was then producing 500 watts. Later it reached one thousand.

In an effort to keep the lines of communication "clear" between the field and home office, Nate wrote to Grady Parrott:

"This is not a careful letter, Grady. I am keenly aware that I do not state things smoothly, don't oil my suggestions properly, etc. I only trust that the Lord will give you grace and allow us something of mutual confidence and understanding. Don't let a little thing like my affinity for an airplane with long wings and consequent prejudices get you and the slide-ruling brethren all unhappy with me. It takes all sorts, doesn't it? I appreciate the latitude that you have always allowed us. We all want results . . . we want missionary materials moved safely, economically, and on schedule. May the Lord give us results by any channel possible whether it be by logarithms, drawing boards, catalogues, and midnight oil or by local experience, hunch, and seat of the pants . . . or a combination of both which we will recognize as being the desired brew. . . . You could probably put my opinions in the bottom of a gallon can, add my opinion of Einstein's theory of relativity, shake the can vigorously, and pour out one gallon of hot air plus negligible quantities of water vapor. . . . I'm not preaching to anyone, Grady, just putting my heart on paper so that you can count the official pulse for me . . . possibly a preclusion to misunderstanding later."

Nate was willing to be frank about his own shortcomings and eager to express his convictions, and demonstrated a desire to work in harness with others.

Finally came word that a second pilot would be added to man the other plane. Meanwhile Nate and Marj carried on the work. Their second term in Ecuador would be even more exciting than the first one.

19

OASIS IN JIVARIA

. . . as swift as the eagle flieth. . . . DEUTERONOMY 28:49

FROM the start Nate had enjoyed the friendship and confidence of Frank and Marie Drown. Frank, who had been reared on an Iowa farm, had met Marie, who came from Berkeley, Michigan, while they were students at Northwestern Schools in Minneapolis. Accepted as missionaries by the Gospel Missionary Union, they volunteered for service among the Jivaro head shrinkers of the eastern jungle of Ecuador.

The Drowns had joined the Ernest Johnsons at Macuma in 1945. They were able to begin their work in the isolated jungle station chiefly through the help of co-operative pilots of the Shell Oil Company, who occasionally flew supplies into the airstrip at Ayuy, a day's hike from Macuma. Later Macuma was serviced with the plane operated by Bob Hart. When this plane crashed, the Drowns were in a tight fix until MAF began its operations in 1948. One of Nate's first flights was to supply Macuma with food.

Frank Drown, like Nate, was a practical down-to-earth missionary. He learned to speak Spanish fluently and then the difficult tribal language of the Jivaros. These Indians have no words for abstract concepts such as "faith," so two words "hear" and "obey" must be used to convey the correct meaning.

The Jivaros are handsome warriors with a high intelligence quotient. They have a keen sense of humor and giggle constantly, either because they are amused or to cover embarrassment or deeper feelings. Another peculiarity is their penchant for spitting.

Through the years the Jivaros have been friendly generally to white men but they are cruel and heartless in their intertribal warfare that has continued for generations. In former years, the victor in these battle-to-the-death encounters would cut off the head of his victim and by employing a mysterious pickling process, shrink the head of the vanquished into a gruesome tsantsa about the size of a baseball. Scientists still are seeking to determine the formula that produces a shrunken head.

When the Spanish conquerors marched down the eastern slopes of the Andes, they met resistance from the Jivaros. On one occasion the leader of a Spanish expedition for gold was captured. The Jivaros pried open the mouth of their captive and poured molten gold down his throat as their cruel reply to Spanish greed.

But by the time the missionaries had arrived, the Jivaros confined their killings to their own people, or in the continuing feuds with neighboring tribes like their distant kin, the Atshuaras.

The lives of the Jivaros, even to this day, are filled with the horror of witchcraft and evil spirits. They live in a constant state of concern—fear that they will be hexed by a witch doctor, fear that they will be pursued by the evil spirits, or fear of sudden death from reprisal raids. Their children are taught to hate, repeating the names of those on the tribal or family black list.

The Jivaros, who have been a seminomadic people, are clever hunters living off the land by killing game and catching fish. They employ seven-foot-long blowguns that accurately send sharp wooden darts, tipped with curare, into the vitals of birds and small game. More recently they have learned to employ shotguns and rifles which they carry with them wherever they go—even to church.

Both men and women have long blue-black hair, although the women do not have elaborate coiffures like the men. The women wear drab, shapeless dresses. Since most of the menial work—which means all of it—is done by the women, the Jivaro braves sit about braiding their hair, adorning themselves with long strings of beads that are brought in from Peru, or painting their faces in the designs of their tribe. They love to talk by the hour, but always, when meeting, go through a strange, formal method of greeting that follows strict patterns. The remainder of the time they hunt or carry on warfare with the enemies about them.

Recognizing that conversions among the Jivaros would mean

their settling down and forming churches, Frank Drown began to teach the Indians the rudiments of agriculture. The Jivaros were quick to learn and Macuma gradually became a sort of experimental jungle farm. In addition, the Drowns and Dorothy Walker, their co-worker, conducted a school for Jivaro children and a clinic for treating their many diseases.

The missionaries, by immersing themselves in the lives of the Jivaros and identifying themselves with all of their joys and sorrows, soon won the confidence of these attractive, keen-minded Indians. A church began to form following the cultural patterns of the Jivaros rather than those of Midwestern Fundamentalism. In a polygamous culture Drown decided that it would be better to accept a converted Jivaro and his wives into the church rather than to enforce monogamy upon them as a test of fellowship. Forcing additional wives to leave their husbands would drive them into immorality and leave them without means of survival.

In due time he taught the Indians to conduct the affairs of the local church, including the standards for discipline, self-support, and evangelism. The Jivaros themselves decided that after a man became a Christian, he could not take additional wives.

In his frequent visits to Macuma, Nate grew in favor with both the missionaries and the Jivaros. Frank said of him:

"He was always conscientious and serious. He was more than just a pilot, he was a spiritual inspiration to us. We were impressed with his fervency, honesty, dependability, and complete devotion to Christ."

The missionaries and officials of the GMU felt that the aviation program meant extending their borders and establishing outstations deep in Jivaro country. Thus it was that even before the Saints went home on furlough, Nate had flown Frank Drown on an aerial survey of the southern and eastern jungle to determine sites of additional stations. In a flight that lasted an hour and a half, they were able to survey a territory that would have required a month of surface travel. Even then, Frank said, he would not "have seen much of anything but river banks."

When an epidemic of influenza struck the community at Macuma, a Jivaro witch doctor made life miserable for the Drowns and Keith Austins who were then working with them. Nate wrote of the incident:

"It is telling on their nerves because a Jivaro killer never comes out in the open. It's always an ambush and this old fellow has killed other whites which is unusual in the Jivaria. He claims that Frank bewitched a boy in his tribe so that he died. A number of times during the nights recently friendly Jivaros have come to warn that the enemies were in the brush nearby."

Later some of the witch doctors themselves were "captured by the spell of the gospel."

"The Jivaro is a funny combination of cold cruelty and rollicking humor," Nate wrote. "They really aren't cruel except that they are made that way by their religion of fear and evil spirits with which they hope somehow to cope with their sin problem. For instance, a witch visited the Macuma Indians a couple of months ago. He was from another section of the forests. For some reason or other he got mad and cursed a certain woman. Women are soulless possessions of the men and are frequently stolen or used in business deals. At any rate the woman who had been cursed died within twenty-four hours. Her husband, brothers, and father then felt duty-bound to avenge her blood because the witch was as guilty as if he had shot her outright. They went over to the other tribe and brutally killed the witch and another fellow and then came back and asked Frank to protect them from expected counter-vengeance. Frank told them that it was their party and they'd have to see it through alone. They wouldn't listen to the gospel, and now they were afraid of the wages of their sin. This happened a couple of months ago so life goes on as usual again but one of these days there will be another killing. It's routine in the Jivaria. There's no end to the killings. They're afraid of being killed and yet they are afraid not to kill if the family obligation or debt, as they call it, for a killing falls their lot to execute. The miserable part is that to pay off these debts, they don't necessarily have to kill the very fellow who killed one of them. Any relative will do. Their consequent fear determines even the construction of their houses which are very little short of military fortresses. They often put traps in the trails for their suspected enemies. Not long ago

Mr. Moffat was out doing visitation work in the jungles. His bare-foot carrier, who was walking in front as they approached a Jivaro clearing, pulled up to a sudden, painful halt. A needle-sharp palm-wood spike was sticking out of the top of his bloody foot."

To aid in the work at Macuma came Roger and Barbara Youderian in 1953. Roger, a native of Montana, had overcome a childhood attack of poliomyelitis to win athletic honors in high school and college. A paratrooper during World War II, he served with distinction in Europe. Like Frank Drown, Roger met his future wife Barbara, a girl from Lansing, Michigan, while they were students at the Northwestern Schools in Minneapolis.

Through letters sent to the States by Marie Drown, the Youderians had become interested in work among the Jivaros. After their marriage they were accepted as GMU missionaries.

While they were studying Spanish at Shell Mera, Roger became acquainted with Nate. Later the Youderians joined the Drowns at Macuma and started the study of the Jivaro language.

In Roj Youderian, Nate discovered another kindred spirit. He recognized that this was an intense man, with great natural abilities, who was a completely dedicated warrior of the cross.

Nate said of him: "Roj displays a real sense of urgency in the task of winning souls." Later Roger suffered from spiritual depression and discouragement, but he and Nate were to have stirring adventures together.

20

CANGAIME AIRSTRIP

. . . they were swifter than eagles. . . . II Samuel 1:23

The GMU mission council continued to seek means of extending their work in the southern jungle. They found that when the Youderians reached the field, Roger wanted "to preach the gospel not where Christ has already been named." So it was that Roger and Barbara were sent from Macuma to the Taisha airstrip which was to be known after that as Wambimi.

When they were settled at Wambimi Roger wrote Nate:

"I walk the strip each time, before you come, to be sure there are no jaguars, tapir, or deer on it. That is the only livestock we have to worry about here. A jaguar hung around our house about an hour the other night telling us what he thought of our invading his territory but we haven't heard him since. He didn't talk to us in a very pleasant tone."

Barbara enclosed in Roj's letter a little poem that read:

> *Wings of help, wings of cheer*
> *Daily contacts we like to hear;*
> *Meat, vitamins, and dessert, too.*
> *Come to us because of you!*

Something of Roger's character was displayed in a subsequent mercy mission in which both he and Nate were enlisted. A Jivaro Indian had been hit by a tree while helping prepare an airstrip at Cangaime, a new outstation eighteen miles from Wambimi. By radio Nate was called to fly in to the new strip to see if he could evacuate the wounded man. Besides being a legitimate call for a mercy flight it was a test case in an area where the gospel had not been preached. But there was the necessity of determining whether the new Indian-built strip would support the planes' wheels

213

without bogging down and perhaps flipping the plane on its back during the landing roll. An interrupting call from Wambimi solved that one. Roger volunteered to hike over the jungle trail from Wambimi to the new strip immediately. Even seasoned Indian trail men said that Roger could not make the distance in a single day, but Roj said he would be at the new strip by 4:00 P.M.

"I asked him to start smudge fires at the cliff end of the strip so that the smoke would warn me of any serious down drafts, caused by the 300-foot drop off," Nate recounted.

It was already ten o'clock in the morning. To cover eighteen miles in six hours on this trail was a big assignment. "But if there was a man out in those woods who could do it, Roger was the man," Nate said.

"At 3:15 P.M. I warmed up the plane and took off for the rendezvous seventy miles away. At 3:55 P.M. I was approaching the new strip, a mere cut in the matted grass and almost invisible until you got right over it," Nate continued. "My heart rejoiced as my eyes spotted smoke drifting skyward from the cliff end of the clearing. There was Roger running from one smudge to another, stirring them up so they'd throw more smoke. He signaled 'Okay' on the condition of the strip. The wind was almost calm, slightly favorable. No down drafts. I went in, committing the operation to the Lord.

"The landing surface was the roughest I've been on for a long time, but firm and perfectly safe. Roj was a ghost of his usual self. He was haggard and pale and sweating profusely. His shirt was in shreds. His heart pounded visibly and he panted for breath as he shouted to the Jivaros instructing them to bring the wounded man as quickly as possible. I had some food for Roj in the plane . . . but he had no appetite for anything but a ripe pineapple which he promptly finished off. He hadn't had anything to eat since we had talked on the radio in the morning. Why? Why, because he could not stop even a minute . . . could not spare himself and still arrive in time."

Nate flew Roger over to Wambimi and then returned to the new airstrip to pick up the wounded Indian. It was getting late in the day. Nate couldn't speak Jivaro so he mixed Spanish with generous proportions of sign language and urged the Indians to hurry.

"Off through the jungles," Nate said, "I could hear the excited calls of the men who were bringing the victim. They carried him on a bamboo pallet slung between shoulder poles. His face was horribly mutilated; . . . bones broken . . . one eye was opaque, probably blind before the accident . . . the other was blood red. He looked so dead that I was shocked to see him move."

In a few minutes the plane was aloft again and headed for Shell Mera.

"Lying beside me on the floor of the plane was a stinking, repulsive, mangled Jivaro Indian," Nate continued. "The sight of the rotten wounds on the disfigured face turned my stomach. Yet I tried to look reassuringly into that one black pupil surrounded by hemorrhaged eyeball. Here was an immortal soul hanging over the brink of hell by a tattered thread. Here was one of the hopelessly lost ones that the Lord Jesus had come to seek and to save . . . a poor old one-eyed killer who rarely had seen or shown any expression of pity. He probably trusted me only because his own people had given him up. Death to him was the horror of uncertainty; the anguish of a starless night forever. He knew nothing of God and less of Calvary. If I could only make it to Shell Mera, maybe Doc Fuller could pull him through the night. The Lord willing, he still might be snatched from the brink.

"The Cruiser was light and at 6000 feet I leveled out and pushed along at 115 miles per hour. The poor fellow was shivering from the cold at that altitude so I took off my shirt and tucked it around him and closed all the cabin ventilators except one near my head which helped dilute the nauseating stench. I kept one reassuring hand on the trembling frame at my side and reflected on Roger's race thru the jungle:

"Suppose he had given up. Suppose he had strained a little less. He was hungry. Suppose he had taken time to eat. I recalled his stories of the war . . . the jump into the unknown over France. I pondered the steel-like tenacity of purpose that characterizes the fellow. What is the drive behind that sort of performance? What is it? What can take a happy-go-lucky prewar lad and forge him into a man capable of that marathon? Well, Roger is a soldier more than a paratrooper. He was convinced that the cause was worth dying for and therefore put no price or value on his own life. He was trained and disciplined. He knew the importance of unswerving conformity to the will of his Captain. Obedience is not a momentary option . . . it is a die-cast decision made beforehand.

"I need to draw some conclusions so that I won't lose the blessing of the experience in the whirl of activities at the base. The answer is surely discipline—guess that's where real disciples come from. How about me now? . . . lot's of room for improvement . . . lots of battles ahead. Discipline-devotion-decision . . . Christ the Captain."

Nate circled for the landing at Shell Mera. He could see the doctor by the side of the airstrip with a stretcher. The plane rolled on to the strip smoothly. Stepping from the plane, Nate said, "Hi, Doc, sure glad you're here. This fellow's a mess."

The Indian lived!

There were also developments in the Quichua area of the jungles. Early one morning Nate flew from Shell Mera to Villano, now an Army base, on a routine courtesy flight for the Ecuadorian government. He had carried no passengers to Villano, just some needed supplies for the soldiers. He had unloaded the Cruiser and climbed back into the plane to take off.

Before he had revved up the engine, soldiers from the base shouted that two wounded Quichua Indians were coming up the jungle trail and needed his help.

An Indian, perspiring and panting, told Nate that a band of Aucas had attacked the Quichua settlement near Villano and had seriously injured a man and his wife.

As Nate was being briefed, other Quichuas appeared carrying the woman, who had been speared in the armpit and lower back. Her husband, still able to walk, had suffered two spear wounds in his chest, another in his thigh, and a hole in one hand as he had tried to ward off one of the deadly shafts.

When Nate had first come to the jungle he had heard of the killer tribe of Aucas who refused contacts with all outsiders, whether Indians or whites. Now he was in the vicinity of an actual Auca attack, not a comfortable thought.

Nate did not stop for further rumination. He arranged for the two injured Indians to be carried to the little plane, making them as comfortable as he could in his makeshift air ambulance. He took off from the grassy jungle airstrip and as soon as he was airborne, spoke into his microphone:

"This is 56 Henry calling Shell Mera. Out of Villano."

Then through the crackle and static, came the businesslike response of his wife Marj:

"Okay, okay, okay, I'm reading you."

"I have two Quichuas with me—a man and a woman who are injured," Nate called. "Have two cots ready in the bodega. This is 56 Henry."

In a matter of minutes the radio speaker at Shell Mera rasped again, louder now. "This is 56 Henry preparing to land at Shell Mera. Over and out."

Following the normal landing pattern, the plane dropped swiftly and surely and touched the runway, then taxied back to the base. Stopping at the hangar, Nate quickly turned over the two injured Indians to his wife and Dorothy Brown, a GMU nurse. They placed the Indians in the storeroom that had been transformed into emergency quarters for the occasion.

When the two nurses had ascertained that the Quichuas needed surgical treatment, arrangements were made to convey them by commercial plane to the HCJB clinic in Quito.

There doctors learned that a speartip had lodged in the woman's spine and had caused temporary paralysis of her legs and lower torso. This situation was complicated by the fact that she was eight months pregnant. An operation was performed to remove the speartip and several days later she gave birth to a normal, but premature baby.

Later the couple was flown back to Shell Mera where they convalesced at the Bible Institute. "We can't talk to the patients directly," Nate wrote, "but our hired couple speak both Spanish and Quichua and converse easily with them. Last night our hired man read the Bible to them in Spanish, interpreting into Quichua as he went along. They had never heard of the Bible. Apparently the truth had not yet found its mark this morning because the man asked if I couldn't fly back out there in the airplane and kill at least one of the Aucas for him. Again the hired man explained that we are not interested in taking life but rather in saving it through the Lord Jesus."

Thus Nate Saint was reminded once again that the dread Auca Indians were still pursuing their old tactics, slipping quietly from the jungle to attack their unsuspecting victims in ambush. The Quichuas injured at Villano were not certain why they had been singled out. They knew that Villano was near Auca territory, but they could only theorize that they had been attacked in reprisal for a raid upon the Auca settlements many years before by the man's grandfather.

To Nate the incident had greater significance. He had come to the jungle as the pilot of an airplane to speed the job of reaching jungle Indians for Jesus Christ—that meant Aucas . . . they too were precious in God's sight.

Nate had often thought about ways of reaching these elusive Aucas. The Villano attack stirred his active imagination. He knew now surer than ever that the stories about the Aucas were more than folklore. They were living somewhere in the jungle just minutes away from one of the mission stations he served.

21

REFEREE IN A WAR

. . . for a bird of the air shall carry the voice. . . . ECCLESIASTES
10:20

IT SEEMED as though the black forces of evil were loath to re-
linquish their hold on the jungle, even though Christianity had
made inroads into many hearts.

Word came to Frank Drown that some of the unconverted
Jivaros in the vicinity had hit the trail intent on staging a retalia-
tion raid on the Atshuaras. This news came right on the heels of
the successful contact Frank and Roger and Nate had made
with Santiaku and his people when the airstrip had been opened
up. Frank feared that the minds of the cautious and suspicious
Atshuaras would relate the two incidents. It could make the missionaries look like traitors and the door so recently opened might
slam shut again for who knows how long.

Refereeing Indian wars was a rather new role for Mission Aviation but Frank called Nate on the short-wave radio. He suggested
that they could lower the plane-to-ground telephone to the
Atshuara chief and permit Frank to warn him of the advancing
war party. This would show them in a practical way that the
missionaries were faithful friends. Nate, however, felt that
Santiaku, never having seen a telephone in his life, wouldn't
know what to do with it. He suggested instead that he rig up a
loud speaker in the plane. Foul weather held up the take-off for
two days. Since it would take the raiders only three days to reach
their destination, less than a day remained to halt the bloodshed.

On the third day it was still cloudy and threatening. Nate
learned by radio that the weather was clearing at Macuma. It was
3:30 P.M., when he started out. In Macuma he picked up Frank
and another missionary, Bill Gibson. They removed the cabin door

of the plane, set up the loud speaker, and took off. As they reached the first Atshuara houses, Frank warned them of the impending attack, giving them the names of the attackers so they would know it was not a hoax.

Circling around the main Atshuara house, Frank spoke to the Indians below by name. They were dumfounded. One woman grabbed a basket of supplies, ran across the clearing, and headed for the bush. Others jumped up and down like college football cheer leaders, Frank repeated the message several times, then suggested that if they heard him, to go into the house as a signal. The reaction to this was a lot of violent arm waving. The missionaries dropped a pair of trousers as a gesture of friendliness and the Indians waved back with blanket in hand as though offering it in exchange. Once more they glided past to lessen the engine noise, repeating the warning again.

It was getting late now, so the missionaries flew back toward Macuma. At the first Jivaro house bordering on Atshuara territory the plane circled as Frank warned the occupants that the Atshuaras had been told of the impending attack and would be ready for the raiders. The Jivaros would know that this meant a deadly ambush.

Back at Macuma the three men decided to make a test to determine the probability of the success or failure of the flight. They circled the Macuma mission stations and Frank talked to the Jivaros on the ground in the same tone of voice he had used on the Atshuaras. If they heard him, he said, they were to lie down as a signal. He had hardly finished the sentence when they dove for the ground. When the plane landed the Jivaros were, almost beside themselves with excitement—they had heard Frank as though he had been standing right beside them.

Later they learned that Catani, the witch doctor who had led the raid, and his companions had heard Frank from the plane and had slipped back sheepishly to their homes. Oddly enough they seemed respectful rather than resentful toward the missionaries who had thwarted their raid.

"We shudder properly," Nate said, "at the thought of these sudden killings in the night or from ambush along the trail, and we feel the need of preaching Christ more than ever."

Some two years later Santiaku, unhappy over the death of his son-in-law, decided that Catani, his old enemy, had bewitched him. Santiaku rounded up his warriors, lay in ambush close to Catani's house, and wounded Mancash, one of Catani's relatives. Catani then retaliated and wounded an Atshuara woman. After a few days, the enraged Santiaku returned with burning vengeance and accomplished his purpose. His men shot Catani's wife and the baby strapped to her back, and fired four bullets into Catani. The baby died instantly . . . his wife the next morning. Catani was flown to Shell Mera and nursed back to health.

"Why did you save his life?" Santiaku asked Frank Drown in criticism of the kind treatment given to his enemy.

"Because we wanted him to hear more of God's Word and to become His child," Frank replied.

"Then preach to him plenty!" Santiaku advised.

Thus the missionary plane was aiding in the opening of the Jivaria to the gospel. The work started at Sucua, Chupientsa, and Macuma had now spread to Wambimi, Cangaime, Pakientsa, and Cumai. Nate had been involved in opening five of these airstrips.

And in the north, in addition to the Tena strip that served Dos Rios, there had been the installation of the airstrip at Pano. Ahjuana had been served for a time. Llushin had been opened by Wycliffe workers, but later was washed away. Nate had also aided in the opening of the Montalvo airstrip, which was a help to the Ecuadorian Army and to Wycliffe workers.

A very important development was the arrival in Ecuador of three young Plymouth Brethren missionaries. Dr. Tidmarsh told Nate they were coming even before he left on furlough. Now they were in Ecuador, getting started in the work for which they had been commissioned by the Lord.

Jim Elliot and Pete Fleming had been brought up in devout Christian homes where the Word of God and prayer was as much a part of their lives as breathing. They had heard the call of the Savior and had learned to walk obediently with Him long before they set foot in Ecuador.

Pete had received his master's degree in English literature from the University of Washington where he was president of the Inter-Varsity group. His heart during this time was turned toward Ecuador.

Jim, the son of a Plymouth Brethren Bible teacher, had been brought up in a happy Christian home in Portland, Oregon, with two brothers and a sister. In high school Jim revealed his gifts in public speaking, then went on to Wheaton College where he met Betty, the tall, talented daughter of Dr. Philip E. Howard, Jr., editor of *The Sunday School Times*. They were drawn to each other but their marriage had to wait for another five years. Jim graduated from Wheaton with high honors, and in the summer of 1950 attended the Summer Institute of Linguistics, conducted by Wycliffe at the University of Oklahoma. There he providentially encountered Dave Cooper, missionary to the Quichuas in Ecuador, and learned first hand about the Aucas. Jim later wrote Dr. Tidmarsh that the Lord had definitely indicated he was to serve in Ecuador.

When Nate returned from his furlough in the spring of 1953, Elliot and Fleming, both still single, had arrived in Ecuador. Ed McCully and his wife Marilou had come to Quito about a year later with their infant son Stevie and were engaged in language study.

Ed and Jim had been close friends at Wheaton and conducted preaching tours together. Ed was the son of Theo McCully, bakery official and later executive secretary of the Christian Business Men's Committee International. An athlete and orator and president of his senior class at Wheaton, Ed later had entered Marquette University law school in his home town of Milwaukee. While working as a night clerk in a hotel, young McCully was able to spend more time in reading Scriptures, and in meditation. This resulted in a decision to give up business as a career and to prepare for the Lord's work. Before going to the field he married Marilou Hobolth, pianist and choir director at the First Baptist Church, Pontiac, Michigan.

The Lord blessed the work of the young men at Shandia as they learned to know the Quichuas, their customs and language. Jim and Pete had taken a survey flight to look for Auca settlements, but no trace of the elusive tribe could be found. They returned to their respective immediate duties.

Nate had been actively promoting the idea of establishing a clinic at Shell Mera that would bring medical aid closer to the needs of the Oriente. Conversations and correspondence with Dr. Fuller in Quito gave further impetus to the project. MAF approved Nate's request to cede a portion of their land to HCJB for the proposed medical buildings.

Soon Dr. Fuller and his wife Elizabeth and their family moved to Shell Mera.

"During the past year," Nate wrote, "we have seen many prayers answered, but one blessing has been outstanding . . . the establishment of a missionary doctor in Shell Mera, next door to the MAF base, and serving this entire needy area.

"During recent months it has been my privilege to help Dr. Fuller get established here. Roger Youderian, Stan Houghton, other missionary colleagues, and I have built a small clinic where the doctor can operate until we get a larger building up for him. We have suspended the MAF work in midstream whenever it did not jeopardize our air-support obligations. Roger has contributed to the construction work so far beyond what was expected that I have felt I should try to relieve him so that he could get back to the Jivaros.

"The medical needs and responses are tremendous. We see, as in an incredible drama, the flow of needy people from all parts of the Oriente by road, by airplane from the mission stations, and by foot from the fast-growing colonies that dot the region. In one afternoon sixty patients were carefully attended. Since Dr. Fuller's coming he has had to do several difficult operations with only crude temporary facilities. For instance, we rigged a #2 photoflood over the operating table for an emergency Caesarian section. We thank God for Dr. Fuller's willingness to do the best he can to save lives even though he doesn't have everything a surgeon ought to have at hand. Tonight, as I am writing this, he is just starting an operation to save the life of an eight-year-old girl with a telescoped intestine.

"On a recent flying clinic one of the doctors walked over to a group of six Jivaro Indians standing near the plane. He listened to their chests and found three of them with advanced tuberculosis of the lungs! At another point on the medical circuit we made the first landing on an airstrip built entirely by Jivaro Indians a day's journey from the nearest mission station. They were led in the project by a Christian Indian from Macuma who had married into that group and was therefore obligated to live there. His motive was to get a strip so that the missionaries could come and preach the gospel to them, but, of course, that didn't carry much weight with the unconverted. However, what did carry weight was the fact that doctors would come. They, like all Indians, have many sick among them and they have learned that the white man's injections run curative circles around the intonations of the witch doctor.

"We had an interesting experience yesterday. I had just finished making the first flight when an emergency call came. (Seems that most of our experiences start with 'when an emergency call came.') This time it was not from the jungles . . . rather it was from Guayaquil, Ecuador's largest city.

"A missionary's wife [Mrs. Abe Dyck] in that city was ill following the stillbirth of her child and the morning report on the radio was not good . . . she was unconscious and considered in a grave condition. Dr. Fuller offered to go over the mountains to Guayaquil to help out if asked. He was asked. I told him I would fly him directly over the Andes to the coastal city. We took off twenty minutes later.

"The mountain valleys were quite clear although the weather was already starting to build up over the ridges at around 15,000 feet. The pass seemed to be choked up with clouds at all levels. They were broken up, though, and a little careful investigation soon showed that we could get through safely. These are rugged mountains and they go up and down with a vengeance. We continued from hole to hole at 14,000 feet after verifying the weather at Guayaquil, now only 70 miles west and 2½ miles down. About 20 miles farther the holes became larger and the various decks of clouds thinner. Within about 10 miles of Guayaquil, we decided to spiral down through a large hole so as not to venture into the airline traffic while still among the clouds. When we got out the bottom of the hole we found we were right smack on course, over the railroad tracks leading to Guayaquil. I am not a crack navigator, but in this case the circumstances were very stimulating to any gift I might have in that field. An hour and forty minutes after take-off we got an okay on the radio from Marj in Shell confirming her receipt of our transmission from Guayaquil.

"It was still only a couple of hours since they had called for a doc from across the Andes. In addition to flying to Guayaquil, Dr. "Ev" had consulted Dr. Paul Roberts in Quito by radio. That doc in turn looked up an article in a medical journal and got the latest data on nonfunctioning kidneys and also got in touch with the U.S.A. by short wave to find out about artificial kidneys. Only three of the machines exist and they seemed to be the only hope left since Mrs. Dyck was already unconscious.

"I left the doc immediately and took off for the mountains, in hopes of maybe making it back to the pass before it closed up completely. . . . Radio contact later revealed that Mrs. Dyck was out of danger. Swift action had saved her life.

"With this much background," Nate continued, "it is unnecessary to tell you of our personal interest in the success of the medical project. We believe that even the most enthusiastic people underestimate the far-reaching implications of this work for the Gospel ministry here in the Oriente. Already we have seen the tall walls of prejudice fall. We are perhaps in a better position to appreciate these gains since we have been here in the gateway during the transition period, feeling the 'before' and 'after' status quo, so to speak. MAF will do everything in its power to make air transportation the bridge needed for reaching Indians through the medical ministry for Christ."

Later the word came that Radio Broadcaster Theodore Epp had contributed the initial gift toward building a full-fledged twenty-five-bed hospital.

There were other basic matters that Nate faced during this period. In the early stages of their work in Ecuador, MAF, through Nate, had transported Wycliffe Bible Translators, included them in the jungle radio network, aided them in medical emergencies, provided hospitality at Shell Merita, and in other ways helped them to get established in the Oriente. But certain differing views of procedure were involved in the aviation outlook of the two organizations. Ultimately, Wycliffe launched its own air program similar to its Jungle Aviation and Radio Service in Peru which would have planes within their own organization. MAF would continue to serve all the other mission boards working in the country. Nate and the missionaries served by MAF in the eastern jungle by this time were sold on the concept of the co-operative program.

Later, Wycliffe constructed its main base, Limon Cocha, in the northeastern part of Ecuador, not far from the borders of both Colombia and Peru, and used Shell Mera as a foothill air base.

Meanwhile Nate's own sister Rachel was stationed at Hacienda Ila first with Katherine Peeke and later Mary Sargeant. She had begun studies of the Warani Auca dialect by working with Dayuma, an Auca woman who had fled from her tribe some years before.

Meanwhile, Nate continued to sparkplug other developments. He was one of the first to suggest that with the increase in the number of jungle stations and the added missionary population resulting from the establishment of the Bible Institute and hospital at Shell Mera, it would be logical to launch a primary school for missionaries' children at Shell Mera. "I believe," he said, "the motive is purely a question of having the children at home in their tender years." He and Roger Youderian drew up plans, discussed the idea with leaders of the Alliance Academy in Quito, and Nate received the approval of his superiors to place the school on the property between the MAF base and hospital. However, the project had to be sidetracked by other more pressing interests and the plan was not consummated.

Still indomitable in his desire to develop a safer plane, Nate was reluctant to drop the idea of converting his little single-engined monoplane to a tri-motored biplane. He tackled one of the problems raised by the aeronautical engineers: the increased "drag" caused by the addition of a set of lower wing panels. To lift this argument out of the realm of the academic he fashioned a set of removable lower wing panels for the MAF plane, and conducted tests as he skimmed a few feet off the ground in the simulated biplane. This brought him a rebuke from the headquarters office . . . involving the manner in which he had proceeded rather than being an objection to the experiments. MAF officials, influenced by engineering counsel, had been less enthusiastic than Nate to the idea of a tri-motored biplane. To their letter, Nate replied:

"Thanks for your frank comments regarding 'Operation Woodswhacker.' I agree with the expressions you wrote. I was aware of what would be at stake if there were an accident. With that in mind I planned not to do anything but 'fast taxi tests' . . . I'll just say . . . 'it happened like this . . . I was taxiing down the runway when a gust hit and . . .' I must admit I am completely defenseless, having ventured whatever confidence I may have built up with you in the past few years. We finished the wing panels and fitted them to the plane in just two weeks and a day. We did nothing to the airplane except put longer bolts in the landing gear and remove the fairings. From there to having the lower wings on ready for use took only twenty minutes. When the thing was set up and ready to test, I took my reputation (and yours) in my hand and decided to go ahead with lift-off tests, staying close to the ground. It was a long gamble on your confidence in me. I reasoned that so favorable an opportunity would probably knock only once.

"As things stand now, I should like very much to mount two empty mock-up nacelles on the new wing panels to test the drag situation. We are looking forward to Jim's visit so that we can show the set-up to him and thus send you a more adequate report by him personally. Let me know your reactions . . . if they aren't too violent . . . /3.&"%$#"$ . . . 8 . . . 9 . . . 10."

Nate also wrote to his father about the biplane:

"I'm sure, Dad, that once you had made up your mind to see missionaries riding in a safer plane, you would, if you were in my place, get the result even without others sharing the initiative and burden. I hope I have learned something in my childhood from your go-get-it determination. I believe it was the thing the Lord sanctified and honored in bringing you the recognition that you in turn used as a testimony for Him.

"I feel like the general who said he liked a certain officer because he 'isn't always trying to convince me that a thing is impossible just because it can't be done.' I think that a discipline of thought and imagination that assures a good result in a small matter can do the same in a more serious one.

"We would be glad if the doubtful and the fearful would pray with us but we would rather, with Gideon, be accompanied by those people who can help us at the risk of disappointment.

"We haven't heard from Mother for awhile, but I guess the building program has just about floored her. We hope that when the carpenter's smoke has cleared away she will still be there . . . another victory added to the many that have seen her through the difficult years with a big family. Mom, we're asking the Lord to drop your bi-focals so that your view will always be by the spiritual side that turns mountains into molehills."

Nate's plan for a safer plane was another project, close as it was to his heart, that he did not see solved. But his number of "wins" far outnumbered his "losses."

22

JUNGLE HANDYMAN

. . . I will trust in the covert of thy wings. PSALM 61:4

WITH burgeoning work in the jungle, the cry for relief was repeated frequently. Nate had pointed out that the addition of the GMU stations in the south and the coming of the Brethren missionaries in the northern jungle necessitated a two-plane and two-pilot operation in Ecuador. Therefore, it was a day of great rejoicing when word came through that Johnny and Ruth Keenan were scheduled to provide this help at Shell Mera. The necessity of obtaining support and equipment, language study, and visa delays did not permit the Keenans to reach Ecuador until the spring of 1955.

"First we want to tell you how well the Keenans are working in," Nate wrote to MAF. "We don't know how we ever got along without them. Johnny is a natural in the saddle, is very teachable, and has picked up the radio technique and routes, and all, very well. He is riding dual on the radio bench and already has one notch in the stock of his soldering gun. Ruth, too, is fitting in very nicely. She's teaching school for the boys . . . finishing the year they could not complete in Costa Rica. We feel that they are surely the Lord's people for this place. I like Johnny's maintenance . . . very methodical and thorough."

Life at Shell Mera moved on with increasing tempo. Both 1954 and 1955 were eventful years. Recognition came to Nate from many quarters for his development of the spiraling-line technique, but he was particularly pleased one day when he received a letter of commendation and a gift of two hundred and fifty dollars from John P. Gaty, vice president and general manager of the Beech Aircraft Corp. of Wichita, Kansas.

Then there were the visitors. One of the most distinguished was

General William K. Harrison, Jr., then commander of the Army's Caribbean forces, who previously had won world-wide attention as the patient negotiator at Panmunjom. General Harrison, who had come to visit the Elliots, gave his personal testimony in the church at Shell Mera. He showed deep interest in the jungle stations and MAF operation. Nate also conducted Dr. William Reyburn, American Bible Society anthropologist and linguist, on an extensive tour of the jungle.

A visitor of another sort was a little girl, accompanied by her mother, who arrived at the Shell Merita gate one day. The girl said she wanted to know more about the way of salvation. She had first heard Nate painfully reading from his Spanish Bible in Puyo in 1949, and later she had contacts with other believers. Nate had the pleasure of introducing her to the Savior.

Philip Jonathan, third child of the Saints, was born at Shell Merita December 28, 1954, with their good friend Ev Fuller and his wife Liz as the attending physician and nurse. Dorothy Walker from Macuma took over Marj's duties for the brief period.

This time Nate arranged for Dr. Fuller to use one of the small bedrooms of the Saint home. Nate saw that all useful equipment was on hand and added an extra feature, a tape recorder.

"This means still more work for my six-armed wife," Nate quipped, and from the start Philip found a big place in his busy father's heart.

By this time the "Brethren boys" had become well established in their stations among the Quichuas. The McCullys, thwarted for a time by a flood that virtually destroyed Shandia, moved there to work with Pete Fleming in the reconstructed premises. Then later they started making weekend preaching trips to the abandoned Shell Camp at Arajuno, just inside Auca territory. They called it "Wawatosa," after Ed's home town, a Milwaukee suburb.

Jim and Betty Elliot had settled at Puyupungu, southeast of Shell Mera, after their marriage. Later they took over the station at Shandia. Pete Fleming had remained in Shandia until his return to the States in 1954 to marry Olive Ainslie, and had brought her back to Quito for language study.

Nate's friendship for the Elliots, the McCullys, and the Flemings increased as they worked together.

To Betty and Jim, Nate was a constant source of practical help, Christian fellowship, and sometimes amusement.

"Nate would laugh at his own jokes before he got halfway through," Betty recalls. "He threw back his head, often blushed, and covered his mouth with his hand when he laughed."

Once Jim said something that Nate didn't hear.

"What was that?" he asked. "Sounded like one of those Old Testament names on the first run through!"

On his visits to Puyupungu, Betty remembers, Nate commented on how pretty the table looked. It was a folding table standing on a mud-floored kitchen, with the simplest of jungle foods upon it. When he saw Betty drying wood in the oven before burning it in the wood stove, he expressed deep interest; he thought it would be a good idea if other junglers would do likewise and save the cost and the hauling of so much kerosene in the airplane.

On overnight stays at Puyupungu, Nate expressed his appreciation for the little things . . . the tiny bamboo-walled room pleased him as much as if it had been a Statler suite.

He liked Betty's gravy. He told his hostess: "Give me some more of those potatoes, will you? Potatoes, after all, are just a vehicle for good gravy!"

Standing on the airstrip at Puyupungu or Shandia, Nate would talk for as long as his schedule permitted. When Jim told him of some answer to prayer or victory in the Quichua work, Nate's face would light up with a smile and he'd say, "Praise God, man, that's our pay, you know. That's what we're here for, and if the gospel isn't getting out through those we serve, we'd better pack up."

Sometimes the alarm on his wrist watch would remind him that he must move along. Then he'd fly off to the next station.

Valerie Elliot was born at Shell Merita and Nate rushed about being helpful. He got up at 3:00 A.M. to turn on the diesel motor, so that there would be no power failure from the hydroelectric plant.

The Elliots and Saints were discussing a baby's crying after Val was born.

"It's a good thing it grates on us as it does," Nate observed. "If it didn't, I guess the poor little yardbirds would die of hunger."

Later he realized that Betty might think he was referring to Valerie's crying.

"Betty, you're just going to have to believe me," he said. "Honestly, I didn't mean just *your* baby."

His observations of Indian life led him to question many of the practices we call civilized, like placing a woman on her back for childbirth. He told the Elliots he wondered if the stooping, kneeling, and squatting of the Indian women was not more in line with nature's plan. He also wondered if the American woman's failure to breast-feed was contributing to the incidence of cancer.

When the McCullys found they dared not have their piano at their damp jungle home, they left the instrument at Shell Merita. Nate loved music and every time Marilou came he would ask her to play his favorite Spanish hymn, *"Tierra Bendita de Palestina"* (Blessed Land of Palestine).

Nate enjoyed music and as a result bought a guitar. Writing to Marj, who was away at the time, he mentioned that he had paid what appeared to be twenty-two dollars for the instrument. Marj wondered why he would spend that much for his amusement when their funds were limited. Later she learned that she misread the letter. The difference between the sign for the Ecuadorian sucre, worth six cents, was the single instead of the double line through the dollar sign. Instead of the guitar costing twenty-two dollars, it had cost only one dollar and thirty-two cents in the American equivalent.

He also played the mouth organ. He wrote his parents:

"This evening after reading of David's pact with Jonathan and flight from the wretched jealousy of Saul, I dug out my mouth organ. I don't know what key it is but somehow it seems the only hymns I can get through without a hitch are the ones Mother used to sing in the kitchen, 'At the Cross, at the Cross, where I first saw the light; Alas and did my Saviour bleed, and did my Sovereign die?' I had hoped to learn to play Marj's accordion but it begins to be clear that my ministry of music will be confined to the mouth organ. It serves to break the quiet of the jungle whenever I get weathered in and have to spend the night on a lonely jungle airstrip. It will never raise goose pimples on anyone else but it serves me as a vehicle of meditation and praise when I am alone with the Lord. I remember, Dad, how you used to play these same precious old hymns on your little mouth organ. It just disappeared between your beard and mustache and the music seemed to come out the end where your hand wobbled out the vibrato, whatever that is."

Ed McCully subscribed to *Time* magazine, which was Nate's favorite periodical. Nate, who received the jungle mail from Quito, would slip the magazine out of the wrapper and read it before taking it to Ed on the next flight. On one occasion he delivered Ed the wrapper with other mail, but had left the magazine at the base.

Ed drew up the following brief in pseudo-legal style on the *Time* wrapper and returned it to Nate:

"*Defendant:* Nathanael Saint.

"*Charge:* Removing *Time* magazine from mail without replacing it.

"*Evidence:* One empty wrapper in said mail.

"*Verdict:* Guilty.

"*Judge's Comment:* In the commitment of said felony, it is always advisable to destroy the evidence."

When Nate dropped in at Shandia, and later at Arajuno, Marilou often would bring him milk and cookies. Besides the regular three meals, he was always ready for a mid-morning, mid-afternoon, or evening snack.

Nate repaired Marilou's washing machine because Ed was a better orator than mechanic. When Ed was stumped, he'd call Nate on the radio and ask for help. Nate would advise him on the air, then conclude by saying, "If you can't get it going, I'll be out in a couple of days."

Nate volunteered "handy-man" help to the other stations as well. He once gave instructions over the radio on how to mix cement. Dorothy Walker and Marian Lowen, in charge of Macuma at the time, were building a shower. When the shower drain failed to work, Nate "diagnosed" the trouble by radio. The girls then removed the solid joints of the bamboo "pipe" and solved the plumbing "riddle."

When Marj was stricken with appendicitis, Nate said to Ed McCully: "Pray for Marj. If anything happened to her I wouldn't be worth anything."

In spite of his own fatigue, he insisted on staying by Marj's hospital bedside. When someone offered to take his place, he replied: "You wouldn't want to cheat me out of this privilege, would you?" Marj's illness caused Nate to reflect on the increasing tempo of their lives. He expressed his thought vividly in a letter to her:

"Life seems entirely too short for the accomplishment of all the things to which we aspire . . . of love and affectionate attention . . . of work and duty. But God grant that each task be oiled and inspired by a proper mixture of the required and the desired—the rough and the lovely—the hurried thought and the detailed expression."

Early in 1955 the McCullys started making definite plans to move from Shandia to Arajuno. In Ed's heart there were two motives for making this change: the opportunity of working among the colony of Quichuas living along the Arajuno river, and the possibility of making a friendly contact with the Aucas. Arajuno had been built on the Auca side of the river to be near the airfield. The Quichuas so respected the river boundary line between themselves and the Aucas that they would not spend the night on the airstrip side of the river. They crossed over only in daylight and then always with their guns.

Nate Saint had helped the McCullys get settled in their new station and hauled aluminum sheets and other building materials needed in the construction of the station.

In a letter dated April 17, 1955, to his parents, Nate wrote:

"The most interesting flight of the recent past was one into the Arajuno strip on the edge of Auca-land. Ed McCully wasn't there but he was hoping to move over with his family next week if I could get enough aluminum sheets flown in to complete the roof on the house the Indians had built for him.

"When I got there bad weather was moving in from the east

with nightfall riding its heels. That meant I'd have to get out of there in a hurry or spend the night. Spending the night was out because of vulnerability to an Auca attack. The Quichuas hadn't seen any signs of Aucas for two weeks, but that was small comfort. After landing I found out the Quichuas had already evacuated to their homes.

"The pathway to Ed's temporary shack was wide so I taxied right up to it, locating the wing right over the door to give shelter from the rain that was now setting in. When I got out of the plane, it was growing dark fast and it was very quiet. The chance of Aucas being in the area was slim but it was there. I recalled that Shell people said that no one carrying a gun had ever been attacked. They apparently have a healthy regard for the strange weapons. I had taken a small revolver on my belt to lend its inhibitive influence to any curious onlookers who might be in the brush. I also made it my business to keep glancing over my shoulder as I unloaded the plane and moved about.

"I felt silly, unloading the plane pretty much with one hand while holding the revolver in the other. I was concerned that the nice little automatic was so trim that the Aucas might not recognize it as a gun. To counter that possibility I felt I should keep it where it could suddenly explain itself with a bang. Of course, I would never shoot a man, unless perhaps in the leg, to stop an obvious close-in threat to my life.

"There having been no contact with these people and no means of communication with them, it seemed to me pointless to think in terms of a heroic martyrdom.

"On the other hand, in order to speed the day when they might hear the gospel, it seemed important to forestall an unfriendly encounter and avoid any bloodshed at all costs. The handier the revolver, the less chance of that sort of unfortunate encounter. Suppose they should come? Suppose I should have to stop one with a wound in the leg? Suppose we hauled him out to the hospital here and got him fixed up, treated him royally and sent him back to his tribe? A lot of things go through a fellow's mind in a situation like that. I'm not justifying my reactions. I'm just reporting on them factually. It's a comforting final thought to realize that we are here on business for the Lord and that He is watching us every moment."

Nate finished unloading the plane and taxied out to the airstrip. In his haste, the plane pushed over a sapling that removed the lens from the left navigation light on the wing tip. Nate reported later that he was glad it was only the light and not the wing "until the fellowship might be a little better with the 'neighbors.'"

As he flew back to Shell Mera, Nate was still musing about his experience.

"In thinking it over afterward," he told his parents, "I suppose the danger faced in that situation was probably less than you face on the highway in front of the house there in the United States. However, if you are interested in adventure and thrills, this has it beat three ways.

"And if we are responsible enough to require of ourselves an intelligent justification of risks faced, what greater justification than to find one's self in the position of supporting a fellow who feels God has called him to live in that situation with his family—to feel one's self bracing shoulders with Ed to make, as it were, a human bridge, over which the gospel might leap the chasm that isolates these savage people.

"The McCullys are now in Arajuno. Last night was their first time on the Auca side of the river. As you know, there are several reasons for their being in that location, but we are hoping that one might result in a friendly contact with the Aucas. (Rachel will be interested.) Meanwhile humanly speaking, they face real danger on that side of the river practically unprotected. I rigged them up a battery-operated light to illuminate the area around the house whenever their dog might bark and also a large electric alarm bell. If a friendly contact is made, it will be a clear manifestation of the Lord's undertaking since there is nothing in recent Auca history to lend hope.

"Ed and Marilou are an unusually gifted couple. Yet God called them to the needs of isolated groups of jungle Indians. I know that many young people feel that since God has blessed them with wonderful personalities and talents the Indians wouldn't appreciate, that means that they aren't called but I'm here as a witness to say that Ed and Marilou are a couple who would eclipse many acclaimed personalities.

"Marilou's piano playing is the finest. Yet her piano is at our house. I've never heard her even mention knowing how to play. I would never have known of Ed's outstanding past and demonstrated abilities had I not been with him at Wheaton. Their lives are a mute challenge to us.

"One of the outstanding inspirations and blessings that is Marj's and mine is the fellowship and privilege of service we enjoy with and for some of God's choicest servants who have counted not their lives dear unto themselves . . . all 27 of them.

"Pray for this Quichua ministry and pray for a friendly contact with the Aucas. It may take years, but it seems to us that Ed and Marilou McCully stand in the most promising position for the needed contact.

"I flew over the hacienda and dropped mail to Rachel the other day. Whenever she can get enough of the language over there at Ila to make it feasible we are all thinking of the possibility of Ed using a tape recording that would play to the jungles every evening . . . just in case there might be curious eyes and ears around."

Thus in the events of daily life the Brethren missionaries and Nate Saint were drawn together. Their friendship deepened when they discovered that they shared a deep desire to reach the Aucas. This was to become the focus of their comradeship and their sense of Christian mission.

23

OPERATION AUCA

. . . under his wings shalt thou trust. . . . PSALM 91:4

IT WAS Monday morning, September 19, 1955. The sun was fast dissipating the chill of the night before. The air was unusually clear. The "modern missionary mule," as Nate called the little yellow airplane, was standing on the gravel between the kitchen door and the small open-sided hangar. Marj had sorted the mail, and boxed the meat and groceries. Nate was stowing the supplies in the plane, weighing and recording each package. Five-year-old Stevie lent a hand. Marj came hurrying from the radio room off the kitchen, Philip in her arms, Kathy trailing behind. Nate kissed Marj good-by, took Philip in his arms briefly, gave Stevie and Kathy each an affectionate squeeze. He climbed into the airplane and pressed the starter button. Marj and Philip opened the gate and waved as he taxied through, across the road and onto the long runway. Kathy and Stevie stood on the grassy bank by the house and watched their Daddy climb away toward the morning sun.

This was September 19, 1955 . . . on January 8, 1956, Nate Saint was to die in a swift hail of long, black, wooden lances.

On that bright September morning as he flew toward Arajuno on the weekly vegetable run, Nate was beginning the last chapter of his life. He had three months and twenty more days to live.

The events that commenced that morning are known to millions as "Operation Auca." The story has gone around the world in *Reader's Digest, Life* magazine, and many other periodicals. It has appeared in ten languages in Elisabeth Elliot's book, *Through Gates of Splendor.* The story, as recorded by Nate on thirty-nine closely typed pages of yellow tissue, of five missionary men who

238

died in their effort to reach the Auca Indians with the gospel, needs no detailed retelling here. Highlights, however, of this last, and biggest event in Nate's life need to be recounted as background for the more intimate, yet untold, facets of his last months on earth.

As Nate buzzed along high above the jungle on that Monday morning, his heart was reaching out to the dark forest where the Aucas lived somewhere in their unknown clearings. "We've got to find them first," he thought. "It's so clear today and I've got a little time. Perhaps . . ."

When Nate climbed out of the plane at Arajuno he greeted Ed with: "How'd you like to go looking for your neighbors?" Big Ed McCully was instantly enthusiastic. A half-hour later they were in the air together. Their search continued until they were almost out of gas. "Then," to repeat again Nate's own words, "a blemish, barely discernible in the jungle, grew into a well-defined pockmark and then into a good-sized clearing covered with well-cleaned manioc. This was it. We had gas enough to hang around for a few minutes, so we hung around. All told, we must have seen about fifteen clearings and a few houses. It was an exciting old time, a time we'd waited for."

Ten days later Nate and Pete Fleming spotted another group of clearings. "We flew down a little river and saw half a dozen big houses with smaller ones around them. There they were, plain as the nose on your face and only fifteen minutes from Ed's place at Arajuno by plane."

Two days later on the evening of October 1, Nate, Ed, Jim, and Johnny Keenan were huddled over a huge map on the living-room floor at Shell Merita. The fellows talked far into the night, and in the kitchen over a cup of cocoa, they decided it was the Lord's time to try to contact the Aucas. They concluded also that their efforts should be carried on in strictest secrecy. As they organized their strategy, they felt sure that if their plans became known there might be a rush of ethnologists and anthropologists and other nonmissionary groups that could obliterate the opportunity to lead the Aucas gently to Christ . . . it might set back for decades the missionary effort among these Stone-Age people.

The four men discussed at length the best methods of approaching the Aucas. They knew that tribal languages are customarily learned most effectively after a tribe has been penetrated, yet they recognized their lack of knowledge of the Auca language as a serious handicap. Nate's sister Rachel at that time knew more Auca words and phrases than any person outside the tribe. The fellows considered taking Rachel into their confidence, but in the end decided against it.

Nate was caught between his deep affection for his sister and his pledge of secrecy. His solution of the problem was to sit down the next day and write a letter to Rachel marked: "To be held until further notice." It read in part:

Dear Sis,

Last night Jim, Ed, Johnny and I reached a hard decision. We decided that, since you were unable to come down here so that we could talk to you personally, it was the Lord's indication to us that we should follow the general plan that has formed in our minds and that is to maintain the following enterprise as secret as practicable.

As you know, the reaching of the Aucas has been on our hearts for a long time. It has been heartening to know that the Lord has laid a specific burden on your heart also and that you are currently engaged in work on their language. For this reason it has been hard to decide not to share with you the efforts that we are about to initiate toward the contacting of these people. Our efforts will be directed toward inspiring confidence in Ed McCully who is, as you know, living within easy reach of the Aucas in two days overland.

I am writing this note now so that you will better understand and so that I will be spared an embarrassed effort to explain it to you after the need for secrecy blows over.

As we see it, you might feel obligated to divulge this information to save me the risks involved. In view of that fact, and since we know that you are already praying for the contacting of these people, we trust God to carry us forward in this effort and you in your efforts to the end that Christ might be known among them.

Affectionately, Nate

Jim Elliot had already met Dayuma, Rachel's informant. The men decided that he should visit her and obtain more basic Auca phrases that they could use in the initial contact with the tribe. Jim had a natural ability with languages supplemented by training in linguistic principles, but most important of all he was fluent in Quichua, the language Dayuma had used since she escaped from her tribe ten years before. Jim recorded neatly on 3 x 5 white cards the many Auca phrases Dayuma gave him.

Presenting gifts has always been a successful method of approaching primitive people. It was natural that the fellows decided to lower gifts in the bucket from the MAF plane using Nate's spiraling-line technique. They felt this method would be better than dropping the gifts—that objects dropped could be misinterpreted. Perhaps the Indians would think the gifts had fallen out of the airplane by accident, but with the line a more intimate contact could be made, one that could hardly be misunderstood. There was one question: Would the Indians approach the "bucket" to take out gifts or untie them from the ground? The fellows thought they would not, at least at first, so characteristically Nate went to work the next morning to design and test an automatic release mechanism. His solution was as simple as it was practical. Two loops of wire were held together by a hook. The hook was held in position by the weight of a broom handle attached to the hook. When the broom handle touched the ground, the hook fell clear and the bucket tied to the lower loop was detached from the line.

Nate didn't sleep much the night before he and Ed made the first gift flight. When they arrived over the village it appeared deserted, but there were plenty of evidences of life in the area. They got the gift overboard with the broom handle mechanism rigged. The gift was a large aluminum kettle with brightly colored streamers attached. Inside they had placed an assortment of colored buttons and a small bag of rock salt.

"We continued circling," Nate wrote, "until the gift was drifting in a small lazy circle below us, ribbons fluttering nicely. Finally the gift appeared to be pretty close to the trees below. Once I believe the ribbons dragged across a tree and hung up momentarily. We held our breath while the kettle lowered toward the earth. It hit about two or three feet from the water directly in line with the path to the house. Finally the line was free and there was our messenger of good will, love and faith two thousand feet below on the sandbar. In a sense we had delivered the first gospel message by sign language to a people who are a quarter of a mile away vertically . . . fifty miles away horizontally . . . and continents and wide seas away psychologically."

On Friday, October 14, 1955, Nate again sat at his old typewriter feeding in sheets of yellow tissue. "I haven't brought the narrative up to the moment," he wrote, "but rather than let the hottest stuff cool off while I catch up, I'm going to go ahead with what just happened today." Paragraph after paragraph of vivid eyewitness description rattled out of the old portable typewriter. They took a machete for a gift on the second visit. A machete is the most prized possession of any jungle primitive. They checked the beach first to see if the big aluminum kettle had been found. It was gone. The binoculars removed any doubt. They saw no one and so again put overboard the gift with broom-handle attachment. As they circled, the high-riding machete was behaving nicely. "Ed was glued to the binoculars," Nate's record continues. "All of a sudden he let out a yell and all but crawled out the open door to get a better look. We were seeing our first Auca. He was running around, not hiding. Pretty soon there were three of them out in front of their big leaf-covered house. They were already watching the dangling prize. We let it down. First it looked as if it would hit the house but it drifted toward the stream. Splash! Then quicker than you could bat an eye, another splash. An Auca had dived after the treasure. Minutes later there must have been a half dozen or eight of the men on the bank examining the prize. Our hearts were grateful. We had not hoped to see this for perhaps months. Of course we wonder what they are thinking."

And thus began the series of thirteen weekly gift-drops as reported by Nate on those thirty-nine pages.

After the second visit the release mechanism was no longer necessary. The Aucas came running to where the prize dangled overhead, "converging like women at a bargain counter." On the sixth visit the Aucas tied a return gift on the line, a beautifully feathered head crown. From that time on, every visit involved an exchange of gifts. And there were other signs of friendly feeling from the clearings below. The "neighbors" cleared land up on

242

the hill to allow the airplane to fly closer. They built high platforms so the "traffic director" could operate from a better vantage point. Nate and Ed were flabbergasted to discover on one flight a three-foot crude model airplane on the roof of an Auca house. With this sort of reaction coming faster than the fellows had dared to hope, they began making plans for the next step.

Nate reported that team members ranged all the way from conservatism to impatience. Jim Elliot was the most eager to press forward in an actual contact with the Indians on the ground. Pete, the conservative of the group, favored working longer with Dayuma to build a bigger vocabulary of Auca words. Ed wanted to establish an airstrip on the Curaray River five miles or so from the Auca clearings. Nate, impressed with the results that were being obtained by the gift-drops, recommended that they keep to that program for a little while longer. Cautious as usual, Nate didn't feel that anything should be done suddenly.

The gift-drops were continued and Nate began a systematic search for a place to land nearer "Terminal City," the code name the fellows had given the Auca village. The only possible landing area would be one of the beaches along the Curaray River that passed within four and one-half miles of the Auca settlement.

As Nate thought of meeting the Aucas face to face, it was a time for careful second thoughts. To a friend, Wilbur Fletcher, attached to a Navy mission station at Guayaquil, Nate wrote:

"We're getting set to contact the Aucas. We are flying over their houses every week. Let me present one of the immediate problems. Suppose we have an engine failure and have to land in one of their clearings. We have to decide whether to defend ourselves or not. In view of the lethal record of these fellows and the past history of encounters, I don't feel we should plan our actions on a no-defense basis. I think we should do everything possible to have enough protection so as to discourage an attack that could result in fatalities. These people are definitely afraid of firearms and have not been known to attack anyone evidently armed except for the ambush of the Cooper expedition. If forced down we could figure on setting up defenses, foxholes, in their clearings. It would be rough going and in the final analysis we would be thrust upon the mercy and care of God, but we feel that a sensible precaution would be to have with us one of those light automatic .22 rifles like your crew men had back here . . . could I buy one of them?

"More important than any precaution we might take we are anxious to operate within the will and providence of God. The Lord has charged us with getting the gospel to every creature and we feel there is nothing to be gained by further delay on the Aucas."

To his parents, Nate sent a veiled prayer request:

"Please pray especially for a project directed at getting the gospel to another isolated group of Indians that as yet have not heard. Pray hard, speculate little, and don't mention it at all. We can't share details until we get the results. The results are very much in the Lord's hands. Don't let your curiosity get you all animated about it, but do pray that God will work on behalf of this particular group of jungle Indians, and pray for us as well as we try to reach them with the gospel."

An inkling of some of the earlier thinking on the approach to the Aucas was contained in a letter to Grady Parrott of MAF, dated October 31:

"The reason for the urgency is the Brethren boys feel that it is time now to move in toward the 'neighbors.' They plan to go downriver to a site just across a couple of ridges from their houses and build a quick airstrip for evacuation in case the contact they make is not friendly. They feel that it is essential to associate themselves with the plane that has been giving these people gifts. I will not plan to spend nights on the strip with the plane, rather I'll commute daily from Arajuno about thirteen minutes away.

"We have been seeing the barefoot (and bare everything else) boys regularly and they take our gifts off the line with evident confidence and have a big old time over what we give them. They seem to look forward to our regular weekly Santa Claus run. We're writing weekly reports on our visits. If we can write it right and if the Lord continues to bless so that it ultimately succeeds, I think it might someday make a booklet with pictures. I'll tell you, it is high adventure, as unreal as any successful novel . . . ha. At present writing we have swooped within fifty feet of these people. They show no signs of fear or hostility. The whole thing is fantastic.

"This type of thing presents a unique opportunity for the airplane to open a closed door, reduce risks to the lives of missionary personnel and then support them in an otherwise almost impossible situation. For me, the objective is dual. Locally, we want to see this new tribe have a chance to know Christ. Beyond that, we want other missions to know what air support can do to reduce the risk of initial contacts with dangerous, primitive people.

"Folks around here suspect what we are up to, but they have no idea how far along we are on it. We think our reason for secrecy is sound. Since recent Auca attacks, there has been some talk of an expedition that would go in armed to the teeth. Chances are, they wouldn't even find the Indians, but if they did there would surely be bloodshed and increased danger for those of us who are willing to labor patiently for a friendly contact for the Lord's sake."

Meanwhile, the regular weekly gift exchange went on. A few paragraphs from the December 10 entry in Nate's journal are worth repeating:

"We flew up over the new clearing on the hill. There were two women there. We dropped a small knife. The head man was down by the house on his platform directing traffic. He had on the red and black checkered shirt we dropped last week. We signaled and shouted to him, indicating that we wanted him to come up to the hilltop. While we circled again he disappeared from the platform. A few minutes later we spotted the old boy's checkered shirt up on the hill, so we made two passes and on the second pass dropped him a pair of pants which he caught in mid-air. (These fellows will be dressed like dudes before we get to see them on the ground.)

"Next, up to house number 4 and the main act. The big shots, four of them, were clad in white T-shirts. Youngsters and women were in the older uniform. The trees that we had tried to get them to cut down by tossing stuff into them were now cut down.

"While passing low, we saw one of the four Big Wheels

holding up a package, roundish and brown. We figured this was our trade item. Ed was feeling pretty rough . . . it had been an unusually strenuous workout. This week we had for them a couple of little bundles of string, a few smaller items, and four 6 x 9 inch portraits of the team members, tinted and bearing the insignia of the operation . . . a drawing of the little yellow airplane. These were glue-mounted on Masonite board.

"When this stuff got down over by the trees, they quickly took it out to the center of the clearing. They went into a 100% huddle over the contents of the white cloth mail sack that carried the mentioned items, except for the fellow who was busy fastening on their gift to us. I saw the gift leave him, drifting upward lazily. I rolled out of the turn and added power. Within three or four seconds the package was swished skyward from them and the last man joined the huddle over the pictures. What wouldn't we have given to see those boys studying out our pictures and see their reactions!

"We headed home with the prize dangling at the end of the line. At Arajuno we set the package down at the edge of the strip, cut the line, and landed. On the ground, I bashed my way through the brush at the edge of the strip while Ed lost his breakfast. This is the first time I've beat him to the prize. (His legs are at least a foot longer than mine.) When I got to the bark-cloth bag, it was moving. Since we had given them a chicken last week I figured this would be a bird, but as I started to peek in a hole the thought of a snake crossed my mind. However, it was a nice parrot in a basket covered with bark. The bird was well tied and was complete with a partially-nibbled banana inside for the trip!"

It was on this same trip that Nate and Ed before arrival in Terminal City had found a beach on the Curaray just four and a half miles from the village. After careful inspection of the approaches, Nate flew low over the beach and "bombed" it with paper sacks of dry paint pigment. By careful timing between the sacks of powder he measured the usable portion of the beach. On a final pass he touched the wheels lightly and decided the surface was hard enough. So from that time on, all plans were focused on using the beach they had named "Palm Beach" for an aerial entry into the territory. The idea of walking in and cutting an airstrip was abandoned. Plans were firmed up rapidly because they felt the next full moon would be the right time. By the following month the rains would begin and the beach would likely be unusable. They started construction of a prefabricated tree house that could be flown in. As agreed to by the others, Nate had asked Roger Youderian to join the team. He had accepted. Pete Fleming was still undecided.

24

CURARAY SANDBAR

. . . they shall mount up with wings as eagles. . . . ISAIAH 40:31

IT WAS the Christmas season . . . always a happy time at Shell Merita. Nate and Marj had dug the Christmas things out of a special barrel where they had been packed for the past year—the little artificial Christmas tree with the folding branches, the boxes of decorations and strings of lights. Gifts were wrapped in bright red and green paper and transferred to a dark corner of the top shelf in the bedroom closet. Nate had made a papier-mâché model of the volcano Sangay to go under the tree. It had a red light on the top and a cotton streamer to indicate the fire and smoke. There was an electric train for Stevie. Nate had added a cardboard box railroad station and made a tunnel for the tracks under Sangay. The smell of Christmas cookies floated through the house.

It was Sunday afternoon, December 18. Nate got out the type-writer and wrote a letter to his and Marj's parents:

Dear Farrises and Saints,

Christmas is in the air in Shell Mera. We are putting up the little tree in the living room and the kids are all excited. The tape recorder is playing the familiar Christmas carols and hymns, and we feel creeping over us the thrill of that great mystery . . . that God should send His only Son to take on our likeness in a stable. Shame on us for getting so used to the story that we fail to get goose pimples when we contemplate such incomprehensible con- descension.

Philip, toddling around, holding on, is just old enough to sense that something special is coming up. We are anxious that the children catch the real significance of it all.

248

This morning in Bible class, in a one-room shack where a whole family lives, it was easy to see why God chose a stable to give His gift. When I asked if God made special preparations for His coming, if He had a palace, if His earthly parents were kings, you could feel the love and confidence as they said "No, He was born of poor people, just like us."

Up at the clinic right now there is a ten-year-old boy who has osteomyelitis in his right leg. The other night when he was in particularly acute pain, Dotty Brown, the nurse, called Marj and me and asked if we could come up to visit him. We felt compelled to shove our work back on the desk and go. It was a blessed opportunity. The boy's mother was in tears, convinced that the boy would be lame the rest of his life. He was crying out, just like I did when I had osteo. We tried to show him (he is a believer) that God has a purpose in everything that comes into our lives. It blessed my own soul to tell him how my pain became so intense that I finally prayed for God to take me out of this world or heal me, at the same time vowing that if He spared my life, it would henceforth belong to Him. My, how I thank God for that day. How many times have I forgotten that vow and how great His patience in reminding me over and over until, by His grace, we know the unspeakable joy of serving Him here.

We cannot think of the humility of His first coming into this cursed, hateful world without thinking of the mode of His coming again when the heavens shall roll up as a scroll and the islands shall be moved and the mountains shaken. And every eye shall see Him and every tongue shall confess that He is Lord of all. And among His redeemed, gathered from the four corners of the earth there shall be some from every tribe and nation on earth. Praise His holy name. And pray with us for the small remaining group in eastern Ecuador who have not yet as much as heard the Name of the Lord Jesus Christ.

May God richly bless each of you. Thanks for your wonderful gifts . . . what more could one ask than good parents who love the Lord and taught us early that we must give ourselves to Him if we are ever to have peace in our hearts and the hope of Glory.

May this season be a time of blessed reflection.

Affectionately,
Nate and Marj

To the letter Marj added a postscript:

P.S. Please continue to pray about the matter we can't name yet. It is of extreme importance especially between now and the middle of January. Nate says he feels a real lack of prayer just because we can't ask for definite prayer. This is the biggest thing yet.

As Nate finished writing the letter to their parents, Marj asked him to come and help with the trimming of the Christmas tree. What with Stevie insisting that each ornament had to be brought to the proper unloading spot by his electric train, and Kathy scolding him for holding up the wheels of progress, and little Philip's chubby fist gravitating like a magnet to the bright colored balls, Marj had her hands full . . . her need for her husband to help was most urgent. But Nate held off, saying that he had one more letter to write . . . a letter that had to be written. He remained in the bedroom, sitting on the edge of the bed with the portable on his lap, the intermittent sound of the keys passing faintly through the door. Finally he appeared in the living room, relaxed and smiling. Handing Marj the letter in his hand, he said, "Honey, you might want to read this before putting it in the file . . . put it with the Auca stuff for later."

When he wrote this letter Nate had 21 days to live. The letter, written for use after the need for secrecy was past, read:

Dear brother in Christ:

It almost seemed that an effort would be made to go downriver to meet our "neighbors" at this season. We might well have been on some lonesome sandbar making mute overtures to a bunch of naked savages while the rest of the world rolled out pomp and merchandise.

During all of our discussions of these curious people, there have always been funny twists, pun-able situations. For instance, in our effort to visit them regularly so that they would expect us on a certain day, we became aware of the fact that they have no week. That fact lends itself easily to jesting in a lighter moment.

But when it came to Christmas I could not help noticing the fact that none of us was in a jesting mood; not because we would miss being with Christian friends and co-laborers in the gospel, but because these witnesses to two hundred silent generations who have gone to their pagan graves without a knowledge of the Lord Jesus Christ . . . these who have never once known the name of Christ, these who survive by killing and die by counterkilling . . . these have no Christmas!

Then as we become nostalgic, thinking of past Christmases . . . as we weigh the future and seek the will of God, does it seem right that we should hazard our lives for just a few savages? As we ask ourselves the question, we realize that it is not the call of needy thousands. Rather it is the simple intimation of the prophetic word that there shall be some from every tribe in His presence in the last day and in our hearts we feel that it is pleasing to Him that we should interest ourselves in making an opening into the Auca prison for Christ.

As we have a high old time this Christmas, may we who know Christ hear the cry of the damned as they hurtle headlong into the Christless night without ever a chance. May we be moved with compassion as our Lord was. May we shed tears of repentance for those whom we have failed to bring out of darkness. Beyond the smiling scenes of Bethlehem may we see the crushing agony of Golgotha. May God give us a new vision of His will concerning the Lost and our responsibility.

Would that we could comprehend the lot of these Stone-Age people who live in mortal fear of ambush on the jungle trail . . . those to whom the bark of a gun means sudden, mysterious death . . . those who think all men in all the world are killers like themselves. If God would grant us the vision, the word "sacrifice" would disappear from our lips and thoughts; we would hate the things that seem now so dear to us; our lives would suddenly be too short, we would despise time-robbing distractions and charge the enemy with *all our energies* in the name of Christ. May God help us to judge ourselves by the eternities that separate the Aucas from a comprehension of Christmas, and Him, Who though He was rich, yet for our sakes became poor so that we might, through His poverty, be made rich.

Lord, God, speak to my own heart and give me to know thy holy will and the joy of walking in it. Amen.

On Christmas night Nate wrote another and final letter to the parents on both sides of the family. He had started it on Christmas Eve but carolers from the Bible Institute at Shell Mera had interrupted him. He wrote:

It has been a wonderful Christmas for us here. Last night (Christmas Eve) for a while there was no one around . . . our house is usually like Times Square on Saturday night. Rachel had retired early and the kids were playing quietly at one thing or another in other parts of the house . . . so Marj and I sat on the day bed in the living room watching the lights on the Christmas tree and reflecting on the goodness of the Lord. It wasn't long until Kathy and Stevie were curled up with their heads on our laps. They looked so good to us in that softly colored light. They were soon fast asleep, as was Philip already in bed.

CONFIDENTIAL: Please be in prayer for a special project the 3rd of January. Please do not mention it even in your correspondence to us because we sometimes pass letters around and word might leak out. We are attempting to contact a primitive group of Indians and the situation is such that the lives of missionaries who make up the team might be endangered by interference. I will be flying in support of the operation. There are four other missionaries involved and I have been privileged to work with them on it. I'm sure your hearts will be thrilled with the reports we are keeping of the Lord's blessing, when we can share them with you.

We feel confident that the Lord is blessing and we shall go forward just one step at a time, looking constantly for clear indications of the blessing of God on each step.

Already months of groundwork have been laid with every encouraging sign . . . we have made heavy investments in paving the way, both financially and in missionary effort.

For now, pray earnestly, especially in the week following the 3rd of January . . . we feel a real need for prevailing prayer help at this time. A sudden move or careless word at this critical stage in the operation could slam the door of hope on people who live in the stone age.

It is extremely difficult to guard your talk about something so interesting and close to you but now it is a must. Remember, tell no one . . . regardless of the confidence you have in them. The other team members are making the same personal sacrifice and we must not betray confidence.

It is a rare privilege that is ours and we believe that God has given us a pattern of approach that holds down missionary risks . . . one that might well help other missionaries in reaching tribes that we believe will be reached before the consummation of the age.

May this New Year be one filled with special blessings and with an increased knowledge of the Lord Jesus. May we all feel His presence and the imminence of His return as never before. God forbid that the incredible rush toward the consummation of all things might become trite as we watch it develop on the world scene. We of the fallen race get used to new things at a fantastic rate. May we see the signs and be watchful. Maranatha.

Love from the five of us,
Nate

Then there was a final letter to the men in the MAF office in California, dated December 29, 1955. It was addressed to "Grady, Charlie, Don, Jim (if there), et al.:"

First off . . . this will be the last opportunity to write before we make an effort to reach the wild boys. The operation is to begin next Tuesday or Wednesday, the Lord willing. We're all glad to be getting under way. The suspense is killing. Please pray definitely for us . . . for safety and for a good solid contact and the beginning of language work and the beginning of an airstrip that would permit direct access to whatever personnel might be working among them. There are very few in this group, yet we're quite sure they are responsible for recent killings. And we trust that successful contact with this group will give us access to the other groups in this area in due time.

The remainder of this letter described trouble with a sticking valve in the Cruiser's engine and repairs to a cracked engine mount. Then Nate added:

May we never take for granted the sweat, toil and tears it takes there in California to make possible our operation here in Shell Mera. May your joy equal ours as we rejoice in the fruit of these labors.

On the morning of Tuesday, January 3, the airstrip at Arajuno took on the appearance of a miniature military invasion on "D-Day." Food supplies, radios, parts for the prefabricated tree house, clothing, gifts for the Indians, utensils, and medical supplies were laid out in neat piles for each of the flights Nate would make.

Nate took only Ed on the first trip to Palm Beach, not wanting to risk the landing with more than one passenger. They got airborne at 8:02 A.M. just two minutes behind the paper schedule set up in advance. Fifteen minutes later they were over the site.

"The fog thinned so that we could safely slip in under it and make an approach," Nate wrote that night. "We went in, simulating a real landing, checked the full length for sticks and other hazards and pulled up. As we came in the second time, we slipped down between the trees in a steep side slip. It felt good as we made the last turn and came to the sand, so I set it down. The right wheel hit within six feet of the water and the left ten feet later. As the weight settled on the wheels, I felt it was soft sand . . . too late to back out now. I hugged the stick back and waited. One softer spot and we'd have been on our nose . . . maybe on our back. It never came."

That was the first landing in Auca territory. Ed stayed there alone as Nate went back for Jim and Roger. It took five flights that day to establish their beachhead. By nightfall the prefabricated house was high in an ironwood tree overlooking the beach. The long wait for visitors began. Nate and Pete spent every day on the beach with the other three, but flew back to Arajuno for the nights, not wanting an unexpected rain to trap the airplane on the sandbar.

From Nate's thirty-nine-page journal, two paragraphs re-create the days of waiting on the strip of sand by the Curaray River:

"The three musketeers had a good night's sleep in the tree house. At 9 P.M. a strong wind swayed the trees and made such sounds that woke up the three men . . . but all were soon asleep again. They had a lighted lantern up there to keep the target well lit. At 5 A.M. they shined the flashlight down on the beach to check a gift machete left the night before. It was gone! For the next fifteen minutes the jungles rang with Auca phrases . . . perhaps with a Midwestern accent. They then shined the light for a closer look. A big leaf had fallen on the knife so as to hide it. Tough!

"Days are spent down on the sand in the sun. Pete's long-sleeved shirt, pants, and straw hat make him look like a beach-comber. Flies keep the rest of us pretty well clad in T-shirts, pants, and tennis shoes. The 'armor' Roj made (breast and tummy plate) out of a gas drum works very well for a stove. While getting steam up on the stew we tossed termite nests on the fire to chase the gnats like the Indians do."

The big day on Palm Beach was Friday, January 6. At eleven-fifteen in the morning three naked Aucas—a young man, a girl, and an older woman—suddenly appeared on the bank of the river opposite Palm Beach. When they hesitated, Jim waded across the stream and led them over to the camp. After a few minutes all were relaxed; the atmosphere was completely friendly. The Aucas stayed all afternoon, eating hamburgers and drinking warm lemonade, and jabbering away as though the fellows could understand every word they said. "George," as the fellows nicknamed the young man, indicated he wanted to fly in the airplane, so Nate flew him over his own village, where he leaned out the open side of the plane (the door was off) and shouted down to the amazement of his friends below.

After the Indians had disappeared again into the forest, the five fellows gave way to jubilation. This successful first meeting was the thing they had longed and prayed for.

Saturday for the five men on the beach was a day of quiet rest and waiting. That evening Nate gathered up all the film and took it back to Arajuno. Sunday morning, January 8, as Nate and Pete prepared to leave for Palm Beach, they reminded the girls, "Pray for us . . . today is the day things will happen."

Back at Shell Mera there was the usual round of Sunday morning activity. Olive Fleming took the children to Sunday school at the Bible Institute so Marj could stay near the radio to listen for Nate's calls. At noon Olive joined Marj in the radio room . . . Nate had said he would call at twelve-thirty. Ruth Keenan in the other MAF house also tuned in. Right on the appointed time, Nate's voice came booming through the interference into the loudspeaker at Shell Mera.

He was airborne when he called. He had just flown over Terminal City and was about to land at Palm Beach. "Have just sighted a commission of ten," Nate informed the girls with suppressed excitement, "it looks like they'll be here for the early afternoon service. Pray for us. This *is* the day! Will contact you next at four-thirty."

At three-twelve Nate's wristwatch was suddenly smashed against a stone and the hands stopped moving as the muddy water of the Curaray River seeped into the broken case.

EPILOGUE

AN HOUR and fifteen minutes after the brutal attack on Palm Beach the first fleeting hint of what had happened reached the wives waiting by radios back at their various mission stations. At four-thirty, the time of the promised contact, the radio receivers were silent.

At Shell Mera Marj put down a little gnawing worry. Radio transmitters break down, she thought, as she continued with the day's routine. But at dusk she turned to the Lord to calm her beating heart. Nate had not flown into Arajuno from Palm Beach as he always had before. Had the plane also broken down? This seemed too much to be coincidence.

Thus began five terrible days of uncertainty. The wives, still hoping that nothing was wrong, decided to wait for morning. It was a long dark night. Johnny Keenan took off with the first light. He flew directly to Palm Beach. His radio report gave sudden sharp substance to the vague fears of the night. He had found Nate's plane sitting in the middle of Palm Beach, its fabric all stripped off. *There was no sign of the fellows.*

Suddenly the secrecy barrier was down. Word spread rapidly. Missionaries and Ecuadorian and United States military personnel organized a search party to go into the Auca territory on foot.

Jerry Hannifin, a *Time* correspondent in Washington, D. C., got the first brief word over the press wires. He already knew of Nate and his jungle flying. Jerry dropped everything to spend hours on the phone persuading the editors of *Life* magazine to send Cornell Capa, one of the world's great photographers, to Ecuador. From New York came two officers of Christian Missions in Many Lands; also hurried to the scene was MAF's president, Grady Parrott.

Nate's brother Sam left a pile of papers forgotten on a conference table in Washington—a badly distorted and third-hand account had made it clear that something was seriously wrong in the far-off jungle. Within a few hours he was on his way to Ecuador.

Back in the States the phones of the several families involved began to ring incessantly. Questions poured in to parents and brothers and sisters who had no answers.

Newspapers across the land blew shreds of information into dramatic, speculative headlines.

Meanwhile, Shell Mera had become the headquarters for rescue efforts. Large military planes flew in with a dismantled helicopter. There were conferences and plans in a constant state of flux in the Saints' large house at Shell Mera. Abe Van Der Puy, down from HCJB in Quito, set up a desk on the piano bench and got out the press releases that informed the anxious world. The Keenan house and the Berean Bible Institute took the overflow.

The wives of the missing men were brought to Shell Mera to await the outcome together. Nate's sister Rachel was also flown in. Then Marilou McCully was flown back to Arajuno to help in the work there.

By Wednesday afternoon two bodies had been sighted from the air. Identification was impossible. Gradually it began to dawn on the military men and other outsiders that they were witnessing something unusual. Under the distressing uncertainty of who was dead and who might still be alive it would have been normal to expect the thin walls of Shell Merita to be carrying the muffled sounds of hysteria. From a purely human point of view one would have expected others to be caring for the wives and Rachel as they waited, hearts breaking with uncontrolled panic. Sedatives should have been the order of the day.

But none of this was taking place. There were some tears shed into pillows at night, but in the hearts of these women a miraculous calm reigned—a quiet readiness to accept whatever the outcome as the will of their heavenly Father.

As that awful week progressed the five wives and Rachel continued to care for the children and prepare the meals for the large crowd of extra people. Marj stuck by her post at the radio from dawn until dark, day after weary day. She brought in weather reports from the outlying stations, kept track of the military and other planes as they flew, and kept a continuous flow of messages going between Shell and the outside world.

On Wednesday evening Betty Elliot wrote a letter to her folks. This letter throws a bright shaft of illumination into the quiet inner pool of a heart where faith was stronger than human fear. Betty's letter can best be read in the light of a poem she had written in her college days.

ALONE WITH THEE

Perhaps some future day, Lord, Thy strong hand
Will lead me to the place where I must stand
Utterly alone.

Alone, O Gracious Lover, but for Thee,
I shall be satisfied if I can see
Jesus only.

I do not know Thy plan for years to come.
My spirit finds in Thee its perfect home,
Sufficiency.

Lord, all my desire is before Thee now;
Lead on—no matter where, no matter how.
I trust in Thee.

On that dark Wednesday night in Shell Mera, January 11, 1956, Betty wrote:

I want you to know that your prayers are being answered moment by moment as regards me—I am ever so conscious of the everlasting arms. As yet we know only that two bodies have been sighted from the air but not identified.

Jim was confident, as was I, of God's leading. There are no regrets.

Nothing was more burning in his heart than that Christ should be named among the Aucas. By life or death, oh, may God get glory to Himself.

Pray that whatever the outcome I may learn the lessons needful. I want to serve the Lord in the future, so pray for His continued grace and guidance. I have no idea what I will do if Jim is dead, but the Lord knows and I am at rest.

We hope for final word tomorrow and trust our loving Father who never wastes anything. All my love,

Betty

The story of the rescue effort, the finding of the bodies in the muddy waters of the Curaray, the hasty burial in a common grave under the tree-house as a violent tropical storm darkened the scene in a fury of wind and rain—all this has been told in detail elsewhere.*

Marj and the other wives and Rachel accepted the final news that all five were dead in the same spirit they had shown through the interminable days of waiting. They gathered that evening with the children in the living room while some of the older men present opened the Bible and read various passages about heaven. Military officers and others in the house sat listening. The women were thankful that their men had been faithful to the Lord. Marilou went to the piano and began to play the song that the men had sung the morning they left for Palm Beach. Then Betty's clear soprano took up the words:

> *We rest on Thee, our Shield and our Defender,*
> *We go not forth alone against the foe.*
> *Strong in Thy Strength, safe in Thy keeping tender,*
> *We rest on Thee, and in Thy name we go.*
>
> *We go in faith, our own great weakness feeling,*
> *And needing more each day Thy grace to know,*
> *Yet from our hearts a song of triumph pealing,*
> *We rest on Thee, and in Thy name we go.*

As Betty and Marilou finished, one military man shook his head and muttered with a choke in his voice: "I've never seen anything like this!"

---

* *Through Gates of Splendor* by Elisabeth Elliot (New York: Harper & Brothers, 1957).

Birth is the beginning and death is the end of the life chronicle of most men. But there are those, like Nate Saint and his four companions, who learn to walk with God and live in the dimension of the eternal. They are in the true spiritual succession of Abel of whom it was said: "He being dead yet speaketh."

For Nate and his four companions there was no sharp line of demarcation between the "martyrdom" of their lives and the "martyrdom" of their deaths. Their witness did not cease with what men call death. For example, the gift-drops to the Aucas were continued regularly by MAF pilots. Oddly enough, there seemed to be no change in the attitude of the jungle tribe toward the fliers. The Aucas appeared to be as friendly and as responsive as they were before the brutal attack on Palm Beach.

Meanwhile, Rachel, who had caught the vision of reaching the Aucas while visiting Nate at Shell Merita, grew more and more fluent in the tribal language with the help of Dayuma. In 1957 Rachel Saint's story was presented on the coast-to-coast television program, "This Is Your Life." Dayuma accompanied her to the States for what they thought was to be a missionary conference. After the surprise TV program, Rachel and Dayuma retired to the seclusion of the Wycliffe Home at Sulphur Springs, Arkansas, for concentrated language study.

As Rachel was building her knowledge of the language, Dayuma was gaining a deeper knowledge of what Christ's death on the Cross could mean in her own life. In due time she confessed her faith in Christ and became the first Auca convert to Christianity.

While Betty Elliot was working with the Tidmarshes at Arajuno in November, 1957, word reached them that two Auca women had come out from their tribe and were staying at a Quichua fishing village six trail-hours away on the Oglán River near the confluence of the Curaray. Leaving at once Betty went into the jungle to meet the Auca women, Mankamu and Mintaka. The latter turned out to be the older women of the trio that visited the men on Palm Beach. Ultimately it was revealed that Mankamu and Mintaka had come out of the jungle seeking Dayuma. Through the years Dayuma's mother had longed for the return of her daughter. Somehow the older woman had gained the idea that

Nate and the MAF plane could provide the means of reaching the lost one. Dayuma's little brother on several occasions had tried to tie himself to the line let down by the plane so that he might be taken by the MAF fliers to Dayuma somewhere outside. The boy had climbed to the top of one of the platforms erected in the Auca settlement to bring him closer to the plane. His climbing motions had puzzled the fliers.

Betty persuaded the two Auca women to return with her to Shandia, where she began intensive study of the tribal language. In the spring of 1958 Rachel and Dayuma returned to Ecuador to collaborate with Betty and her charges. Some months later Mankamu and Mintaka decided they should return to their tribe. They told the missionaries they had promised their families before they left that they would return when the kapok was ripe. Dayuma, who had been away from her people for twelve years, decided to accompany them. Thus on September 8, 1958, the three Auca women struck out on the jungle trail, carrying three puppies and food for the trek.

For a time it appeared that the jungle had swallowed up the three but on September 28, Betty Elliot and Marj Saint, who was visiting her for a brief period during the absence of the Tidmarshes, got breathtaking news from a Quichua who arrived out of the jungle. His first words were a noncommittal greeting.

"Didn't you bring us any news about the Aucas?" Betty asked him.

"Oh, yes," he said with a casual shrug, "they have come and brought others with them. They have stopped down at the river to bathe."

As Marj, Betty, and four-year-old Valerie rushed out to the opening of the trail, they heard someone singing "Jesus Loves Me!" with an Auca accent. It was Dayuma, followed by Mankamu, Mintaka, and seven other Aucas.

They brought the first news from inside the Auca settlement. Dayuma also brought the long-awaited word that the Aucas wanted Rachel and Betty to visit them. Thus Nate's sister Rachel, Jim Elliot's wife Betty, and daughter Valerie, accompanied by

261

the ten Aucas and several Quichua carriers, walked into the Auca settlement on October 8, 1958.

The Aucas welcomed them to the two simple thatched houses they had built for them and soon all were sharing their jungle meat and manioc.

At the time of this writing, Rachel and Betty and Valerie have lived quietly among the Aucas for six months, sitting in the evenings around the fire with Kimo, Monga, Nimunga, and others of the Auca men who had hurled those long black wooden lances on that warm Sunday afternoon only three years before.

The goal of the five martyrs had been accomplished by two women and a tiny girl.

When Marj Saint, in New York, finished checking the previous chapters of this book, she wrote a letter to her children. This book would not be complete without this final summing-up:

My darling children,

The story of your father's life has now been written. A few years ago there would have been no need to write these things, but there came a day when I had to tell you our Daddy wasn't coming back to live with us—he had gone with four of his friends to live with Jesus in heaven.

You often asked Daddy to tell you about his boyhood. And now, more than before, you want to know everything—the things he told me when you were asleep—how he learned to fly—and why we came to Ecuador to live. The story is yours now, recorded here for you and others who may want to read about our "Jungle Pilot."

Kathy, you are a big girl now—you are Mommy's helper and companion. You have your Daddy's clear blue eyes with the built-in twinkle. Your golden hair looks just like a lock of your Daddy's baby hair that Grandpa Saint gave me on our wedding day.

Stevie, though you are only eight, you are the man of the house. So often when I see you walk or listen to you talk, I think to myself, "He's just a miniature of the life-size man that the Lord gave me." There are times when your little face is serious—you seem to be thinking thoughts far beyond your years. There are other times when you make us all laugh as your Daddy did so often.

And Philip, my four-year-old bundle of love, it's easy to guess whose boy you are. You make everything fly like an airplane—everything from a piece of carrot on the end of your fork to the bar of soap in your bath.

Some day, my precious jewels, your hearts will be even more tender and your minds more curious than now. Then you will ask, "Why did my Daddy go among those savage Aucas?" The very best answer I can give you is to recall the night Daddy read you the story of Noah from the Old Testament, and to remind you how Daddy prayed afterward that he, like Noah, would be faithful and do all that God commanded him to do.

Your Daddy wrote to our friends the Michaels only a month before he was killed. You won't understand all the letter said until you are older, but one paragraph I must include anyway. It reads:

"Congratulations on the arrival of another man to garrison the Michael fort. May God bless and use him in what surely looks like the gravest epoch man has faced since the flood. When I look at our children, I think that these little ones are particularly blessed of God, for it may be their privilege to lay down their lives for Christ's sake. These are terrible, yet wonderful days in which to be a witness on the world scene."

You see, what Daddy thought might be God's plan for you, became God's plan for him. For a long time you children have prayed for the Aucas. Now Auntie Rachel and Auntie Betty are living down in the jungle with the Aucas. Someday, perhaps soon, you may meet some of the men who killed Daddy. Daddy would want you to love them and thank our heavenly Father that our prayers for these Indians are being answered.

It is my heart's desire, Kathy, Stevie, and Philip, that this biography will help you, and others who read it, to see the importance of knowing God's will for your lives and of following Him in simple obedience.

Love,
Mother

MAF pilots are still challenged with situations like the ones Nate Saint faced. But today's frontiers have expanded to include dynamic national churches needing help. Can the men of MAF meet that challenge? The nature of the specific task is often different from "Operation Auca." But the demand for persistence, planning and dedication is at least equal. Pray for them daily.